Socialism Vanquished, Socialism Challenged

Socialism Vanquished, Socialism Challenged

Eastern Europe and China, 1989–2009

EDITED BY NINA BANDELJ
and
DOROTHY J. SOLINGER

OXFORD
UNIVERSITY PRESS

OXFORD

UNIVERSITY PRESS

Oxford University Press is a department of the University of Oxford.
It furthers the University's objective of excellence in research, scholarship,
and education by publishing worldwide.

Oxford New York

Auckland Cape Town Dar es Salaam Hong Kong Karachi
Kuala Lumpur Madrid Melbourne Mexico City Nairobi
New Delhi Shanghai Taipei Toronto

With offices in

Argentina Austria Brazil Chile Czech Republic France Greece
Guatemala Hungary Italy Japan Poland Portugal Singapore
South Korea Switzerland Thailand Turkey Ukraine Vietnam

Oxford is a registered trademark of Oxford University Press
in the UK and certain other countries.

Published in the United States of America by
Oxford University Press
198 Madison Avenue, New York, NY 10016

Library of Congress Cataloging-in-Publication Data
Socialism vanquished, socialism challenged: Eastern Europe and
China, 1989–2009 / edited by Nina Bandelj and Dorothy J. Solinger.
p. cm.
Includes bibliographical references and index.
ISBN 978–0–19–989597–7 (hardback)—ISBN 978–0–19–989596–0 (pbk.)
1. Europe, Eastern—Politics and government—1989– 2. Post-communism—Europe,
Eastern. 3. Europe, Eastern—Economic policy—1989– 4. China—Politics and
government—1976–2002. 5. China—Politics and government—2002– 6. Post-communism—
China. 7. China—Economic policy—1976–2000. 8. China—Economic policy—2000–
I. Bandelj, Nina. II. Solinger, Dorothy J.
JN96.A58S64 2012
320.94709′049—dc23
2011047404

ISBN 978–0–19–989597–7
ISBN 978–0–19–989596–0

1 3 5 7 9 8 6 4 2
Printed in the United States of America
on acid-free paper

CONTENTS

ACKNOWLEDGMENTS

This volume is the product of a conference convened in November 2009 on the 20th anniversary of the fall of the Berlin Wall. The meeting was organized and held in commemoration of that event and to evoke the memory of the popular protests that broke out seven months earlier across China—with their largest manifestation at Tiananmen Square in Beijing. Our first objective was to appraise the longer-term outcomes of these spectacular episodes; a second aim was to draw comparisons across fields of activity—in politics, economics, culture, and state-society relations—in these two disparate parts of the globe. In one, state socialism as it had been known for decades was vanquished, obliterated; in the other, under the name if not really the substance of socialism, it limps forward, though under challenge. As editors, we have learned a great deal in the process; we hope that readers of this volume will have the same experience.

Of all those who must be thanked, the authors come first. We were fortunate to work with a group of creative and highly knowledgeable scholars whose contributions we celebrate along with the publication of the book. Much gratitude goes to these people, for their hard work, their insights, and their patience through a number of rounds of revision.

The original meeting included others whose papers, while stimulating and valuable, in the end did not fit as well into the project we envisioned as the ten papers we selected did. These scholars are Leszek Balcerowicz, Martin Dimitrov, Wade Jacoby, Antoni Kaminski, Bartlomiej Kaminski, David Laitin, Victor Nee, David Stark, Ivan Szelenyi, Daniel Treisman, and Jeffrey Wasserstrom. We thank all of them for their contributions, both written and oral, at the conference. We also appreciate the job done by discussants Ewa Balcerowicz, Thomas Bernstein, Lei Guang, Barbara Heyns, Kate Merkel-Hess, Kenneth Pomeranz, David Smith, and Yuliya Tverdova. Thomas Bernstein also assisted with the introduction to the volume and with writing the proposal that earned us funds to hold the gathering. Marek Kaminski and Su Yang served on the organizing committee, as did Thomas Bernstein, David Smith, and Yuliya Tverdova.

So much of the supportive work that made the venture possible was done by Elizabeth Sowers, who took time from her own doctoral research to help with the coordination of and the logistics for the meeting and also with a great many of the tasks involved in the preparation of the final manuscript. Paul Morgan also took time from his own work to assist in formatting the figures in the book.

Certainly we would never have been able to hold the meeting without generous funding from the University of California, Irvine, Center for the Study of Democracy (CSD) and from the American Council of Learned Societies. The idea to hold the conference came from the then director of the CSD, Bernard Grofman. We are much indebted to his designating our conference the "signature conference" of the year for the center. We also gratefully acknowledge support from the University of California, Irvine's Office of Research, Center for Asian Studies, Department of Sociology, Department of Political Science, International Studies Program, and the University of California Multi-Campus Research Program in World History.

Finally, this book could never have come into existence without the hard work and excellent support we received from our editor and his assistant at the press, David McBride and Caelyn Cobb. We also appreciate the fine reviews done for us by two (originally) anonymous readers, one of whom turned out to be Meg Rithmire.

Now that the countries of the Eastern European region no longer are labeled "socialist," it is sometimes claimed that scholars can no more pit the structures and activities of these nations against those of China for comparative purposes. We hope that this collection will lay that claim to rest and, perhaps, inspire more works on this fascinating theme, the aftermath of the great twentieth-century experiment in established, state-sponsored socialism.

ABOUT THE CONTRIBUTORS

Nina Bandelj is associate professor of sociology at the University of California, Irvine. Her research examines the social and cultural bases of economic phenomena, and social change in postsocialist Europe. Bandelj has published in the *American Sociological Review, Social Forces, Theory and Society,* and *Socio-Economic Review,* among other journals. She is the author of *From Communists to Foreign Capitalists: The Social Foundations of Foreign Direct Investment in Postsocialist Europe* (Princeton University Press, 2008), *Economy and State: A Sociological Perspective* (with Elizabeth Sowers, Polity Press, 2010), and editor of *Economic Sociology of Work* (Emerald Publishing, 2009) and *The Cultural Wealth of Nations* (with Frederick F. Wherry, Stanford University Press, 2011).

József Böröcz is professor of sociology at Rutgers, The State University of New Jersey, with additional affiliations at the Center for Migration and Development at Princeton University and the Institute for Political Studies of the Hungarian Academy of Sciences. He is the author of the award-winning *The European Union and Global Social Change: A Critical Geopolitical Economic Analysis* (London: Routledge, 2009 and 2010) and *Leisure Migration: A Sociological Study on Tourism* (Cambridge, UK: Pergamon Press, 1996). His recent work addresses the complexities of (post-)state socialism and the crises of global capitalism.

Valerie Bunce is professor of government and the Aaron Binenkorb Chair of International Studies at Cornell University. She received her doctorate in political science at the University of Michigan in 1976. Her most recent publications include *Defeating Authoritarian Leaders in Postcommunist Countries* (Cambridge University Press, 2011), which she coauthored with Sharon Wolchik, and *Democracy and Authoritarianism in the Postcommunist World* (Cambridge University Press, 2009), which she coedited with Michael McFaul and Kathryn Stoner-Weiss. She is a member of the American Academy of Arts and Sciences, and she has served as vice president of the American Political Science Association and president of the Association for Slavic, East European and Eurasian Studies.

Joseph Fewsmith is professor of international relations and political science and director of the Boston University Center for the Study of Asia. He is also an associate of the John King Fairbank Center for East Asian Studies at Harvard University. Fewsmith is author and editor of six books, including, most recently, *China Today, China Tomorrow* (2010) and *China Since Tiananmen* (2nd ed., 2008). He is also one of the seven regular contributors to *China Leadership Monitor*, a quarterly web publication analyzing current developments in China. He has written more than 100 articles, which have appeared in such journals as *The China Quarterly, Asian Survey, Comparative Studies in Society and History, The China Journal, The Journal of Contemporary China,* and *Modern China.*

Theodore P. Gerber is professor of sociology at the University of Wisconsin, Madison. His research examines socioeconomic stratification, demographic processes, education, labor markets, public opinion, and social change in contemporary Russia and other former Soviet republics. He has authored or coauthored 45 published articles, which have appeared in the *American Sociological Review, American Journal of Sociology, Demography, Annual Review of Sociology, Social Forces, Foreign Affairs, International Security, Sociology of Education,* and other scholarly journals or edited volumes. His work has been funded by the National Science Foundation, the National Academy of Education, and the National Council for East European and Eurasian Research.

Yasheng Huang is professor of political economy and international management and holds the International Program Professorship in Chinese Economy and Business at the Sloan School of Management, Massachusetts Institute of Technology. He also holds a special-term professorship at the School of Management at Fudan University, the School of Management at Xi'an Jiaotong University, and the School of Public Administration at Zhejiang University and an honorary professorship at Hunan University. His previous appointments include faculty positions at the University of Michigan and Harvard University. His most recent book is *Capitalism with Chinese Characteristics* (Cambridge, 2008).

Barry Naughton is an economist and So Kwanlok Professor at the Graduate School of International Relations and Pacific Studies (IR/PS) at the University of California, San Diego. His most recent book is *The Chinese Economy: Transitions and Growth,* a comprehensive survey of the Chinese economy published by MIT Press in 2007. Naughton publishes extensively on China's economy and political economy, including topics related to market transition, industry, and technology. His first book, *Growing Out of the Plan: Chinese Economic Reform, 1978–1993,* won the Masayoshi Ohira Memorial Prize in 1995. Naughton received his PhD in economics from Yale University.

Akos Rona-Tas is associate professor of sociology at the University of California, San Diego, and a research associate at Met@risk, INRA, Paris. He is the author of the book *Great Surprise of the Small Transformation: Demise of Communism and Rise of the Private Sector in Hungary,* several articles in journals including the *American Sociological Review, American Journal of Sociology, Theory and Society, Socio-Economic Review, Social Science Research,* and *Research on Sociology of Organizations,* as well as various chapters in edited volumes. His current research is on credit and risk analysis.

Dorothy J. Solinger is professor of political science at the University of California, Irvine. She was simultaneously senior adjunct research scholar at the Weatherhead East Asian Institute, Columbia University, from 1991 to 2008. Her most recent book is *States' Gains, Labor's Losses* (Cornell University Press, 2009), which was selected as an Outstanding Academic Title by *Choice* magazine; her book *Contesting Citizenship in Urban China* (University of California Press, 1999) won the Joseph R. Levenson Prize of the Association for Asian Studies for being the best book on twentieth-century China published in 1999. Her current work is on urban poverty in China. She is the author of six single-authored books and editor or coeditor of five other books; she also wrote more than 90 book chapters and articles published in *The China Quarterly, Comparative Politics, World Politics,* and *Modern China,* among other academic journals.

Yang Su is associate professor of sociology at University of California, Irvine. He is the author of *Collective Killings in Rural China during the Cultural Revolution* (University of Cambridge Press, 2011). His recent research work includes "Street as Courtroom: State Accommodation of Labor Protest in South China" (with Xin He, *Law and Society Review,* 2010) and "Adapt or Voice: Class, Guanxi and Protest Perception in Urban China" (with Shizheng Feng, *Journal of Asian Studies,* 2013).

Katherine Verdery is the Julien J. Studley Distinguished Professor of Anthropology at the Graduate Center, City University of New York. She has conducted fieldwork primarily in Romania, on ethnic and national identity, the workings of socialism and the transition from it, the state, and property. Her books include: *Transylvanian Villagers* (1983), *National Ideology under Socialism* (1991), *What Was Socialism, and What Comes Next?* (1996), *The Political Lives of Dead Bodies* (1999), *The Vanishing Hectare* (2003), and *Peasants under Siege* (with Gail Kligman, 2011). Currently she is writing a field memoir based on her Romanian Secret Police file.

Wang Feng is a professor of sociology at the University of California, Irvine, and currently a senior fellow at the Brookings Institution and the director of the Brookings-Tsinghua Center for Public Policy in Beijing. Professor Wang is an expert on China's social and demographic change and on comparative demographic and social history. His recent work on social inequality in China includes *Boundaries and Categories, Rising Inequality in Post-Socialist Urban China* (Stanford University Press, 2008), and *Creating Wealth and Poverty in Post-Socialist China* (coedited with Deborah Davis, Stanford University Press, 2009), and his work on demographic change in China includes "The Demographic Factor in China's Transitions" (with Andrew Mason, included in Loren Brandt and Thomas Rawski, eds., *China's Great Economic Transformations*, Cambridge University Press, 2008).

Robert P. Weller is professor and chair of anthropology and a research associate at the Institute on Culture, Religion and World Affairs at Boston University. He is the author of *Alternate Civilities: Chinese Culture and the Prospects for Democracy* (1999) and *Discovering Nature: Globalization and Environmental Culture in China and Taiwan* (2006). His next book, currently in press and coauthored with Adam Seligman, is *Rethinking Pluralism: Ritual, Experience, and Ambiguity*. Weller's present research focuses on the role of religion in creating public social benefits in Chinese communities in China, Malaysia, and Taiwan.

Sharon L. Wolchik is professor of political science and international affairs at George Washington University. She has published numerous articles and several books on Central and East European politics and is the author, with Valerie J. Bunce, of *Defeating Authoritarian Leaders in Postcommunist Countries* (Cambridge University Press, 2011). She recently completed a summer fellowship at the Woodrow Wilson International Center for Scholars focusing on links between activists in the electoral revolutions in the postcommunist world and in the Middle East and North Africa. She is also currently comparing mass mobilizations in communist and postcommunist Europe and Eurasia with recent protests in the Middle East and North Africa with Valerie Bunce.

Socialism Vanquished, Socialism Challenged

Introduction

Postsocialist Trajectories in Comparative Perspective

NINA BANDELJ AND DOROTHY J. SOLINGER

The events of 1989 stimulated what—by virtue of their vast geographic scope as well as their foundational challenges—turned out to be among the most dramatic transformations of both political and economic institutions in the twentieth century: the collapse of communist regimes and socialist economies in the Soviet Union and its satellite states, on the one hand, and a crisis that set the stage for what became a deepening yet also a partial reorientation of already initiated, path-breaking changes in China, on the other hand. However unlikely the prospects for a fundamental reconfiguration of regimes may have seemed at the outset, it soon became apparent that the Central and East European countries, Russia and the rest of the former Soviet bloc, and China at that point had all embarked on what became nothing short of revolutionary changes over the subsequent two decades. The mission of this volume is to provide a set of in-depth, interdisciplinary treatments of some of the issues at the center of the political, economic, and social transformations that unfolded in these nations over the two decades from 1989 to 2009.

The book was born when an ensemble of leading scholars prepared papers for a late 2009 conference on the broad theme of postsocialist developmental trajectories out of socialism, each in accord with his or her own disciplinary calling and regional specialization. Each appraised one of the following themes in one or more of the countries in question: how politics has been reinstitutionalized, how state-societal relations have been recast, how economic systems have performed at the macro level, how economic behavior has been reoriented at the micro level, and how social institutions have changed. For each of these five topics—political institutions, state-society relations, economic systems, economic behavior, and social institutions—we have a pair, one chapter on several countries from the former Soviet bloc followed by one on China.

In macro terms, the collection addresses the large query that guided our project: Just how much—and in what ways—did the earth-rattling events of 1989 matter for the 20 years that ensued in their wake in what are currently the countries of Central and Eastern Europe, the new states of the Former Soviet Union, and in the People's Republic of China (PRC)? In what disparate forms did these momentous happenings leave an imprint? We start by reviewing previous scholarship, highlighting distinctive, relevant contributions already made in the literature on the political, economic, and social transformations that took place after 1989. While this research has been voluminous, at the same time, it has rarely drawn comparisons across this sizable region nor has it simultaneously pitted the experiences of the countries of the former Soviet bloc against those that have evolved over this time in China. Our volume takes on precisely this mission; our conclusion is that the role of the state in the two halves of our comparison—that is, the former Soviet bloc and China—has evolved in substantially different ways since 1989. Our venture yields a picture of a strengthened state since 1989 in China next to one that has undergone retrenchment in the formerly communist European and Eurasian countries. We offer a brief summary discussion of these issues in the volume's postscript.

Two caveats are in order. First, we recognize that the contributing scholars whose specialty is China tended to take on ambitious chunks of behavior in their appraisals, while those writing on Eastern Europe examined concrete, empirically rooted alterations that took place over the 20 years, and they present more specific, fine-grained analyses of particular processes and events instead. These dissimilar approaches reflect the differential accessibility of the respective societies and their rulerships, and, related to China's relative elusiveness, the disparate styles of scholarship in Soviet-Eastern European studies versus in China studies. Second, we do not strive to present a comprehensive coverage of every pertinent topic for each place discussed; rather, we have aimed at offering telling probes into our five thematic areas of inquiry. Following a brief literature review, the last section of this introduction provides a summary of the chapters, with both of these sections grouped in accord with each of our themes.

Systemic Change: A Review of the Literature

Political Transformations

The wave of communist regime collapses in Central and Eastern Europe after 1989 were startling to external observers who all had failed to anticipate such dramatic change. It is notable that only a few years before 1989 Samuel Huntington (1984) had concluded that democratization was less likely to occur in Eastern Europe than elsewhere in the world. In retrospect, scholars have tried to make sense of how communist downfall came about there; they have researched how the democratization that happened can be used to reevaluate assumptions and arguments developed on the basis of other historical cases; and they have investigated the causes for the disparate outcomes in different countries within the former Soviet region following 1989.

While social scientists have produced an extensive body of literature proposing explanations for the causes that drove the regimes' demise in the former Soviet Union and its satellite states, there are no clear answers. Debate has arisen over whether the breakdown was inevitable because of internal, mostly economic, contradictions within the system writ large or whether it was due instead to historical contingencies beyond that system's control. Moreover, it has been asked, is this a query whose answer can be generalized? If not, why not (Szelenyi and Szelenyi 1994; Walder 1994; Verdery 1996; Bunce 1999; Kaminski 1999)? For Sovietologists in particular, the inquiry has been about why the 70-year-old Soviet Union unraveled in so short a period of time, since, though it had major problems as of 1985, these did not appear to constitute a threatening crisis of survival (Whitefield 1993; Brown 1996, 2007; Hough 1997; Odom 1998; Solnick 1998; English 2000; Hahn 2002; Kotkin 2003).

Scholarly research has also examined how the transitions from communism occurred and the impact of these moves. Based on the experiences of countries in Latin America and South Europe that initiated what has been dubbed the "third wave of democratization" (Huntington 1991), it was hypothesized that regime changes in Central and Eastern Europe that were achieved through negotiations eventuated in power-sharing arrangements between elite factions (Linz and Stepan 1996). While early empirical studies found support for this so-called pacted-transition hypothesis (Welsh 1994), Michael McFaul (2002) has argued that when we take into account the whole socialist region, including those former Soviet bloc countries that have been less successful at democratization, and then examine the persistence of dictatorship as well as the emergence of democracy, we see that it was the noncooperative, rather than the negotiated, transitions that turned out to be most effective. According to McFaul (2002), the process transpired as a simple power game: "Democracy emerged...in countries where democrats enjoyed a decisive power advantage." This interpretation is in line with Valerie Bunce's (2003) conclusion that the most successful transitions in the postcommunist context involved a sharp break with the old order.

In addition to the importance of power shifts among elites as an aspect of understanding communist regime collapse, there are other internal, domestic factors that researchers have addressed. Some look at the role that the masses and that collective protest performed in political change (McSweeney and Tempest 1993; Ekiert and Kubik 1999). Other scholars have stressed external influences, including the political opportunity for oppositional challenges created by the loosening of the Soviet grip on the satellite states once Mikhail Gorbachev came to power (Niklasson 1994; Bunce 1999) and the "demonstration effect," whereby circumstances in neighboring countries appear to have influenced domestic behavior (de Nevers 2003).

Yet another critical external factor was the role of international organizations (Zielonka and Pravda 2001; Wejnert 2005); in particular, the European Union (EU) has played a major part in fostering democratization in Central and Eastern Europe, and also in the Baltic countries of Estonia, Latvia, and Lithuania (Hyde-Price 1994; Kurtz and Barnes 2002; Schimmelfennig and Sedelmeier 2005; Grabbe 2006; Schimmelfennig et al. 2006). Soon after 1989, as many as ten postcommunist East European countries set out upon EU preaccession reforms, a process that was followed by accession negotiations. Applying the pressure of conditionality, the EU "routinely vetted candidate countries for their democratic credentials" (Cirtautas and Schimmelfennig 2010) and demanded their compliance with EU legislation (*acquis communautaire*) before they were permitted to become members in one or the other of two historic EU enlargements, the first in 2005 and the second in 2007. The culminating alignment of their legal systems with those in the western half of the continent meant that the EU left an important imprint, not just on the new political systems but also on what became the altered economic and social policies of Central and Eastern Europe and of the Baltic states.

While we do not address this issue in the present volume, we take note here of a body of scholarship that examines the nature of nascent democracy in Central and Eastern Europe. Writers on this topic find that early efforts were marked by the creation of a plethora of political parties as well as by the regeneration and persistence of communist parties. For instance, in the second or third round of elections, former communist parties returned to power in Poland, Hungary, Lithuania, and Bulgaria (Orenstein 1998; Grzymala-Busse 2002). The widespread appeal of nationalist parties in all the postsocialist European countries, with the exception of Hungary, was another trend; analysts discovered that these parties also often won representation in government (Verdery 1996).

More recently, Grzymala-Busse (2007) documented a divergence in the patterns of political party consolidation across the region, from the two-bloc party competition that took root in the Czech Republic and in Hungary to the constantly reconfiguring party systems in Latvia and Poland. Extant explanations target variation in electoral institutions (where these exist), voter and constituency cleavages, and specific political legacies to account for these differences. One of the persistent foci in discussing political transformations in the former Soviet bloc countries has been historical legacies, or path dependence, and how "resource endowments and institutions that precede the choice of democratic institutions have a distinct impact on the observable political process under the new democratic regime" (Kitschelt et al. 1999; see also Ekiert and Hanson 2003).

The democratization of Central and Eastern Europe has not been matched in the former Soviet Union republics, with the exception of the Baltic states. Even in the core state of the former Soviet Union, Russia, an early experiment with democracy (1906–1917) was short lived, and the country steadily mutated in the direction of authoritarian rule thereafter. Why such a divergence? Did democratic institutions abort in Russia because the time of their intended birth was simultaneous with a near economic collapse, such that infant political institutions were simply discredited from the start? Or, in contrast to what happened in some Eastern European states, is the best explanation that there was a near lack of historical experience with democracy in Russia and an underdevelopment of civil society? Or, again, was it the peculiar nature of economic reforms in Russia in the 1990s and a resulting concentration of economic power in the hands of a few oligarchs that led to the resurgence of overriding state power under Vladimir Putin? Trying yet one more avenue of exploration, do we see a replay of the nineteenth-century cultural controversies between Slavophiles and Westernizers, in which Slavophiles rejected the West and sought to establish a uniquely Russian style of rule, as some maintain? All these possibilities have been put forward as explanations (Orttung 1995; Tismeanu ed. 1995; Connor 1996; Cook 1997, 2007; McFaul et al. 2004; Evans et al. 2005; Fish 2005).

When we look at China, we have an entirely different puzzle to unravel. Researchers investigating that country have attempted to plumb the roots not of a downfall but instead of the surprising endurance of communist rule there, attempting to account for the sources of the legitimacy that props up the party and its power, or, if not legitimacy, then to discover some other roots of socialism's longevity there (O'Brien 1990; Shirk 1993; Solinger 1993; Walder 1995; Goldman and MacFarquhar 1999; Wank 1999; Fewsmith 2001; Peerenboom 2002; Perry and Selden 2003; Gries and Rosen 2004; Naughton and Yang 2004; Pei 2006; Li 2007; Tsai, K. 2007; Tsai, L. 2007). All manner of transformation has occurred in China, including what could be termed political changes—such as the generalized shift from what amounted to totalitarian rule under Mao Zedong to what is much better termed authoritarian rule after his death. But the socialist system persists, at least in grand structure, in rhetoric, and, most critically, in the persistence of rule by the Communist Party. Scholars have studied not just the nature of and the processes permitting and under-girding the tenacity of old institutions and practices but have also debated the reasons for this durability. Some examine lesser changes in the institutions, even as the overall formal framework endures (O'Brien 1990; Shirk 1993; Solinger 1993; Fewsmith 1994; Naughton 1995; White et al. 1996; Oi and Walder 1999; Solinger 1999; Fewsmith 2001; Peerenboom 2002; Dickson 2003; Sun 2004; Yang 2004; Gallagher 2005; Pei 2006; Li 2007; Naughton 2007; Tsai, K. 2007; Li and Ong 2008).

Despite the regime's failure to fall, scholars have disagreed about whether it is tottering under the cumulative weight of official corruption, an unwork-able legal system, regional inequalities, at best only partially genuine electoral reforms at the local levels, accumulating social pressures arising from rapid modernizing reforms, and frightening income gaps (Pei 2006). Quite a dif-ferent perspective, however, asks whether, instead, the Chinese state might be starting to show promising signs of political reform (Peerenboom 2002; Naughton and Yang 2004; Yang 2004; Goldman 2006; Li 2007; Tsai 2007; Mertha 2008). A recent set of essays tracing the lasting influences of what its editors term "Maoism" concludes that tactics introduced during the revolu-tionary and early postrevolutionary periods—from the 1920s through the 1950s—such as local experimentation, flexibility and ad hoc adjustments, and successful tension management—might account for the regime's endurance (Heilmann and Perry 2011). Perhaps the most influential piece to emerge to date is Andrew Nathan's (2003) short musings on what he labeled China's "authoritarian resilience," in which he tags such features as regularized party meetings and predictable succession mechanisms as helping to construct a kind of regime legitimacy that is shoring up an extension of life for the Communist Party.

Economic Transformations

The revolutionary demonstrations of 1989 that produced the collapse of com-munist regimes throughout the former Soviet bloc were followed by a range of proposals about how to transform socialist economies. The debate on this issue can be characterized as one between "shock therapy" reform—in which liberalization and privatization are undertaken simultaneously, speedily, and comprehensively—and a much more gradualist approach.

Neoliberal economists from the West who offered advice to these countries argued for hasty and holistic changes, with a goal to creating markets quickly by eliminating state command of the economy and wiping out the supposed irrationalities of redistribution. These advisers emphasized that the most effi-cient way of organizing an economy is by means of a self-regulating market, and so they encouraged societies that had ousted communists to develop a private property rights regime swiftly through mass privatization. According to economic theory, the release of price and currency controls, the withdrawal of state subsidies, and the liberalization of trade would act to give rise to an economic system largely free of governmental control. That new system, then, was to be coordinated purely by market prices and competition, with a clear incentive structure inducing efficient corporate governance and a rapid restructuring of firms (Boycko, Shleifer, and Vishny 1995).

Advocates of the gradualist approach, on the other hand, criticized shock-therapy recommendations for their authors' assumption that externally manipulated alterations could be induced into these economies as if on a tabula rasa foundation. These analysts argued that it was unlikely that a simple institutional vacuum would be left after the removal of socialist institutions; they also questioned the premise that market institutions could be designed via a blueprint at the systemic level. To this second group of specialists, the process of change was not about destruction and rebuilding *ab initio* but rather about a piecemeal construction of market institutions, which would take time and require the state to play a role. The process would also depend on experimentation and evolutionary learning and incorporate existing social and economic networks and practices (Stark and Bruszt 1998). As sociologist David Stark (1992) famously put it, capitalism should be built not on but with the ruins of socialism.

The shock therapy view of postsocialist transformation rested mainly on the conviction that "markets [will] spring up as soon as central planning bureaucrats vacate the field," as a prominent economic adviser to the region, Jeffrey Sachs (1993: xxi), put it. In contrast, economic sociologists studying economic changes in Central and Eastern Europe and in the former Soviet Union maintained that the state would have to continue to play a critical role in postsocialism, even if it no longer exercised the direct power over economic production and distribution that it had wielded in the past. Aside from ensuring private property rights, postsocialist states would also have to regulate enterprise restructuring (King and Sznajder 2006), provide institutional underpinning for consumer markets (Guseva 2008), and institutionalize the demand for foreign direct investment (Bandelj 2009), according to this second view.

The involvement of former state officials in the process of privatization provided breeding ground for political capitalism (Staniszkis 1991) and corruption, a problem that occurred more extensively in Russia than in Central and Eastern Europe. The Russian nomenklatura elite, in abandoning socialism, managed to retain power, as its members plunged into insider privatization while paying little heed to first fashioning the necessary political and legal institutional framework that markets require for healthy functioning. State officials in Russia lacked the tools to monitor market behavior; they did, however, have the clout to engage in predatory practices (Nolan 1996; Frye 2000; Hough 2001; Rutland 2001; Barnes 2006). A way of making sense of this process is to view the collapse of the socialist state in Russia as having resulted in an involution of society that brought anarchy to production while introducing barter alongside market exchange in the process (Burawoy 1996; Woodruff 1999; Southworth 2004). These developments amount to what King and Szelenyi (2005) have called a neopatrimonial postcommunist system, in contrast to what they term the neoliberal system that unfolded in Central Europe.

Despite the difference in type of economic transition, all of the former Soviet bloc countries suffered major economic downturns immediately after 1989. Still, in the first decade after 1989, the period of the so-called first phase of reforms (O'Dwyer and Kovalcik 2007), the Central and East European countries were markedly more successful economically than Russia was, where, for instance, economic managers did not succeed in passing the 1989 gross domestic product (GDP) level until 2007 (Szelenyi and Wilk 2010).

As opposed to what took place in these other states, from the outset the process of undertaking economic reforms in China was quite different. In general, it is safe to say that in the nations once bound to the Soviet Union economic changes were aimed at rapidly transforming the economy in a market-based direction. In China, by way of contrast, the reforms were gradual and piecemeal, with the result that the economy "grew out of the plan," to quote Barry Naughton's famous phrase.

After the death of the nearly omnipotent revolutionary, Mao Zedong, his successor, Deng Xiaoping, initiated economic reforms in 1979. A progressive accumulation of measures that state leaders installed to loosen the plan was directed at a liberalization and decentralization of the Chinese economy, although both of these processes remained at least at first strongly supervised by the communist state. Early steps included a redesign of the organization of agricultural production and the creation, in 1980, of four special economic zones to promote foreign investment on highly attractive terms. These moves set into motion a process that, within a decade, had created the sprouts of a capitalist-like economy.

With the mid-1990s, further important reforms were enacted, such as fostering a unified internal and external exchange rate, setting uniform tax rates irrespective of enterprises' ownership status, and restructuring state-owned enterprises (Naughton 2007). Following the first steps initially taken in 1979, the country was increasingly opened up to foreign investment as time went by. While there had been practically no foreign companies in China before the 1980s, by the new millennium the country had become the most popular destination for direct foreign investment in the world (Wang 2001).

As a consequence, the degree of state ownership in the Chinese economy steadily decreased over the years. By mid-1995, 90,000 small state-owned enterprises had been transferred to the nonstate sector by merger, sale, or lease. Despite larger steps toward privatization over time, the ongoing existence of growth plans—even if much more "indicative" as compared with the mandatory plans of the past—exemplifies the substantial control and direction that the state still has over the economy. Given this ongoing state involvement and the government's persistent favoritism toward state enterprises, many observers resist labeling the Chinese economy as full marketized (Gallagher 2005). Nonetheless, or perhaps precisely because of such state direction, the economy managed to grow steadily at an average rate of 10 percent per annum for most of the period.

Thus, the reforms spearheaded continuous rapid economic growth, propelling China into the ranks of the top world economies in terms of nominal GDP value. All told, this pattern of growth challenges conventional wisdom, which holds that clearly defined and enforced private property rights are essential to economic growth. From that perspective, enormous economic success, despite the persistence of state ownership of major productive assets, presents a conundrum. Part of the answer here lies in the leadership's use of a form of state-affiliated private ownership paired with a steadily growing reliance on markets. Together these factors help to account for the achievements observed.

Social Transformations

A third strand of research on postsocialist transformations, especially in sociology, is about their social consequences. At the core of this segment of inquiry is the so-called market transition debate about who the winners and who the losers have been in the path to a market economy. Victor Nee (1989) provided one of the first statements to frame this controversy, theorizing that success in the new market economies depends on human capital rather than on the political capital that once made for an advantage in the former, redistributive socialist system. On this basis, Nee predicted that system transition would bring declining returns to communist political elites. Nevertheless, several subsequent studies of stratification in Central and Eastern Europe and Russia have found that the elite of the old regime has been able to convert its political capital into an economic advantage and has even benefited from ongoing social changes (Staniszkis 1991; Rona-Tas 1994; Szelenyi and Kostello 1996; Hellman 1998; Gerber and Hout 1998; Gerber 2002). Work on China has also documented that the possession of prereform political power can easily be used for building up one's economic power (Ding 2000a, 2000b; Walder 2003).

Connected to the role that the former elite was able to play following market reforms is a more general debate about the emergence of new forms of social inequality after 1989. Although socialism did not erase all inequalities (Szelenyi 1978), especially those between the nomenklatura and the rest of the society, scholars overwhelmingly agree that inequality was substantially lower during socialism—when private ownership had been eliminated—than it was in other systems at comparable levels of industrial development (Heyns 2005). In addition to its basis in public ownership, this relative equality was largely the outcome of socialist guarantees of full employment, universal pensions, and free education and health care.

In the first decade after 1989, most Eastern European countries retained relatively extensive systems of social protection, at least as compared to what obtained in the developing countries in Latin America and East Asia (Haggard and Kaufman 2008), perhaps because the first-phase reforms in Central and Eastern Europe aimed more at building market institutions than at designing what would have been more politically controversial reworkings of social institutions. After 2000, however, leaders in these countries realized that alterations in welfare and other social institutions were necessary, even if they would be unpopular, and they went on to undertake them (Szelenyi and Wilk 2010). By 2009, 20 years after 1989, postsocialist states had significantly retrenched their social provisions compared to what they had offered in their socialist pasts; they were also registering higher levels of income inequality than any of them had seen before.

It is notable that, despite other differences between the former Soviet bloc states and China, the significant amount of privatization that took place in them all must be connected to the surges in inequality they share today. Bandelj and Mahutga (2010) found that, in the period between 1990 and 2000, income inequality rose more in those Central and Eastern European countries that had more substantially expanded the private sector and that had more vigorously abandoned the institutions of the old redistributive state. Inequalities were also higher in states with larger proportions of ethnonational minorities whose members were subjected to various forms of discrimination. Bandelj and Mahutga also demonstrated that those countries that opened more widely to foreign capital penetration became more unequal. In reviewing the literature on postsocialist inequalities, Barbara Heyns (2005) concluded that inequalities by age, education, health status, and across the urban-rural divide increased in the first decade after 1989, while gender differences appear to have declined (but see Krizkova et al. 2010 on contrasting evidence for gender wage inequality).

Also in China, market reforms have come with gross inequalities, even if they almost immediately brought new prosperity to the countryside, eliminating poverty for approximately 200 million people within less than two decades. A phenomenal rise in living standards took place for almost every population group, as well as huge increases in GDP per capita (Brandt and Rawski 2008). But these improvements also widened the gap between the richest and the poorest, most notably between urban and rural areas, where the ratio of urban to rural incomes has become somewhere in the range of 3.3 to 1 (Davis and Wang 2008). The country has also seen new and ever-expanding income gaps among regions, along with the emergence and formation of what for post-1949 China are novel social strata, such as state-affiliated private entrepreneurs (Khan and Riskin 2001; Bernstein and Lu 2003; Dickson 2003; K. Tsai 2007; Wang 2008; Hu and Wang 1999).

But it was only in the second decade or so after 1989 that clear winners and losers emerged. As in Russia, the winners have been mainly comprised of so-labeled red capitalists, or communist party members who had gone into business (Hellman 1998). There is a growing literature on resistance to the regime on the part of the losers (and sometimes also from middle-class elements, who perceive that their immediate economic interests are endangered) in China (Perry 2002; Bernstein and Lu 2003; Perry and Selden 2003; O'Brien and Li 2006; Lee 2007; Hurst 2009). Not only have regional inequalities persisted, despite political elites' efforts to bolster the economies of the poorer areas (Wang and Hu 1999), but even intraurban inequalities have become enormous, in a marked contrast with the past (Wu et al. 2010).

The Present Volume

This brief review of 20 years of scholarship on political, economic, and social issues in postsocialist European and Eurasian countries and in China highlights some of the central issues that can guide comparisons of the situations in places where socialism, at least in name and pretense, has so far lasted with the numerous countries where it has not: the functions and nature of older versus emergent institutions in precipitating collapse or in sustaining dominance; in paving the way for fundamental change or in allowing for adaptation within continuity; and in facilitating the accumulation of new power and the creation of new pockets of wealth, or in maintaining in submission those historically disadvantaged and even in creating new axes of inequality.

While it turned out that the chapters addressed most of these issues, the volume unavoidably was shaped by the interests and specialties of its individual contributors. As is usually the case, the researchers' present interests, plus their respective methodological approaches, fashioned the way each of them conceptualized the outcomes of the sweeping changes that unfolded over a 20-year interval between circumstances in the pivotal year 1989 and those in these places two decades later. The tendency of Eastern Europeanists to theorize about a subset of the polities that were once a part of the Soviet bloc, on the one hand, and China specialists having only the one country to cover, on the other, made the level of country detail in the comparisons uneven and the degree of ambition among the parts of the whole enterprise somewhat unbalanced.

Nonetheless, it was possible to tease out from this group of treatments five thematic clusters that organize our broad comparison of political, economic, and social developments in the countries of the former Soviet bloc, on the one hand, and China, on the other. These five clusters, forming the five sections of the volume, are: reinstitutionalizing politics, recasting state-society relations, reforming economic systems, transforming economic behavior, and reshaping social institutions.

The activity associated with the first theme, reinstitutionalizing politics, veered in diametrically opposed directions in the two regions, with the nations comprising the European segment swerving toward democracy—if not all simultaneously or fully—as part of a grand process spurred by the diffusion that Bunce and Wolchik delineate in their chapter in the present volume. But in China, though intellectuals were aware of what went on overseas, no receptivity or replication of any political consequence was permitted to take place. Retaining their dominance, China's leaders saw to it that any politically edged cultural or intellectual connections its populace forged abroad during the 1980s were far briefer in time, more limited in scope, and more distant in space as compared with linkages abroad that intellectuals in Eastern Europe were weaving at the same time. Besides, the possibilities for learning from abroad were greatly undermined when people in China who were involved in any kind of external politically colored liaisons had to face ongoing resistance and repression and constant warnings from officials even before 1989.

Once what was happening at Tiananmen Square in 1989 became associated in the leadership's view with democracy—a competing political system that threatened the continuity of party rule—all alternative "political options" were "closed off," to quote Fewsmith's contribution to this project. Though at several points in the 1980s local elections were pioneered in China, they were just at the village or urban district levels, and to this day, nationwide, voting has remained stuck in the grass roots (except for scattered experiments in a few townships, the level just above the villages).

Yet in postsocialist Europe it was precisely elections themselves, along with mass protests, that pushed the turnover forward, write Bunce and Wolchik. While "key players" could defect from the ruling party, survive, and even add weight to the force of the protest in Central and Eastern Europe, when top

Chinese party leader Zhao Ziyang expressed sympathy for the dissenters, his once-colleagues repudiated him, allowing him just to retain his party membership but removing him from all his positions and placing him under house arrest, which continued until his death. As Naughton points out in his chapter, "Tiananmen brought the contradiction [that is, a deep split within the leadership that had lain just beneath the surface in the politics of the 1980s] into the open."

As for the second theme, recasting state-societal relations, again we find antithetical outcomes, in both cases molded by what were variously changed states. True, underlying both Verdery and Weller's chapters in part 2 of this volume is a picture of a state correcting—or endeavoring to correct—former tyranny as it tries to pursue governance in a changed environment. Both authors also portray tinkerings with the truth. But despite these perhaps superficial likenesses, the upshot of the efforts amounted to quite contrasting routes out of totalitarianism for the polities involved. In China, this takes the form of a willingness of the leadership (usually just at local levels) to wink at societal formations its members consider innocuous, pretending they do not exist. But in Central and Eastern Europe, in the words of Verdery, "lustration promotes a form of truth that is absolutist," as it aims at (though, alas, does not achieve) a new measure of "governmental transparency." For the procedure, Verdery asserts, perversely serves to "render politics more opaque."

By a not wholly dissimilar logic—in both cases, things are not what they seem to be—what Weller labels China's new "responsive authoritarianism" or "authoritarian corporatism" entails false registrations (in which the owners of private firms register their businesses as collective ones, for instance) and pretense, in the interest of gaining popular feedback. While Chinese nongovernmental activists in the fields of religion and the environment "push the margins of the law," the "cleansing" and banning rituals of Central and Eastern Europe represent an effort at creating a rule of law from scratch in an allegedly more "pure" polity, according to Verdery. In the process, "the instruments of state power and surveillance [are brought] directly into the hands of any citizen," as a new style of blackballing becomes "a weapon for competition," in Verdery's words. While Weller writes of citizens becoming apolitical within a purposely anti-Maoist atmosphere of "depoliticization," Verdery's subjects, ordinary citizens, have been mutated from being powerless objects into being "part of the surveillance," in a kind of ultrapoliticization. One could characterize the difference here as a case of citizens being prodded to become institutionalized actors in Eastern Europe—ironically as participants in a witch hunt of sorts—versus citizens acting only at the sufferance of the state's officials in China.

The third section of the book, on reforming economic systems, focuses on the macro dimension of transforming postsocialist economies. Borocz's exposition in this part of the book offers data to underpin a claim that economies in all of the countries that made up the Soviet bloc contracted almost immediately upon the collapse of socialism, while only some of them rebounded. Naughton's piece, to the contrary, outlines a story of nearly continuous high-speed growth in China. Especially after 1992, a re-energized state launched harsh marketizing reforms, imposing costs on vulnerable populations, in the interest of reinforcing the state and the party and of fortifying the power of those who managed these institutions, reasserting the capacity of the leadership for repression in the process.

Part 4, on transforming economic behavior, turns to microeconomic factors and reveals a similar opposition between less and more intrusive and effective states. Rona-Tas finds that the introduction of capitalist consumer credit was possible solely because the "role of the state [in the economy] was curtailed." Variously, in China, according to Huang, while private ownership and competition have been permitted to exist, favoritism of many sorts undergirds the ongoing superiority of the state sector and its enormous enterprises, significantly undercutting the opportunities and the growth rates of private firms. Granted, both of these research sites have been witnessing the birth of various styles of capitalism. But in China this is a new economic system that is spreading on a much larger Chinese canvas, where giant-sized state firms still dominate the critical sectors. In Central and Eastern Europe, to the contrary, the economic system as a whole has been totally altered, severely cutting back the role of the state as this happens.

The fifth and last component of the volume concerns reshaping social institutions, with the word *institutions* used in the broad, social scientific sense of established, repetitive, and predictable norms and practices. Gerber's analysis of marriage and fertility patterns is best described by what he characterizes as "the demise of state socialism," the "destruction" of old institutions and policies. In contrast to this, we see a Chinese polity buoyed, as Wang and Su phrase it, by the "rising might of the Chinese economy," the result of the "expanded influence of the Chinese state over the economy." While Rona-Tas sees the demise of state welfare as the engine for redistribution in Central and Eastern Europe, Wang and Su uncover an upswing in governmental welfare spending in China, though both sites have shared a conspicuous surge in social inequality.

***

Since the transformative events of 1989, scholars have queried the nature and the variable processes of the political, economic, and social transformations that have taken place in nations once—versus places yet—ruled by communist parties. While many an analyst has attempted to detail the character of the transformations in specific countries and others have provided comparisons within the former Soviet bloc, little research has ventured specifically to compare and find contrasts among the broad socialist regions of the Former Soviet Union and Central and Eastern Europe, on one side, and the PRC, on the other. Based on reflections made two decades after 1989, this volume engages in just such an inquiry.

Our broad comparisons across several substantive areas in very diverse regions will provide the grounds for making a general statement about the varied roles of the state in disparate postsocialist trajectories in the years after 1989. All told, the chapters collected display not differences in degree across the fields of inquiry but instead, much more broadly, significant and marked divergences. Dividing once socialist states and societies that went on to install democracy from a place that (at least at the level of discourse and continuing communist party preeminence) has remained "socialist," 1989 was about more than a wholesale transformation of regime type across all these countries. It was also a moment that laid the groundwork for the spectacle of a sturdy state in China, and, by comparison, of a much diminished one in the former Soviet bloc, with all the disparities in economic and social life that this gross dissimilarity has entailed. We summarize these differences, along with lessons about the fate of the postsocialist state, in a short postscript to the book.

References

Bandelj, Nina. 2009. "The Global Economy as Instituted Process: The Case of Central and Eastern Europe." *American Sociological Review* 74:128–149.

Bandelj, Nina and Matthew C. Mahutga. 2010. "How Socio-Economic Changes Shape Income Inequality in Central and Eastern Europe." *Social Forces* 88(5):2133–2161.

Barnes, Andrew. 2006. *Owning Russia: The Struggle over Factories, Farms, and Power.* Ithaca, N.Y.: Cornell University Press.

Bernstein, Thomas P. and Xiaobo Lu. 2003. *Taxation without Representation in Contemporary Rural China.* New York: Cambridge University Press.

Blanchard, Olivier, Rudiger Dornbusch, Paul Krugman, Richard Layard, and Lawrence Summers. 1991. *Reform in Eastern Europe.* Cambridge, Mass.: Cambridge University Press.

Borocz, Jozsef. 2000. "Informality Rules." *East European Politics and Societies* 14(2):348–380.

Boycko, Maxim, Andrei Shleifer, and Robert Vishny. 1995. *Privatizing Russia.* Cambridge, Mass.: The MIT Press.

Brandt, Loren and Thomas G. Rawski, eds. 2008. *China's Great Economic Transformation.* New York: Cambridge University Press.

Brown, Archie. 1996. *The Gorbachev Factor.* New York: Oxford University Press.

———. 2007. *Seven Years That Changed the World: Perestroika in Perspective.* New York: Oxford University Press.

Bunce, Valerie 1999. *Subversive Institutions: Collapse of Socialism and the State.* Cambridge, U.K.: Cambridge University Press.

Bunce, Valerie. 2003. "Rethinking Recent Democratization: Lessons from the Postcommunist Experience." *World Politics* 55(2):167–192.

Burawoy, Michael. 1996. "The State and Economic Involution: Russia through a Chinese Lens." *World Development* 24(6):1105–1117.

Cirtautas, Arista Maria and Frank Schimmelfennig. 2010. "Europeanisation before and after Accession: Conditionality, Legacies and Compliance." *Europe-Asia Studies* 62(3):421–441.

Connor, Walter D. 1996. *Tattered Banners: Labor, Conflict and Corporatism in Post-Communist Russia.* Boulder, Colo.: Westview Press.

Cook, Linda J. 1997. *Labor and Liberalization: Trade Unions in the New Russia.* New York: Twentieth Century Fund.

———. 2007. *Postcommunist Welfare States: Reform Politics in Russia and Eastern Europe.* Ithaca, N.Y.: Cornell University Press.

Davis, Deborah and Wang, Feng, eds. 2008. *Creating Wealth and Poverty in Post-Socialist China.* Palo Alto, Calif.: Stanford University Press.

de Nevers, Renee. 2003. *Comrades No More: The Seeds of Change in Eastern Europe.* Cambridge, Mass.: The MIT Press.

Dickson, Bruce. 2003. *Red Capitalists in China: The Party, Private Entrepreneurs and Prospects for Political Change.* New York: Cambridge University Press.

Ding, Xueliang. 2000a. "Systemic Irregularity and Spontaneous Property Transformation in the Chinese Financial System." *The China Quarterly* 163:655–676.

———. 2000b. "The Informal Asset Stripping of Chinese State Firms." *The China Journal* 43:1–28.

Ekiert, Grzegorz and Stephen Hanson. 2003. *Capitalism and Democracy in Central and Eastern Europe: Assessing the Legacy of Communist Rule.* New York: Cambridge University Press.

Ekiert, Grzegorz and Jan Kubik. 1999. *Rebellious Civil Society: Popular Protest and Democratic Consolidation in Poland, 1989–1993.* Ann Arbor: University of Michigan Press.

English, Robert D. 2000. *Russia and the Idea of the West: Gorbachev, Intellectuals and the End of the Cold War.* New York: Columbia University Press.

Evans, Alfred B. et al. 2005. *Russian Civil Society: A Critical Assessment.* Armonk, N.Y.: M. E. Sharpe.

Fewsmith, Joseph. 1994. *Dilemmas of Reform in China: Political Conflict and Economic Debate.* Armonk, N.Y.: M. E. Sharpe.

———. 2001. *China Since Tiananmen: The Politics of Transition.* New York: Cambridge University Press.

———. 2005. *Democracy Derailed: The Failure of Open Politics.* New York: Cambridge University Press.

Frye, Timothy. 2000. *Brokers and Bureaucrats: Building Market Institutions in Russia.* Ann Arbor: University of Michigan Press.

Gallagher, Mary. 2005. *Contagious Capitalism: Globalization and the Politics of Labor in China.* Princeton, N.J.: Princeton University Press.

Gerber, Theodore P. 2002. "Structural Change and Post-socialist Stratification: Labor Market Transitions in Contemporary Russia." *American Sociological Review* 67:629–659.

Gerber, Theodore P. and Michael Hout. 1998. "More Shock than Therapy: Market Transition, Employment, and Income in Russia, 1991–1995." *American Journal of Sociology* 104(1):1–50.

Goldman, Merle. 2006. *From Comrade to Citizen.* Cambridge, Mass.: Harvard University Press.

Goldman, Merle and Roderick MacFarquhar. 1999. *The Paradoxes of Post-Mao Reform in China.* Cambridge, Mass.: Harvard University Press.

Grabbe, Heather. 2006. *The EU's Transformative Power: Europeanization through Conditionality in Central and Eastern Europe.* Basingstoke, U.K.: Palgrave Macmillan.

Gries, Peter Hayes and Stanley Rosen, eds. 2004. *State and Society in 21st Century China: Crisis, Contention and Legitimation.* New York: Routledge/Curzon.

Grzymala-Busse, Anna M. 2002. *Redeeming the Communist Past: The Regeneration of Communist Parties in East Central Europe*. Cambridge, U.K.: Cambridge University Press.

———. 2007. *Rebuilding Leviathan: Party Competition and State Exploitation in Post-Communist Democracies*. Cambridge, U.K.: Cambridge University Press.

Guseva, Alya. 2008. *Into the Red: The Birth of the Credit Card Market in Postcommunist Russia*. Stanford, Calif.: Stanford University Press.

Haggard. Stephan and Robert R. Kaufman. 2008. *Development, Democracy, and Welfare States: Latin America, East Asia, and Eastern Europe*. Princeton, N.J.: Princeton University Press.

Hahn, Gordon. 2002. *Russia's Revolution from Above: Reform, Transition, and Revolution in the Fall of the Soviet Communist Regime*. New Brunswick, N.J.: Transaction Publishers.

Heilmann, Sebastian and Elizabeth J. Perry, eds., 2011. *Mao's Invisible Hand: The Political Foundations of Adaptive Governance in China*. Cambridge, Mass.: Harvard University Press.

Hellman, Joel S. 1998. "Winners Take All: the Politics of Partial Reform in Postcommunist Transitions." *World Politics* 50(2): 203–234.

Heyns, Barbara. 2005. "Emerging Inequalities in Central and Eastern Europe." *Annual Review of Sociology* 31:163–197.

Hough, Jerry F. 1997. *Democratization and Revolution in the USSR, 1985–1991*. Washington, D.C.: Brookings Institution Press.

———. 2001. *The Logic of Economic Reform in Russia*. Washington, D.C.: Brookings Institution Press.

Huntington, Samuel P. 1984. "Will More Countries Become Democratic?" *Political Science Quarterly* 99:193–218.

———. 1991. *The Third Wave: Democratization in the Late 20th Century*. Norman: University of Oklahoma Press.

Hurst, William. 2009. *The Chinese Worker after Socialism*. New York: Cambridge University Press.

Hyde-Price, Adrian G. V. 1994. "Democratization in Eastern Europe: The External Dimension." In *Democratization in Eastern Europe: Domestic and International Perspectives*, Geoffrey Pridham and Tatu Vanhanen, eds., 220–255. London: Routledge.

Kaminski, Marek M. 1999. "How Communism Could Have Been Saved: Formal Analysis of Electoral Bargaining in Poland 1989." *Public Choice* 98:83–109.

Khan, Azizur and Carl Riskin 2001. *Inequality and Poverty in China in the Age of Globalization*. New York: Oxford University Press.

King, Lawrence P., and Ivan Szelenyi. 2005. "Postcommunist Economic Systems." In *Handbook of Economic Sociology*, Neil Smelser and Richard Swedberg, eds., 206–232. Princeton, N.J.: Princeton University Press.

King, Lawrence, and Aleksandra Sznajder. 2006. "The State-Led Transition to Liberal Capitalism: Neoclassical, Organizational, World Systems, and Social Structural Explanations of Poland's Economic Success." *American Journal of Sociology* 112(3):751-801.

Kitschelt, Herbert, Zdenka Mansfeldova, Radoslaw Markowski, and Gabor Toka, eds. 1999. *Post-Communist Party Systems: Competition, Representation, and Inter-Party Cooperation*. Cambridge, U.K.: Cambridge University Press.

Kotkin, Stephen. 2003. *Armageddon Averted: The Soviet Collapse, 1970–2007*. New York: Oxford University Press.

Krizkova, Alena, Andrew Penner, and Trond Petersen. 2010. "The Legacy of Equality and the Weakness of Law: Within-Job Gender Wage Inequality in the Czech Republic." *European Sociological Review* 26:83–95.

Kurtz, Marcus and Andrew Barnes. 2002. "The Political Foundations of Post-Communist Regimes: Marketization, Agrarian Legacies, or International Influences." *Comparative Political Studies* 35(5):524–553.

Lee, Ching Kwan. 2007. *Against the Law: Labor Protests in China's Rustbelt and Sunbelt.* Berkeley: University of California Press.

Li, Cheng, ed. 2007. *China's Changing Political Landscape: Prospects for Democracy.* Washington, D.C.: The Brookings Institution Press.

Linz, Juan and Alfred Stepan. 1996. *Problems of Democratic Transition and Consolidation.* Baltimore, Md.: Johns Hopkins University Press.

McFaul, Michael. 2002. "The Fourth Wave of Democracy and Dictatorship: Noncooperative Transitions in the Postcommunist World." *World Politics* 54(2):212–244.

McFaul, Michael M, et al. 2004. *Between Dictatorship and Democracy: Russian Post-Communist Reforms.* Washington, D.C.: Carnegie Endowment for International Peace.

McSweeney, Dean and Clive Tempest. 1993. "The Political Science of Democratic Transition in Eastern Europe." *Political Studies* (September):408–419.

Mertha, Andrew C. 2008. *China's Water Warriors: Citizen Action and Policy Change.* Ithaca, N.Y.: Cornell University Press.

Nathan, Andrew J. 2003. "Authoritarian Resilience," *Journal of Democracy* 14(1):6–17.

Naughton, Barry J. and Dali L. Yang, eds. 2004. *Holding China Together: China's Economic Transitions and Growth.* New York: Cambridge University Press.

Naughton, Barry. 1995. *Growing out of the Plan: China's Economic Reform, 1978–1993.* New York: Cambridge University Press.

———. 2007. *The Chinese Economy: Transitions and Growth.* Cambridge, Mass.: MIT Press.

Nee, Victor. 1989. "A Theory of Market Transition: From Redistribution to Markets in State Socialism." *American Sociological Review* 54:663–681.

Niklasson, Tomas. 1994. "The Soviet Union and Eastern Europe, 1988–9: Interactions between Domestic Change and Foreign Policy." In *Democratization in Eastern Europe: Domestic and International Perspectives,* Geoffrey Pridham and Tatu Vanhanen, eds., 191–219. London: Routledge.

Nolan, Peter. 1996. *China's Rise, Russia's Fall: Politics, Economics, and Planning in the Transition from Stalinism.* New York: St. Martin's Press.

O'Brien, Kevin J. 1990. *Reform without Liberalization: China's National People's Congress and the Politics of Institutional Change.* New York: Cambridge University Press.

O'Brien, Kevin J. and Lianjiang Li. 2006. *Rightful Resistance in Rural China.* New York: Cambridge University Press.

O'Dwyer, Conor and Branislav Kovalcik 2007. "And the Last Shall Be First: Party System Institutionalization and Second-Generation Economic Reform in Postcommunist Europe." *Studies in Comparative International Development* 41(4):3–26.

Odom, William. 1998. *The Collapse of the Soviet Military* New Haven, Conn.: Yale University Press.

Oi, Jean C. and Andrew G. Walder, eds. 1999. *Property Rights and Economic Reform in China.* Palo Alto, Calif.: Stanford University Press.

Orenstein, Mitchell. 1998. "A Genealogy of Communist Successor Parties in East-Central Europe and the Determinants of Their Success." *East European Politics and Societies* 12(3):472–499.

Orttung, Robert. 1995. *From Leningrad to St. Petersburg.* New York: Palgrave MacMillan.

Peerenboom, Randall. 2002. *China's Long March toward the Rule of Law.* New York: Cambridge University Press.

Pei, Minxin. 2006. *China's Trapped Transition.* Cambridge, Mass.: Harvard University Press.

Perry, Elizabeth J. 2002. *Challenging the Mandate of Heaven: Social Protest and State Power in China.* Armonk, N.Y.: M. E. Sharpe.

Perry, Elizabeth J. and Mark Selden, eds. 2003. *Chinese Society: Conflict and Resistance.* London, U.K.: Routledge/Curzon.

Rona-Tas, Akos. 1994. "The First Shall Be Last? Entrepreneurship and Communist Cadres in the Transition from Socialism." *American Journal of Sociology* 100:40–69.

———. 1997. *The Great Surprise of the Small Transformation*. Ann Arbor: University of Michigan Press.

Rutland, Peter, ed. 2001. *Business and the State in Contemporary Russia*. Boulder, Colo.: Westview Press.

Sachs, Jeffrey. 1993. *Poland's Jump to the Market Economy*. Cambridge, Mass.: The MIT Press.

Schimmelfennig, Frank and Ulrich Sedelmeier. 2005. *The Europeanization of Central and Eastern Europe*. Ithaca, N.Y.: Cornell University Press.

Schimmelfennig, Frank, Stefan Engert, and Heiko Knoebel. 2006. *International Socialization in Europe: European Organizations, Political Conditionality, and Democratic Change*. Basingstoke, U.K.: Palgrave Macmillan.

Shirk, Susan. 1993. *The Political Logic of Economic Reform in China*. Berkeley, Calif.: University of California Press.

Solinger, Dorothy J. 1993. *China's Transition from Socialism*. Armonk, N.Y.: M. E. Sharpe.

———. 1999. *Contesting Citizenship in Urban China: Peasants Migrants, the State and the Logic of the Market*. Berkeley, Calif.: University of California Press.

Solnick, Steve. 1998. *Stealing the State: Control and Collapse in Soviet Institutions*. Cambridge, Mass.: Harvard University Press.

Southworth, Caleb. 2004. "The Development of Post-Soviet Neo-Paternalism in Two Enterprises in Bashkortostan: How Familial-Type Management Moves Firms and Workers away from Labor Markets." In *Russian Transformations: Challenging the Global Narrative*, Leo McCann, ed., 191–208. London: Routledge.

Staniszkis, Jedwiga. 1991. *The Dynamics of Breakthrough*. Berkeley, Calif.: University of California Press.

Stark, David. 1992. "Path Dependence and Privatization Strategies in East Central Europe." *East European Societies and Politics* 6(1):17–54.

Stark, David and Laszlo Bruszt. 1998. *Postsocialist Pathways: Transforming Politics and Property in East Central Europe*. Cambridge, Mass.: Cambridge University Press.

Sun, Yan. 2004. *The Market and Corruption in Contemporary China*. Ithaca, N.Y.: Cornell University Press.

Szelenyi, Ivan. 1978. "Social Inequalities in State Socialist Redistributive Economies." *International Journal of Comparative Sociology* 19:63–87.

Szelenyi, Ivan and Balazs Szelenyi. 1994. "Why Socialism Failed: Toward a Theory of System Breakdown—Causes of Disintegration of East European State Socialism." *Theory and Society* 23(2):211–231.

Szelenyi, Ivan and Eric Kostello. 1996. "The Market Transition Debate: Toward a Synthesis?" *American Journal of Sociology* 101(4):1082–1096.

Szelenyi, Ivan and Katarzyna Wilk. 2010. "Institutional Transformation in European Post-Communist Regimes." In the *Oxford Handbook of Comparative Institutional Analysis*, edited by Glenn Morgan, John Campbell, Colin Crouch, Ove Kai Pedersen and Richard Withley, 565–586. Oxford, UK: Oxford University Press.

Tismeanu, Vladimir. 1995 *Political Culture and Civil Society in Russia and the New States of Eurasia*. Armonk, N.Y.: M. E.Sharpe.

Tsai, Kellee. 2007. *Capitalists without Democracy: The Private Sector in Contemporary China*. Ithaca, N.Y.: Cornell University Press.

Tsai, Lily L. 2007. *Accountability without Democracy: Solidary Groups and Public Goods Provision in Rural China*. New York: Cambridge University Press.

Verdery, Katherine. 1996. *What was Socialism and What Comes Next?* Princeton, N.J.: Princeton University Press.

Walder, Andrew G. 1994. "The Decline of Communist Power: Elements of a Theory of Institutional Change." *Theory and Society* 23:297–323.

———, ed. 1995. *The Waning of the Communist State: Economic Origins of Political Decline in China and Hungary*. Berkeley, Calif.: University of California Press.

Wang, Feng. 2008. *Boundaries and Categories: Rising Inequality in Post-Socialist Urban China.* Palo Alto, Calif.: Stanford University Press.

Wang, Hongying. 2001. *Weak State, Strong Networks: The Institutional Dynamics of Foreign Direct Investment in China.* London: Oxford University Press.

Wang, Shaoguang and Hu Angang. 1999. *The Political Economy of Uneven Development: The Case of China.* Armonk, N.Y.: M.E. Sharpe.

Wank, David L. 1999. *Commodifying Communism: Business, Trust, and Politics in a Chinese City.* New York: Cambridge University Press.

Wejnert, Barbara. 2005. "Diffusion, Development, and Democracy: 1800–1999." *American Sociological Review* 70(1):53–81.

Welsh, Helga A. 1994. "Political Transition Processes in Central and Eastern Europe." *Comparative Politics* 26(4):379–394.

White, Gordon, Jude A. Howell and Shang Xiaoyuan. 1996. *In Search of Civil Society: Market Reform and Social Change in Contemporary China.* New York: Oxford University Press.

Whitefield, Stephen. 1993. *Industrial Power and the Soviet State.* New York: Oxford University Press.

Woodruff, David. 1999. *Money Unmade: Barter and the Fate of Russian Capitalism.* Ithaca, N.Y.: Cornell University Press.

Wu, Fulong, Chris Webster, Shenjing He, and Yuting Liu. 2010. *Urban Poverty in China.* Cheltenham, U.K.: Edward Elgar.

Yang, Dali L. 2004. *Remaking the Chinese Leviathan: Market Transition and the Politics of Governance in China.* Palo Alto, Calif.: Stanford University Press.

Zhang, Li and Aihwa Ong, eds. 2008. *Privatizing China.* Ithaca, N.Y.: Cornell University Press.

Zielonka, Jan and Alex Pravda, eds. 2001. *Democratic Consolidation in Eastern Europe. Volume 2: International and Transnational Factors.* Oxford, U.K.: Oxford University Press.

PART I

REINSTITUTIONALIZING POLITICS

1

1989 and Its Aftermath

Two Waves of Democratic Change in Postcommunist
Europe and Eurasia

VALERIE BUNCE AND SHARON L. WOLCHIK

"The large-scale involvement of citizens in political life, images of
town squares packed with people, along with occasions of euphoria,
brought back memories of November 1989, when the communist
regime in Czechoslovakia collapsed."
          —Martin Butora (2007:40) on the 1998 Slovak election

"Diffusion is the process whereby past events make future events
more likely."
          —Pamela Oliver and Daniel Meyers (2003:174)

It has become customary to think of 1989 in two related ways, as the year when
the communist experiment ended and the year when communist regimes were
succeeded by democratic political orders. However, there are three problems
with this shorthand summary of what happened in 1989 and the political
changes that followed in the wake of that momentous year. First, some communist regimes survived—most obviously, as Fewsmith discusses in this
volume, China, despite the significant challenges to the regime posed by the
protests that took place in Tiananmen Square in 1989. Second, as the introductory essay to this volume highlights, the regime consequences of 1989 in
the Soviet Union and Eastern Europe (to use the Cold War designation of the
region) were far more varied than the simple replacement of communism with
democracy. In practice, the successor regimes ran the gamut from dictatorship
to democracy, including a large number of regimes that combined elements of
the two political systems (see, especially, Bunce 1999a; Frye 2010). Finally,
1989 was one of two rounds of democratic change that took place in this part of
the world over the past 20 years. From 1996 to 1998, a second wave of democratization began in Romania, Bulgaria, and Slovakia, which then moved to

Table 1.1 **Wave 1: 1989 to 1992**

State	1992 Regime Type	Post-1992 Regime Type
Bulgaria (a)	democracy	+
Czech Republic	democracy	+
Hungary	democracy	+
Lithuania	democracy	+
Poland	democracy	+
Slovakia (b)	democracy	+
Slovenia	democracy	+
Albania	hybrid	0
Armenia	hybrid	−
Azerbaijan	hybrid	−
Belarus	hybrid	−
Croatia (b)	hybrid	−
Estonia	hybrid	+
Kazakhstan	hybrid	−
Kyrgyzstan	hybrid	−
Latvia	hybrid	+
Macedonia	hybrid	0
Moldova	hybrid	0
Romania (a)	hybrid	+
Russia	hybrid	−
Serbia (b)	hybrid	−
Ukraine (b)	hybrid	−
Bosnia	authoritarian	+
Georgia (b)	authoritarian	+
Tajikistan	authoritarian	−
Turkmenistan	authoritarian	−
Uzbekistan	authoritarian	−

Notes: (a) The improvements in democratic performance took place in response to pivotal elections and membership in the European Union. (b) Democratic performance actually declined in all of these cases after 1992, but improved following electoral victories by the opposition.

Source: Bunce 1999a: 756–793.

Croatia, Serbia, Georgia, Ukraine, and Kyrgyzstan from 2000 to 2005 (Bunce and Wolchik, 2010a, 2011).

The purpose of this chapter is to compare these two waves of democratic change (see tables 1.1 and 1.2 for a summary). Two questions will guide our inquiry.[1] First, how similar and different were these two waves—in the

Table 1.2 **Wave 2: 1996 to 2008**

State	Electoral Year	Opposition Victory	Regime Type at Point of Departure	Regime Type after Electoral Breakthrough
Armenia	2003, 2008	no	hybrid	hybrid
Azerbaijan	2003, 2005	no	hybrid	authoritarian
Belarus	2001, 2006	no	authoritarian	authoritarian
Bulgaria	1997	yes	democracy	consolidated democracy
Croatia	2000	yes	hybrid	democracy
Georgia	2003	yes	hybrid	hybrid
Kyrgyzstan	2005	yes	hybrid	hybrid/authoritarian
Romania	1996	yes	hybrid	democracy
Slovakia	1998	yes	hybrid	democracy
Serbia	2000	yes	authoritarian	democracy
Ukraine	2004	yes	hybrid	democracy

Source: Freedom House table, which is on their website: http://www.freedomhouse.org/template.cfm?page=439.

processes involved and in their political consequences? Second, what do the answers to this question tell us about political trends in the region over the past 20 years and, at a more theoretical level, about democratization and diffusion?

Wave 1: The Collapse of Communism

There is a sizeable literature on the events that occurred from 1987 to 1990 and our discussion, as a result, will summarize the main elements of what happened (see, for example, Stokes 1993; Joppke 1995; Bunce 1999b; Brown 2000; Glenn 2001 Beissinger 2002). While the beginning of communism's demise in the Soviet Union and Eastern Europe is hard to pinpoint, especially in view of the important role of Solidarity's rise in Poland in 1980, it can nonetheless be argued that the mass protests that eventually led to the disintegration of these regimes and the breakup of three of these states began in two places: in the Soviet Union in 1987, with the rise of popular fronts in support of perestroika in Russia and the Baltic states, and in Slovenia with the rise of a student movement that, by entering the forbidden zone of military affairs, took on both the Yugoslav state and the regime (see Mastnak 1994). Protests then broke out in Poland in fall 1988 (much to the consternation of Lech Walesa, who was losing control over his movement) and culminated in an unprecedented round-table between the opposition and the party in the early months of 1989 that focused on ending the political stalemate in Poland, in place since martial law was declared in 1981, through the creation of a transitional regime that added some competitive political features to authoritarian rule in Poland. However, semicompetitive elections in June 1989 had produced by August of that year, an unthinkable development, the formation of an opposition-led government that then laid the groundwork for a rapid transition to democracy.

The Polish precedent, coupled with the considerable loosening of strictures on political change in Eastern Europe as a result of the Gorbachev reforms, was powerful enough to lead in late summer 1989 to a roundtable in Hungary, which was different in important respects from its Polish counterpart. It was not televised, it featured a more elaborate and specialized set of working groups, and it involved more detailed planning for a democratic future, including fully competitive elections to be held in the following year. In fall 1989, massive protests broke out in East Germany, which were then followed by similar developments in Czechoslovakia, with participants there speaking directly of demonstration effects. Protests, albeit much smaller, then followed in Bulgaria, Romania, and Albania. In the course of these developments, moreover, protests within the Soviet Union continued and spread, as they did within Yugoslavia, where the Slovenian developments influenced, by all accounts, subsequent mass mobilization in Croatia and Serbia, in particular.

Mass Mobilization and Electoral Revolutions

The second wave of citizen confrontations with authoritarian rule in this region occurred from 1996 to 2005 (for a more detailed analysis, see Bunce and Wolchik 2006, 2009, 2010a, 2011).[2] This wave began with four interconnected political struggles in Serbia, Bulgaria, Romania, and Slovakia from 1996 to 1998, countries that provided a regional hothouse for political change, because of the combination of democratic deficits, active and interactive oppositions, and shared borders. From 1996 to 1997, there were massive three-month-long protests in Serbia—protests that were motivated by Slobodan Milošević's attempt to deny the opposition its significant victories in many of the local elections that took place in 1996 (Lazić and Nikolić 1999; Thomas 1999; Pavlovic 2005). These protests, as in the cases that followed in their footsteps, built on previous rounds of political protest—in the Serbian case going back to the early 1980s and in Romania, Bulgaria, and Slovakia to 1989 (and even during the communist period, as in the miners' strikes in Romania during the 1980s). As James O'Brien, who served as the Washington-based coordinator of US assistance to Serbian opposition groups from 1999 to 2000, put it: "We built on the plumbing of the past" (interview, November 16, 2006, Washington, D.C.). While the Serbian protests of this period failed in their objective in the short term, they contributed in important ways to the subsequent and successful electoral challenge to Milošević's rule that took place in fall 2000 (see also Bieber 2003; Pribicevic 2004).

The second set of struggles occurred in Romania, where the liberal opposition finally came together and ran a sophisticated political campaign that succeeded in 1996 in replacing the former communist incumbent president (who came back to power in 2000) with a candidate with far stronger liberal credentials and commitments (see Bunce and Wolchik 2011). The third set of struggles took place in Bulgaria at roughly the same time (see Petrova 2009). In Bulgaria, the protests occurring in Serbia were influential, in particular, in bringing labor and other groups into the streets. While slow to respond and, to some degree, shamed by the spontaneity of their own citizenry, Bulgarian intellectuals and leaders of the opposition finally recognized, especially given the poor performance of the incumbent regime, that such protests could lead to a new election and pave the way for the Union of Democratic Forces (which, prior to this time, would be better characterized as a fractious ensemble) to return to power (which it did in 1997). Although the cohesion of the Bulgarian liberal opposition proved to be temporary and its effectiveness limited (as in the Romanian story as well), its victory, again as in Romania, served as a decisive political turning point—as indicated, for example, by the consistent improvements in Freedom House scores following these pivotal elections in both countries (see Kurekova 2006; Ganev 2007).

The same generalization applies to the fourth participant in the story of the spread of election-based approach to democratic change: Slovakia (see Bunce and Wolchik 2009, 2011, Ch. 3; Forbrig and Demes, 2007). It was in that country where all the components of what can be termed the electoral model of defeating authoritarian leaders came together. Thus, a variety of players, including leaders of the Slovak, Bulgarian, and Romanian oppositions, the US ambassadors to Slovakia and the Czech Republic, "graduates" of the Romanian and Bulgarian turnarounds, and representatives of organizations such as the International Republican Institute, the National Democratic Institute, Freedom House, the National Endowment for Democracy, and the Foundation for Civil Society, combined forces to create the OK98 campaign that led to the defeat of Vladimir Mečiar in the 1998 Slovak parliamentary elections. This model, which functioned as the political innovation that diffused throughout the region, included such components as the formation of a cohesive opposition; pressures on election commissions to improve their procedures and render them more transparent; ambitious campaigns by the opposition and their civil society allies to register voters, advertise the costs of the incumbent regime, and get out the vote; and the deployment of both domestic and international election monitors, as well as exit polls, to provide quick feedback on turnout during election day, to catalogue election day abuses by the regime, and to provide evidence of actual voter preferences (see Hyde 2007 on other consequences).

Once fully articulated and successful when implemented in Slovakia in 1998, the electoral model was then applied in a number of competitive authoritarian regimes (see Levitsky and Way 2002, 2010; Diamond 2002; Schedler 2006; Way and Levitsky 2009). Its first stop in the regional diffusion process was in Croatia in 2000, where the death of the long-serving dictator, Franjo Tudjman, in 1999 had weakened the governing party and provided an opportunity for the opposition to win power. In this case, as in the others that preceded it, the electoral outcome produced a smooth transition. The Croatian opposition also benefited (as would Serbia later in the same year) from assistance provided by the Slovak opposition and the electoral playbook it devised in collaboration with regional and Western actors, along with some earlier successes in local elections and earlier actions by the hardline regime to prevent the translation of voter preferences into representative governments. As in Slovakia, and somewhat in contrast to the situation in Bulgaria and Romania after these pivotal elections, the Croatian electoral shift had dramatic effects on democratization. A political corner was turned.

Later in 2000, the model of using elections to mount ambitious challenges to authoritarian rule moved to Serbia (see Bunce and Wolchik 2009; Bunce and Wolchik 2011). While the implementation of the electoral model was as careful and thoroughgoing as it had been in Slovakia and Croatia, there were, nonetheless, some differences that distinguish Serbia from these other cases. One was that the struggle against Milošević was severely constrained by the increasingly heavy authoritarian hand of the regime. Thus, for example, there were no external election monitors in Serbia in the fall 2000 elections and the media were closely controlled by Milošević. However, there was one similarity to Slovakia: the key role played by young people and their organizations, such as Otpor, in Serbia.

The Serbian presidential election of 2000 was a turning point for elections as democratizing agents, because the incumbent regime had been in power much longer and was far more authoritarian than the earlier sites for such revolutions had been and because these characteristics meant that the regime refused to cede power once the election and the tabulations of the vote, both fraudulent and accurate, had concluded (Goati, 2001). This action sparked massive political protests. Protestors succeeded in taking control over the capital and forcing Milošević to resign. As in Croatia, the result was a regime change and not just a change in government (see, especially, Licht 2007 for developments after 2000 in Serbia).

The Georgian opposition then followed suit in the 2003 parliamentary elections—though this produced, it is important to recognize, a coup d'état by the opposition, since the long-serving president, Eduard Shevardnadze, left office without having been up for reelection (see Welt 2009 and Bunce and Wolchik 2011). In Georgia, the political context was less constraining than in Serbia, especially given the lackluster campaign by Shevardnadze's allies, the defection of so many key players from the ruling group to the opposition (such as Mikheil Saakashvili, the current president), the relative openness of the Georgian media, the formation of a youth group in support of political change (Kmara) that worked closely with the Georgian opposition around Saakashvili, and the presence of a significant number of local and international election monitors (Karumidze and Wertsch 2005). As with the other cases, moreover, it was clear that the Georgian opposition modeled its campaign on the previous electoral breakthroughs in the region and benefited as well as from various kinds of support from the Open Society Foundation and various other US nongovernmental organizations as well as US government assistance efforts (see Cooley and Ron 2002; Devdariani 2003).

The next successful democratizing election occurred in Ukraine a year later (see, in particular, Kuzio 2005; Kubicek 2005; Wilson 2005; Way 2005a, 2005b; Aslund and McFaul 2006; and Bunce and Wolchik 2011). As in the Georgian case, a single charismatic politician—in this case, Viktor Yushchenko—played a critical role. As in both the Georgian and Serbian cases, the successful political breakthrough exploited a record of a leadership that had grown increasingly corrupt, careless, and violent; benefited from defections from the ruling circles; built on earlier rounds of protests and recent successes in local elections; and reached out to diverse groups, with young people playing nearly as important a role as in Serbia with Otpor, the youth organization that had formed in 1997 in response to growing political repression and figured so prominently in the ouster of Milošević. Moreover, as in Serbia and Georgia, political protests after the election (which were larger and longer lasting than those in Serbia) were again necessary to force the authoritarian incumbent to admit defeat. More distinctive to the Ukrainian case, however, was the breakdown of central control over the media during the campaign and especially during the protests and the remarkable role of the Supreme Court, which supported the opposition's argument that the elections had been fraudulent and had to be repeated.

Significant electoral challenges to authoritarian incumbents, coupled with mass demonstrations challenging the official electoral results, also occurred in a number of other countries in the region, including Kyrgyzstan in 2005, where President Askar Akaev panicked in the face of protests following the parliamentary election and left office (see Radnitz 2009) and in a series of presidential and parliamentary elections that took place in Armenia, Azerbaijan, and Belarus from 2001 to 2008, where the common result was that authoritarian incumbents or their anointed successors remained in power in the face of popular protests over electoral fraud (see Valiyev 2006; Silitski, 2009; Bunce and Wolchik 2009, 2010a, 2011). What made these cases of election-based protests against authoritarian rule similar to one another, but different from the earlier challenges to authoritarian leaders, were two factors. First, the collaborative networks that brought together graduates of earlier and successful electoral confrontations with dictators, Western democracy promoters, and local opposition groups and that played such a pivotal role in breaking with authoritarian rule in Slovakia, Croatia, Serbia, Georgia, and Ukraine from 1998 to 2004 were far less present and influential in Armenia, Azerbaijan, and Belarus. Second, the electoral model was not fully deployed in these three countries. This was, in part, because of a thinning out of transnational networks but also because of preemptive strikes on the part of authoritarian rulers (who were watching electoral change in the neighborhood with interest equal to that of the opposition) and failures on the part of oppositions, given their own limitations and those imposed by the regime, to construct sufficiently large coalitions and mount sufficiently ambitious political campaigns and electoral monitoring programs.

Comparing the Two Processes of Democratic Change

We can now step back from the details of these two waves of democratization in postcommunist Europe and Eurasia and compare the processes involved. The two waves diverged from each other in some important respects, aside from the obvious one of timing. First, while both were confined to the same region, the two rounds of democratic change took place in different sites. Thus, if we focus on the countries involved, we find that a somewhat different group of countries served as the focus of the two waves—though there was overlap in the cases of Bulgaria, Romania, Slovakia, and Ukraine. The second wave concentrated on states that functioned as the semiperiphery of the first wave such as Ukraine, Georgia, and the Balkans (except for Slovenia), where mobilizations against communism had occurred in 1989 but where, in contrast to the "early risers" (to borrow from Beissinger 2002), such as Poland, Czechoslovakia, and the

Baltic states, the protests were smaller, later to appear, and less able to produce fully democratic polities because of weaker civil societies, a less experienced opposition, and in many cases the divisions generated by competition among communists, the democratic opposition, and illiberal nationalists. In this sense, the second wave of democratization picked up where the first wave left off. At the same time, regime sites varied as well, with communism serving as the common focus of the first wave and authoritarian regimes, hybrid systems, or fragile democracies serving as the focus of the second.

The other major difference between these two processes of democratic change was in the mode of transition. In 1989, as Nina Bandelj and Dorothy Solinger have argued in their introductory essay in this volume, there were two modes (which were often combined): mass protests against communist party rule and pacted transitions between authoritarians and democrats. In the second wave, elections always served as the mechanism for democratic change— a mechanism that was unavailable during communism because of the absence of contested elections (though Hungary had introduced competition in local elections during the last years of the Kadar regime). Thus, voting results, rather than the less predictable and fixed in time processes of people taking to the street or the more orchestrated processes of agreements forged at roundtables, served as the basis for turnover in political leadership in the second wave. Moreover, the process of turnover was more gradual in the first round, despite the seeming suddenness of the collapse of communism, because new rules of the political game had to be devised and elections subsequently held before the regime change and, thus, the organization of political power and how it was exercised, could be institutionalized. In the second wave, largely because new constitutions were already in place and multiple elections had already been held, the transition could take place more rapidly.

These differences aside, however, there were many similarities between these two waves of democratic change. First, both rounds focused on the same project: ending authoritarian rule. It is often forgotten that a necessary, but by no means sufficient condition for the replacement of dictatorship with democracy is removing authoritarian leaders from office. Stated differently, dictators rarely become democrats, though communist leaders and parties can quickly redefine themselves when, as in Slovenia and Hungary in particular in the first wave, they recognize that their hegemony has ended and that it is in their interest to go along with rapidly changing political developments on the ground. Moreover, the best predictor of democratic change in the postcommunist region over the past 20 years has been elections that led to a turnover in leadership as a result of the victory of the democratic opposition (Bunce 1994; Fish 1998; Bunce 2006; for similar arguments taking a longer-term and global perspective on this question, see Hadenius and Teorell 2007).

A second similarity was the role of popular mobilization in ending autocratic rule. Most obviously in the case of 1989, we are referring to the impact
of popular protests on regime collapse in both the Soviet Union and Eastern
Europe, beginning in 1987. However, popular mobilization was also critical in
the second wave, not just in the sense that postelection protests were necessary to force a transfer of power in the more authoritarian countries of Serbia,
Georgia, Ukraine, and Kyrgyzstan but also in the sense that heightened
public involvement in the pivotal elections, including expanded turnout
among the young, made the key difference in what were close elections in
Slovakia in 1998, Serbia in 2000, and Ukraine in 2004. Thus, the patterns
exhibited in both waves put to rest the argument, common in analyses of the
transitions to democracy in Spain and Latin America in the 1970s and 1980s,
that regime transition through mass protests is less likely to produce full-scale
and sustainable democracy than pacted transitions that give more structure to
the dynamic and that reassure authoritarians while giving democrats opportunities to compete for power (though pacting between authoritarians and
democrats also took place in the postcommunist region but sometimes led, as
in Central Asia, to authoritarian, not democratic outcomes; see Jones Luong
2002; Bunce, 2000, 2003.

A third similarity is in the role of international diffusion in both rounds
of challenges to authoritarian rule wherein new ideas, institutions, policies,
models, or repertoires of behavior spread from their point of origin to new
and usually neighboring sites—for example, from one enterprise, governing
unit, or nongovernmental organization to others (see, for example, Brinks and
Coppedge 2006; Markoff 1996; Ackerman and Duvall 2000; Beissinger 2002;
Beissinger 2007; Bockman and Eyal 2002; Tarrow 2005; Tarrow and della
Porta 2005; Wehnert 2005; Gleditsch and Ward 2006; Bunce and Wolchik
2006, 2009, 2010b; Simmons, Dobbin, and Garrett 2008; Weyland 2009a,
2009b). Diffusion, therefore, implies that innovations spread not just because
similar local circumstances give rise to similar responses but also because
of influences located outside these units. In this sense, "[d]iffusion is the
process whereby past events make future events more likely" (Oliver and
Meyers 2003).

What we find in both rounds of collective action aimed against nondemocratic incumbents is a classic pattern of diffusion; that is, within each wave of
change there were relatively similar repertoires of innovative behaviors that
were adopted by key actors in a lagged fashion in a number of countries that
were in a position to influence one another as a result of being located in the
same region and often sharing common borders. Moreover, each wave was fore-
shadowed by a clear expansion in international opportunities for democratic
change—opportunities that were exploited, albeit to varying degrees, by local

democratic activists and everyday citizens. Here, we refer, for example, to the role of the Helsinki Process and the Gorbachev reforms in the first wave, and in the second the rise, beginning in the early 1990s, of an international democracy promotion community that provided important assistance to democratic activists in the postcommunist region (see Thomas 2001; Mendelson and Glenn 2002; Carothers 2004; Vachudova 2005; Bunce and Wolchik 2006b; Finkel, et al. 2006; Bunce, McFaul and Stoner-Weiss 2009). Just as important for both rounds, but more influential in the second, was a transnational factor: the development of regionally based opposition networks that collaborated closely with one another in support of a showdown with incumbent authoritarian regimes. While these networks benefited primarily from what could be termed a more "permissive" international environment in the first round, in the second wave international (including regional) actors played a more active role by supporting the development of civil society, an open media, and free and fair elections; encouraging the unity of the opposition as well as ties between the opposition and civil society groups; providing training and support with respect to campaign techniques; and offering strong and public criticisms of authoritarian incumbents when they attempted to steal elections.

Finally and also typical of the way international diffusion works, the spread of democratic change within the region was uneven in both waves. Thus, citizens in some countries participated in this diffusion dynamic, whereas those in other countries did not. Why did this happen? We would argue that a similar set of factors came into play in both waves and that these factors shed light in turn on a key theme in this volume: the contrasting regime and state trajectories that materialized in Europe, Eurasia, and China after 1989. In particular, if oppositions could learn from one another by monitoring precedents in the neighborhood, so could authoritarians (see, for instance, Fish 2005; Gershman and Allen 2006; Herd 2005; Kimmage 2005; Benardo and Neier 2006; Chivers 2006; NED 2006; Weier 2006; Koshkovsky 2007; Spector and Krickovic 2007; Hassner 2008; McFaul and Stoner-Weiss 2008; Silitski 2009; Bunce and Wolchik 2010a; Bunce and Wolchik 2010b; and Bunce and Wolchik 2011, ch. 7).

The double-edged impact of the diffusion dynamic was particularly important for two reasons. First, the innovations were profoundly subversive of the status quo, rather than modest variations on it. This was, in short, a high stakes game. Second, many authoritarian leaders in the region, such as those in Russia, Azerbaijan, Armenia, Belarus, and Kazakhstan, were in a more advantageous position to resist change because, for example, they were more repressive, they were more popular, their economies were performing better, their civil societies and opposition parties were weaker, and their countries were more removed geographically from these explosive events. Because of these considerations, many of which also benefited the leadership in China, as Joseph Fewsmith notes in chapter 2 of this volume, they had the time and the resources, along with the knowledge of what could happen to them, to prepare for electoral challenges to their power.

In this sense, local receptivity to change had two consequences—influencing the ability of authoritarians and democrats to draw lessons from the diffusion dynamic and determining whether and, if so, when in the dynamic major challenges to authoritarian rule would be attempted, as well as the outcome of those efforts (see, especially, Way 2005b, 2008; Bunce and Wolchik 2006, 2009, 2010b, 2011; Stoner-Weiss 2009; and Levitsky and Way 2010). Not all hybrid or authoritarian regimes, in short, are equally good candidates for major and successful challenges to their continuation in power.

In the case of the second wave, moreover, two additional constraints on collective action against regimes presented themselves as the wave of electoral confrontations with authoritarian leaders moved from the Balkans to the former Soviet Union. One constraint was, as already noted, a fraying of the transnational network as it spread to locales further and further removed from Central and southeastern Europe, where it had originated and where its members had benefited from shared borders, established contacts among oppositions, and the accumulation among US democracy promoters, in particular, of rich experiences drawn from multiple postings in the states of Eastern and Central Europe as well as, in some cases, earlier postings in Latin America (and see Finkel, Perez-Linan and Seligson 2007).

The other significant constraint was a change in US policies in regard to democracy promotion. Energy politics, strategic geopolitical location, and the victory of Hamas in Palestine in 2006 reduced the priority the United States attached to, for example, the defeat of dictators in Azerbaijan, Armenia, Russia, and Kazakhstan. The Belarusian dictatorship, however, is an exception to these generalizations. The United States, along with the EU, has been extremely critical of the Lukashenka regime and has provided consistent support for free and fair elections and for the development of civil society in that country.

Similarities and Differences in Political Outcomes

We can now turn to the second question of interest in this chapter: how and how much these challenges to authoritarian rule affected subsequent political trajectories. Because each wave contributed new democracies to the region and because the democracies that arose in the first wave were remarkably durable, the number of democracies in postcommunist Europe and Eurasia has increased markedly over the past 20 years, although there was also an increase in the number of countries that were not free. For example, using Freedom House scores to measure this change, we find that, while in 1993 to 1994 (the early stages of the transition and the first year following the breakup of the Soviet, Yugoslav, and Czechoslovak states), 26 percent of the regimes in the region were free (or seven countries), 52 percent were partly free (14 countries), and 22 percent were not free (six countries; see also table 1.1). By contrast, in 2009 the comparable figures were 46 percent (13 countries), 29 percent (seven countries), and 25 percent (eight countries). Just as important is another clear pattern: With the exceptions of Estonia and Latvia, which moved by the second half of the 1990s from partly free to free as a result of improvements in their minority policies, it has only been through the political processes defining these two waves—that is, popular mobilizations against communism and electoral contests that empowered the democratic opposition—that regimes in this region have improved significantly with respect to their democratic performance. While membership in the EU has played an important role in consolidating new democracies in the region, because of the stringent requirements of membership, the extension of assistance, and, as a result, the strengthening of local forces in support of democratic change (see Jacoby and Vachudova 2005), the EU has not been able (or, for that matter, willing), to take the more radical and difficult step of replacing authoritarians with democrats (despite the argument that Vachudova 2005 has made, for example, in regard to the impact of the desire to join the EU on democratic change in countries such as Slovakia).

In comparing the regime effects of the two waves, we discover surprisingly similar political developments after both sets of confrontations between authoritarians and their opponents. While both rounds produced significant democratic change, they nonetheless had diverse political consequences. Thus, following the first wave of political change, communist regimes were succeeded in relatively quick order by the formation of full-scale democracies (as in Poland, Hungary, Slovenia, the Baltic states, and Czechoslovakia); hybrid regimes that straddled democracy and dictatorship (as in Romania, Albania, Armenia, Croatia, Azerbaijan, Belarus, Georgia, Ukraine, Moldova, Kazakhstan, and Russia); and, as in most of the Central Asian states, highly authoritarian regimes that allowed almost no room for opposition or civil society activism. Popular mobilization played an important role in the collapse of communism in most of the regimes that fell into the first two groups but not in those countries, such as Uzbekistan, Turkmenistan, and Tajikistan, that followed the third political pathway. Thus, public protests were associated with the formation of regimes that were at the least more liberal than their communist predecessors—though some were, of course, fully liberal. At least in the early stages of the transition, therefore, popular mobilization never led to dictatorial orders, though some of the hybrid regimes, such as Azerbaijan, Kazakhstan, and Russia, began to move by the late 1990s in a much more authoritarian direction.

Just as striking is another pattern. The most common type of regime to emerge from communism was neither democracy nor dictatorship but hybrid regimes. These regimes feature, for example, uneven rule of law, some limitations on civil liberties and political rights, and electoral competition but on an uneven playing field that favors authoritarians over democrats (see table 1.1). Regimes of this type tend to combine competition for office with authoritarian political practices.

At the same time, as is typical of diffusion dynamics, the most dramatic regime shifts in a democratic direction occurred in those states where the regional wave of popular mobilizations began, as opposed to those where such mobilizations occurred at a later stage. The contrast here, for example, is between Poland, Slovenia, and the Baltic states, on the one hand, and Romania, Bulgaria, and Albania, on the other. There are exceptions to this conclusion, such as Russia, Armenia, Azerbaijan, and Georgia, all of which were "early risers." In all four cases, state and regime formation went hand in hand with the onset of wars over boundaries.

In the second wave, we also find divergent regime trajectories following the defeat of authoritarian leaders (see table 1.2). For example, while Bulgaria, Romania, Slovakia, Croatia, Serbia, and Ukraine were all ranked fully free in the years following the electoral breakthroughs of 1996 to 2004, the democratic gains that occurred after the pivotal elections in Georgia and Kyrgyzstan were far more modest. In particular, while Kyrgyzstan moved from not free to partly free, Georgia, under the leadership of Saakashvili, after an initial improvement returned to its longtime ranking of partly free.

Once again, moreover, the most successful cases of democratic breakthroughs were in the earlier rather than the later stages of the wave (though Ukraine is an exception). Just as important is another consideration: The elections that produced a turnover in Georgia and Kyrgyzstan, unlike the other elections in the second wave, were for the parliament, not for the presidency—though they served in both of these cases as a pretext for ending the long rule of Shevardnadze and Akaev, respectively.

The largest democratic gain was in Serbia,which fell in the middle of the wave of electoral mobilizations against authoritarian rule (though the changes in Ukraine and Croatia were also significant). In some ways, this pattern is also similar to 1989. Just as the first wave started in the most liberal communist regimes—that is, in Slovenia, Poland, and Hungary—and then, in part because of demonstration effects, moved to the more challenging political contexts of hardline East Germany and Czechoslovakia, so the second wave began in more democratic regimes, such as Bulgaria, Romania, and Slovakia and then moved to the far more hostile political environments of Croatia and especially Serbia, where successful electoral breakthroughs had dramatic effects on democratic development. Thus, it was in the early and middle stages of both waves (with Ukraine as an exception) when democratic results were the most pronounced. This was largely because, despite differences in regime contexts, such as whether the communist regime was soft- or hardline and whether the postcommunist regime was free, partly free, or not free, political struggles had produced relatively strong civil societies and democratic oppositions.

Conclusions

Just as there have been several rounds of democratic change in the eastern half of Europe since 1989 and these waves of change have contributed over the past two decades to a remarkable expansion of democratic political systems in the region, so each wave has had nonetheless variable regime effects. Democratization, therefore, has been an uneven process in terms of geography and timing.

Democratization has been propelled by three mechanisms: popular protests, pacts between authoritarians and democrats, and elections. There has been, therefore, no single road to democracy in postcommunist Europe and Eurasia. Just as importantly, none of these three modes of transition seems to be superior in terms of its ability to deliver democratic improvements. If this conclusion flies in the face of earlier studies of democratization during the third wave that led to a strong preference on the part of scholars for pacting as the best approach to democratic change (see Huntington 1991), so it supports their more general argument that specific and unusual actions taken by individuals and groups, rather than more structural or long-term processes, have played a critical role in democratic development in the region. Recognizing the importance of agency in bringing about the ouster of authoritarian rulers, however, the likelihood that political change, including a democratic breakthrough brought about by democratizing elections, would translate into democratic progress rested on more long-term developments in the areas of civil society, opposition politics, and regime vulnerability—whether during the communist era or during postcommunism.

While different in some of their details, the two waves of democratic change in Europe and Eurasia followed relatively predictable diffusion patterns. Each wave of democratic transformation, while influencing politics in a large number of states, nonetheless failed to transform the entire region. This is less surprising for the second wave, given the expansion of the number of states in the region, significant differences in local politics and economics, and the ease for authoritarian incumbents of learning lessons from previous experiences in the region about how and how not to conduct elections (see Dawisha and Deets 2006)—though these points beg the important question of why eight electoral breakthroughs happened. However, the uneven impact of the first wave is more surprising, because the number of states was much smaller, there was a regional hegemon in a position (by accident, as well as design) to influence change, and communism had created relatively similar political and economic orders that were presumably equally ripe for change and had provided a similar stock of factors supporting democratic change.

Also typical of diffusion dynamics were the variations in regime trajectories following successful challenges to authoritarian rule. As each wave progressed, it moved from more to less hospitable political environments and also from contexts in which authoritarians were taken by surprise to contexts in which they, along with the opposition, were forewarned and forearmed. As a result, just as each wave ended, so over the course of each wave democratic change was less and less evident after successful challenges to authoritarian rule.

Finally, it can be argued that we can extend our arguments about these waves of democratic change in postcommunist Europe and Eurasia to the durability of authoritarian rule in China. Here, it is important to recognize that none of the building blocks of the democratic changes discussed in this chapter was available in China. In particular, as chapter 2 in this volume illustrates, the protests in China in 1989 were not the culmination, as in many of the cases in Eastern and Central Europe and in parts of the former Soviet Union in the same period, of long-term struggles between regime and society. In this sense, while 1989 in China was sudden, it was far less so in the region of interest in this chapter. The crackdown in 1989 prevented oppositions in China not just from winning power but also from providing a model of success that would be available for later anti-authoritarian struggles. Third, because of the failure of 1989 to bring down communism in China, there was no hybrid regime that provided electoral opportunities for oppositions to win power (although China has been experimenting with competition in local elections). Instead, as Fewsmith discusses in chapter 2, the threat 1989 posed, like the developments in postcommunist Europe and Eurasia , has increased the vigilance of the leadership in regard to any threat to the power of the communist party's leading role.

As Fewsmith notes, there are significant barriers to the diffusion of democratic change in China—for example, the country's distance from the epicenter of the 1989 struggles in the Soviet Union and Eastern Europe and the absence of a Soviet bloc-like organization that could facilitate the cross-national spread of dissent and common approaches to demands for democratic change, while transforming the struggle against the regime into a struggle that combined liberalism and nationalism. The ability of the Chinese state to buy popular acquiescence in if not genuine support of the regime through economic growth and undermine collective action through marketization, make use of citizens' fear of coercion, and benefit from hard administrative boundaries that contain protest and focus unrest on local governments rather than on Beijing are equally as important. In this sense, if perhaps the most remarkable feature of democratic change in postcommunist Europe and Eurasia has been the role of cross-national diffusion in these developments, then perhaps the most significant contributor to authoritarianism in China has been the ability of the Chinese Communist Party to insulate the country from the influences of diffusion and therefore from demands for democratic change.

Notes

1. There is a third question that could be addressed, why there were two waves of democratic change. A full answer to this question would double the length of this chapter. Two factors played a role. One was that not all countries in this region were ideally and, thus, equally positioned in political and economic terms to support a transition to democracy after communism fell. The other was that, while hybrid regimes provided opportunities for democratic change as a result of electoral competition, they were not equally supportive of opposition victories. See, in particular, Bunce 1999a; Frye 2010; Bunce and Wolchik 2010a and 2011.

2. The data we bring to bear on these questions include information gleaned from more than 200 interviews conducted with domestic and international participants in the 1996 Romanian election, the 1997 Bulgarian election, the 1998 Slovak election, the 2000 elections in Croatia and Serbia, the 2003 election in Georgia, the 2004 election in Ukraine, and the 2005 election in Kyrgyzstan. In addition, we also interviewed participants in a group of elections that, although featuring significant postelection protests, led to the victory of authoritarian incumbents or their designated successors: Armenia in 2003 and 2008, Azerbaijan in 2003 and 2005, and Belarus in 2006 (see Bunce and Wolchik, 2011). Our analysis of the 1989 mobilizations is based not just on the large number of studies on this topic but also on our earlier work on communist politics and research in the Open Society Archives in Budapest, carried out in March 2006.

References

Ackerman, Peter and Jack Duvall. 2000. *A Force More Powerful: A Century of Nonviolent Conflict.* New York: Palgrave.

Aslund, Anders and Michael McFaul, eds. 2006. *Revolution in Orange: The Origins of the Ukrainian Democratic Breakthrough.* Washington, D.C.: Carnegie Endowment.

"The Backlash against Democracy Assistance: A Report Prepared by the National Endowment for Democracy for Senator Richard G. Lugar, Chairman, Committee on Foreign Relations, U.S. Senate, June 8." 2006. National Endowment for Democracy, Washington, D.C.

Beissinger, Mark. 2007. "Structure and Example in Modular Political Phenomena: The Diffusion of Bulldozer, Rose, Orange and Tulip Revolutions." *Perspectives on Politics* 5(2):259–276.

_____. 2002. *Nationalist Mobilization and the Collapse of the Soviet State* Cambridge, U.K.: Cambridge University Press.

Benardo, Leonard and Aryeh Neier. 2006. "Russia: The Persecution of Civil Society." *New York Review of Books* 53(7):35–37.

Bieber, Florian. 2003. "The Serbian Transition and Civil Society: Roots of the Delayed Transition in Serbia." *International Journal of Politics, Culture and Society* 17:73–90.

Bockman, Johanna and Gil Eyal. 2002. "Eastern Europe as a Laboratory for Economic Knowledge: The Transnational Roots of Neoliberalism." *American Journal of Sociology* 108(1):310–352.

Brinks, Daniel and Michael Coppedge. 2006. "Diffusion Is No Illusion: Neighbor Emulation in the Third Wave of Democracy." *Comparative Political Studies* 39(7):1–23.

Brown, Archie. 2000. "Transnational Influences in the Transition from Communism." *Post-Soviet Affairs* 16(2):177–200.

Bunce, Valerie. 1994. "Sequencing Political and Economic Reforms." In *East-Central European Economies in Transition*, edited by John Hardt and Richard Kaufman, eds., 46–63. Washington, D.C.: Joint Economic Committee.

_____. 1999a. "The Political Economy of Postsocialism." *Slavic Review* 58(4):756–793.

_____. 1999b. *Subversive Institutions: The Design and the Destruction of Socialism and the State.* New York: Cambridge University Press.

_____. 2000. "Comparative Democratization: Big and Bounded Generalizations." *Comparative Political Studies* 33(6–7):703–734.

_____. 2003. "Rethinking Recent Democratization: Lessons from the Postcommunist Experience." *World Politics* 55(2):167–192.

_____. 2006 "East European Democratization: Global Patterns and Postcommunist Dynamics." *Orbis* 50(4):601–620.

Bunce, Valerie, Michael McFaul, and Kathryn Stoner-Weiss, eds. 2009. *Democracy and Authoritarianism in the Postcommunist World*. Cambridge, U.K.: Cambridge University Press.

Bunce, Valerie J. and Sharon L. Wolchik. 2011. *Defeating Authoritarian Leaders in Postcommunist Countries.* New York: Cambridge University Press.

_____. 2006. "Favorable Conditions and Electoral Revolutions." *Journal of Democracy* 17:7–18.

_____. 2009. "Defining and Domesticating the Electoral Model: A Comparison of Slovakia and Serbia." In *Democracy and Authoritarianism in the Postcommunist World*, edited by Valerie Bunce, Michael McFaul, and Kathryn Stoner-Weiss, eds., 134–154. Cambridge, U.K.: Cambridge University Press.

_____. 2010a. "Defeating Dictators: Electoral Change and Stability in Competitive Authoritarian Regimes." *World Politics* 62(1):43–86.

_____. 2010b. "Transnational Networks, Diffusion Dynamics, and Electoral Change in the Postcommunist World." In *The Diffusion of Social Movements*, Rebecca Kotlins Givan, Sarah A. Soule, and Kenneth M. Roberts, eds., 140–162. Cambridge, U.K.: Cambridge University Press.

Butora, Martin. 2007. "OK98: A Campaign of Slovak NGOs for Free and Fair Elections." In *Reclaiming Democracy: Civil Society and Electoral Change in Central and Eastern Europe*, Joerg Forbrig and Pavol Demes, eds., 21–52. Washington, D.C.: German Marshall Fund.

Carothers, Thomas. 2004. *Critical Missions: Essays on Democracy Promotion*. Washington, D.C.: Carnegie Endowment.

Chivers, C. J. 2006. "Kremlin Puts Foreign Private Organizations on Notice." *New York Times*, October 20:A8.

Cooley, Alexander and James Ron. 2002. "The NGO Scramble: Organizational Insecurity and the Political Economy of Transnational Action." *International Security* 27:5–39.

Devdariani, Jaba. 2003. "The Impact of International Assistance." IDEA Website and Conference, May 2003.

Diamond, Larry. 2002. "Thinking about Hybrid Regimes." *Journal of Democracy* 13:21–35.

"Eastern European Dissidents Appeal on Hungarian Revolution Anniversary," *RAD BR 0151*, October 28, 1986.

Finkel, Steven E., Anibal Perez-Linan, and Mitchell Seligson. 2007. "The Effects of U.S. Foreign Assistance on Democracy Building." *World Politics* 59(3): 404–439.

Finkel, Steven F., Anibal Perez-Linan, Mitchell A. Seligson, and Dinorah Azpuru. 2006. "Effects of US Foreign Assistance on Democracy Building: Results of a Cross-National Quantitative Study." *Final Report, USAID*, January 12, version no. 34. http://www.usaid.gov/our_work/democracy_and_governance/publications/pdfs/impact_of_democracy_assistance.pdf.

Fish, M. Steven. 2005. *Democracy Derailed in Russia. The Failure of Open Politics.* Cambridge, U.K.: Cambridge University Press.

———. "Democratization's Prerequisites." *Post-Soviet Affairs* 14 (July–September, 1998): 212–247.

Forbrig, Joerg and Pavol Demes, eds. 2007. *Reclaiming Democracy: Civil Society and Electoral Change in Central and Eastern Europe.* Washington, D.C.: German Marshall Fund.

Frye, Timothy. 2010. *Building States and Markets after Communism: The Perils of Polarized Democracy.* New York: Cambridge University Press.

Ganev, Venelin. 2007. *Preying on the State: State Transformation in Postcommunist Bulgaria (1989–1997).* Ithaca, N.Y.: Cornell University Press.

Gershman, Carl and Allen, Michael. 2006. "The Assault on Democracy Assistance." *Journal of Democracy* 17(2):36–51.

Gleditsch, Kristian Skrede and Michael D. Ward. 2006. "Diffusion and the International Context of Democratization." *International Organization* 60(4):911–933.

Glenn, John III. 2001. *Framing Democracy: Civil Society and Civic Movements in Eastern Europe.* Palo Alto, Calif.: Stanford University Press.

Goati, Vladimir. 2001. "The Nature of the Order and the October Overthrow in Serbia." In *R/evolution and Order: Serbia after October 2000*, Ivana Spasic and Milan Subotic, eds., 45–58. Belgrade: Beograd Institute for Philosophy and Sociology.

Hadenius, Axel and Jan Teorell. 2007. "Pathways from Authoritarianism." *Journal of Democracy* 18(1):143–156.

Hassner, Pierre. 2008. "Russia's Transition to Autocracy." *Journal of Democracy* 19:5–15.

Huntington, Samuel. 1991. *The Third Wave: Democratization in the Late Twentieth Century.* Norman: University of Oklahoma Press.

Hyde, Susan. 2007. "The Observer Effect in International Politics: Evidence from a Natural Experiment." *World Politics* 60(1):37–63.

Jones Luong, Pauline. 2002. *Institutional Change and Political Continuity in Post-Soviet Central Asia: Power, Perceptions and Pacts.* Cambridge, U.K.: Cambridge University Press.

Joppke, Christian. 1995. *East German Dissidents and the Revolution of 1989: Social Movement in a Leninist Regime.* New York: New York University Press.

Karumidze, Zurab and James V. Wertsch, eds. 2005. *Enough! The Rose Revolution in the Republic of Georgia 2003.* New York: Nova Science Publishers.

Kimmage, Daniel. 2005. "Analysis: Nipping Oranges and Roses in the Bud—Post-Soviet Elites Against Revolution." *Radio Free Europe/Radio Liberty*, January 21.

Kitschelt, Herbert. 2003. "Accounting for Postcommunist Regime Diversity: What Counts as a Good Cause?" In *Capitalism and Democracy in Central and Eastern Europe: Assessing the Legacy of Communist Rule*, Grzegorz Ekiert and Stephen Hanson, eds., 613–634. Cambridge, U.K.: Cambridge University Press.

Koshkovsky, Sophia. 2007. "Kremlin Secures Price Controls on Food Items before Elections." *New York Times,* October 25. http://www.nytimes.com/2007/10/25/world/europe/25moscow.html?pagewanted=print

Kubicek, Paul. 2005. "The European Union and Democratization in Ukraine." *Communist and Post-Communist Studies* 38:269–292.

Kurekova, Lucia. 2006. *Electoral Revolutions and Their Socio-Economic Impact: Bulgaria and Slovakia in Comparative Perspective.* Masters thesis, Department of International Relations and European Studies, Central European University.

Kuzio, Taras. 2005. "From Kuchma to Yushchenko: Orange Revolution in Ukraine." *Problems of Postcommunism* 52:29–44.

Lazić, Mladen and Liljana Nikolić. 1999. *Protest in Belgrade: Winter of Discontent.* Budapest, New York: Central European University Press.

Levitsky, Steven and Lucan A. Way. 2010. *Competitive Authoritarianism: The Origins and Evolution of Hybrid Regimes in the Post-Cold War Era.* New York: Cambridge University Press.

———. 2002. "The Rise of Competitive Authoritarianism." *Journal of Democracy* 13(2):51–65.

Licht, Sonja. 2007. "Serbia between Autocratic and Democratic Transition: A Case Study." Paper presented at the Project on Democratic Transitions, Seminar II: Lessons Learned and Testing Their Applicability. Foreign Policy Research Institute, Philadelphia, February 22–24.

Mastnak, Tomaz. 1994. "From Social Movements to National Sovereignty." In *Independent Slovenia: Origins, Movements, Prospects,* Jill Benderly and Evan Kraft, eds., 93–112. New York: St. Martin's Press.

McFaul, Michael and Kathryn Stoner-Weiss. 2008. "The Myth of the Authoritarian Model: How Putin's Crackdown Holds Russia Back." *Foreign Affairs* 87(1):68–84

Mendelson, Sarah Elizabeth and John K. Glenn. 2002. *The Power and Limits of NGOs: A Critical Look at Building Democracy in Eastern Europe and Eurasia.* New York: Columbia University Press.

Miller, Eric. 2004. "Georgia's New Start." *Problems of Communism* 51(2):12–21.

Oliver, Pamela E. and Daniel J. Meyers, 2003. "Networks, Diffusion, and Collective Cycles of Action." In *Social Movements and Networks: Relational Approaches o Collective Action,* Doug McAdam, ed., 173–192. Oxford, U.K.: Oxford University Press.

Pavlovic, Dusan. 2005. *Akteri I modeli: ogledi o politici u Srbiji pod Milosevic.* Belgrade: B92.

Petrova, Tsvetlana. 2009. "A Post-Communist Transition in Two Acts: The 1996–197 Anti-Government Struggle in Bulgaria as a Bridge between the First and Second Waves of Transition in Eastern Europe." In *Democracy and Authoritarianism in the Postcommunist World,* Valerie Bunce, Michael McFaul, and Kathryn Stoner-Weiss, eds., 107–133. Cambridge, U.K.: Cambridge University Press.

Pribicevic, Ognjen. 2004. "Serbia after Milosevic." *Southeast Europe and Black Sea Studies* 4(1):107–118.

Radnitz, Scott. 2009. "A Horse of a Different Color: Revolution and Regression in Kyrgyzstan." In *Democracy and Authoritarianism in the Postcommunist World,* Valerie Bunce, Michael McFaul, and Kathryn Stoner-Weiss, eds., 300–324. Cambridge, U.K.: Cambridge University Press.

Schedler, Andreas, ed. 2006. *Electoral Authoritarianism: The Dynamics of Unfree Competition.* Boulder, Colo.: Lynne Rienner.

Silitski, Vitali. 2009. "Contagion Deferred: Preemptive Authoritarianism in the Former Soviet Union (the Case of Belarus)." In *Democracy and Authoritarianism in the Postcommunist World,* Valerie Bunce, Michael McFaul, and Kathryn Stoner-Weiss, eds., 274–299. Cambridge, U.K.: Cambridge University Press.

———. 2005. *The Long Road from Tyranny: Post-Communist Authoritarianism and Struggle for Democracy in Serbia and Belarus.* Unpublished book manuscript.

Simmons, Beth, Frank Dobbin, and Geoffrey Garrett. 2008. *The Global Diffusion of Markets and Democracy*. Cambridge, U.K.: Cambridge University Press.

Spector, Regine A. and Andrej Krickovic. 2007. *The Anti-Revolutionary Toolkit*. Unpublished manuscript, University of California, Berkeley, Department of Political Science and Institute for International Studies, March 7.

Stokes, Gale. 1993. *The Walls Came Tumbling Down: The Collapse of Communism in Eastern Europe*. Oxford, U.K.: Oxford University Press.

Stoner-Weiss, Kathryn. 2009. "Comparing Oranges and Apples: The Internal and External Dimensions of Russia's Backslide from Democracy." In *Democracy and Authoritarianism in the Postcommunist World*, Valerie Bunce, Michael McFaul, and Kathryn Stoner-Weiss, eds., 253–273. Cambridge, U.K.: Cambridge University Press.

Tarrow, Sidney. 2005. *The New Transnational Activism*. Cambridge, U.K.: Cambridge University Press.

Tarrow, Sidney and della Porta, Donatella. 2005. "Globalization, Complex Internationalism and Transnational Contention." In *Transnational Protest and Global Activism*, edited by Donatella della Porta and Sidney Tarrow, eds., 227–246. Lanham, Md.: Rowman and Littlefield.

Thomas, Daniel. 2001. *The Helsinki Effect: International Norms, Human Rights, and the Demise of Communism*. Princeton, N.J.: Princeton University Press.

Thomas, Robert. 1999. *The Politics of Serbia in the 1990s*. New York: Columbia University Press.

Vachudova, Milada. 2005. *Europe Undivided: Democracy, Leverage and Integration after Communism*. Oxford, U.K.: Oxford University Press.

Valiyev, Anar M. 2006. "Parliamentary Elections in Azerbaijan: A Failed Revolution." *Problems of Postcommunism* 53(3): 17–35.

Way, Lucan. 2008. "The Real Causes of the Color Revolutions." *Journal of Democracy* 19(3):55–69.

———. 2005a. "Authoritarian State-Building and the Sources of Regime Competitiveness in the Fourth Wave: The Cases of Belarus, Moldova, Russia and Ukraine." *World Politics* 57:231–261

———. 2005b. "Ukraine's Orange Revolution: Kuchma's Failed Authoritarianism." *Journal of Democracy* 16:131–145.

Weyland, Kurt. 2009a. "Diffusion Dynamics in European and Latin American Democratization." Paper presented at the 105th annual meeting of the American Political Science Association, Toronto, September 3–6.

———. 2009b. "The Diffusion of Revolution: '1848' in Europe and Latin America." *International Organization* 63(3):391–423.

Wehnert, Barbara. 2005. "Diffusion and Development of Democracy, 1800–1999." *American Sociological Review* 70(1):53–81.

Weier, Fred. 2006. "'Color Revolutions' Wane: Russia Asserts Its Influence Ahead of Elections in Belarus and Ukraine." *Christian Science Monitor,* May 7.

Welt, Corey. 2009. "Regime Weakness and Electoral Breakthrough in Georgia." In

Democracy and Authoritarianism in the Postcommunist World, Valerie Bunce, Michael McFaul, and Kathryn Stoner-Weiss, eds., 115–188. Cambridge, U.K.: Cambridge University Press.

Wilson, Andrew. 2005. *Virtual Politics: Faking Democracy in the Post-Soviet World*. New Haven, Conn.: Yale University Press.

2

China Politics 20 Years Later

JOSEPH FEWSMITH

In 1989, students mourning the death of Hu Yaobang (胡耀邦), former general secretary of the Chinese Communist Party (CCP), occupied Tiananmen Square, protested corruption and official profiteering (*guandao* 官倒), and demanded that their unofficial student organization be recognized by the government and permitted to enter into discussions with officials. The CCP split; moderates accepted some accommodation with the students, but conservatives were convinced that if they compromised at all with the students, the CCP would, sooner or later, be driven from power. As Premier Li Peng (李鹏) put it, "They will try to establish a multiparty government, force the Communist Party to step down, and subvert the socialist People's Republic. This is their objective, and they will not stop until they reach this objective" (Li [1989] 2005). Determined to demonstrate their strength to both students and cadres throughout the party, the leadership used force to crack down and put the then general secretary, Zhao Ziyang (赵紫阳), under house arrest. Twenty years later, the CCP had not withdrawn its insistence of eight years earlier that its decision was correct; it seems clear that as of that time the party still had no intention of revisiting the matter (Eckholm and Rosenthal 2001).

There were many reasons why China, unlike Eastern Europe, did not democratize 20 years ago, but there were also reasons why in the late 1980s many people were discussing the need for political reform. Many of the factors that made political reform seem important then are still at play today. The very dynamic of reform touched off the issues that would lead to demands for political reform. When Deng Xiaoping (邓小平) returned to power, he adopted the slogan "seek truth from facts" and emphasized the criterion of "practice." These slogans were necessary levers in Deng's drive to move China away from the highly ideological Maoist era when the Maoist call for "self-reliance" was taken as a reason not to trade with the outside world, when Cultural Revolution slogans about how it was better to eat socialist weeds than capitalist grass prevented economic reform, and when the labeling of intellectuals as the "stinking ninth category" prevented the development of science and technology and the training of a new generation in colleges and universities. But in raising the demand to seek truth from facts and the criterion of practice, Deng was doing more than reorienting the CCP's policies; he was changing the relationship of the party to the society. What he was doing, whether he was conscious of it or not, was admitting the limits of ideological knowledge.

This limitation was addressed expressly by the party's ideological authority, Hu Qiaomu (胡桥木), in a critical speech on the economy in 1978. There were, Hu said, objective economic laws, and if the party did not adequately comprehend and act in accordance with those laws, there would be severe costs to pay—as the party had discovered to its chagrin in the Cultural Revolution and in the Great Leap Forward before that (Hu 1978). Hu's admission that there were objective laws external to Marxism began a process of understanding Marxism-Leninism as an epistemology rather than as a complete ideological system (though, ironically, Hu Qiaomu would object to General Secretary Hu Yaobang taking this line of thought yet further in his 1983 speech commemorating the centennial of Marx's death (Hu 1983). The turn from solipsism[1] to epistemology opens the door to experts, who are specialists in interpreting objective laws, and expertise does not depend (at least in theory) on being a party member or an official. Perhaps non-Marxist economists had something to teach the party about those "objective laws" of economics. Given the pressing need to improve China's economy, the practice of economics became less and less dominated by Marxist ideologues—setting off disputes about the role of Marxist economics that continue to this day (Liu 2005:4–11).

Of course, once the party gave up its solipsistic claim to truth, there was inevitably room for leaders in other fields of inquiry to claim that they, too, were subject to objective laws, and, because of that, experts, not the party (and certainly not party ideologues), were the best interpreters of those laws. This is what Tang Tsou called the "sociological postulate," which Tsou paraphrased as, "Every sphere of social life has its special characteristics (*tedian* 特点) and is governed by special laws of an objective nature. Political leadership can and should create general conditions and a framework favorable to the operation of these laws. It can use these laws to promote the desired development. But it cannot violate these laws without suffering serious consequences" (Tsou 1986:220). Thus, there were soon discussions about the laws governing journalism, sociology, writing, and other fields.

This jettisoning of solipsistic knowledge and the readjustment of the party's relation with society marked an irreversible turn. To put it in the terms Kenneth Jowitt has used, as a Leninist party adopts reform it gives up the "exclusive orientation" toward society that it adopted in its revolutionary days in favor of "inclusionary" policy that attempts to shore up legitimacy by co-opting societal interests. But this process undermines the legitimacy of the party just as the pluralization of societal interests threatens the coherence of the party (Jowitt 1975:69–96).

The changing relationship between the Party and society challenged Party legitimacy in more direct ways as well. Rural reform made agriculture more productive, freed up labor for non-agricultural purposes (such as township and village enterprises), and led to the breakup of the communes. However, this reform inevitably generated conflict between villagers and village cadres because it changed an indirect and hidden tax system into a direct and overt one. Prior to the adoption of the Household Responsibility System (HRS), peasants had turned over the grain they had grown to village cadres who then sold it to state grain stations. The revenue received—minus deductions for expenses (if the village had advanced the peasants seed or fertilizer, for instance) and taxes (to cover cadre salaries, but never made explicit)—was turned over to peasant households. With the adoption of the HRS, however, payment went directly to the peasants—which made tax payments visible and made relations between cadres and peasants difficult. Tax collection became contentious. It was such issues that led to the adoption in 1987 of the Organic Law of Villagers' Committees, which authorized village elections (Li and O'Brien 1999:129–144).

It was not just the countryside that presented challenges to the political order; ideological objections in the CCP to economic reform, the dominance of the state-owned economy, and the lack of a professional bureaucracy all hindered economic reform and made the central leadership look to political reform for possible solutions. In 1986 Deng Xiaoping saw political reform as necessary for continued economic reform: Without it, he claimed, "administrative organs will expand, there will be more people than needed, [there will be] bureaucratism, inefficiency, blaming of each other; one place will decentralize power while another takes it back, and inevitably these will be an obstacle to economic reform and create a drag on economic development" (Deng 1993:160).

The Thirteenth Party Congress in 1987 marked the high point of efforts to introduce political reform. Although Deng Xiaoping repeatedly warned against introducing any "Western-style" political reform, the congress report nevertheless created a distinction between political cadres and professional cadres, a step that, if pursued, might have led to a stronger and more professional civil service (Zhao 2009:274). The report also called for the separation of party and government and the corresponding removal of "party groups" from government bureaucracies. Given China's millennial-old tradition of civil service, these actions seemed to mark out a potentially viable approach.

In the context of the political realities of the times, however, the separation of party and state seemed only to create two centers of authority, with inevitable conflicts over power and policy. The notion seemed to threaten a large party bureaucracy that had deeply entrenched interests. In any event, it would have been a long-term effort to pull off such a reform, and the Tiananmen crisis only a year and a half later ended this possibility. The leadership of the party was again stressed.

Thus, like their counterparts in Eastern Europe, Chinese intellectuals spent much of the reform era exploring ideological formulations that would, they hoped, prevent China from ever repeating the national nightmare of the Cultural Revolution and would open up space for personal freedom. Many of their ideas derived from discussions and practices in Eastern Europe, so there was certainly some diffusion. At least in broad terms, the reform trends in China paralleled those in Eastern Europe at the same time—the movement to relegitimize the party through co-optation and inclusion and efforts to reform the economy, professionalize the bureaucracy, and introduce at least some democratic practices. There was also a diffusion of ideas from East Asia, where the Philippines democratized in 1986, Taiwan lifted its ban on opposition parties in 1986, and South Korea held competitive elections for president in 1987 (see chapter 1, which discusses these themes in the Eastern European context). All these influences fed into Chinese discussions in the 1980s and informed student demonstrators in 1989, but they did not lead to democratization in China.

Part of the reason China did not democratize the way Eastern Europe did is simply that these discussions had a shorter history in China. Whereas Eastern Europeans had been considering reforms of different sorts since the 1950s, such discussions could only get under way in China after Deng Xiaoping came to power in the late 1970s. Moreover, although China was definitely the recipient of many ideas coming from throughout the world, China was certainly not integrated culturally and intellectually with other countries the way Eastern European countries were with their Western European neighbors; there were fewer linkages (Levitsky and Way 2010). Unlike European countries that had interacted with one another and saw one another as sharing a common culture, China was much more *sui generis*. One does not have to invoke hoary images of the "middle kingdom" and the tribute system to suggest that China's size and history made it much less likely to be swayed by arguments circulating in both Asia and Europe.

This resistance to external ideas and practices is more compelling when one distinguishes between intellectuals and party cadres, particularly high-level party cadres. Whereas intellectuals and students were readily taken by notions of democracy, the party elite was not. Deng Xiaoping and most of the leadership that had returned to power with him were victims of the Cultural Revolution-era Red Guards who had denounced and sometimes tortured them under the slogan of "big democracy." It was not surprising given this history that the provision for "big democracy" was removed from the 1982 constitution. Although reform-minded intellectuals and some party officials were inspired by Gorbachev's adoption of perestroika and glasnost, the top leaders of the CCP were threatened by such developments.

If part of the Chinese immunity to the diffusion of democratic ideas and movements was rooted in still raw memories of the Cultural Revolution, part could also be attributed to the fact that China was still ruled by first-generation revolutionary leaders. Although Deng Xiaoping called himself the "core" of the "second generation" of leaders, he was really the second core of the first generation. He was only 11 years younger than Mao Zedong and had participated in all the great events of the revolution: the Jiangxi Soviet, the Long March, the War of Resistance, and the Civil War of the late 1940s. Moreover, although he and his colleagues were frustrated by both the chaos and the lack of economic development under Mao, they still believed that the hierarchical CCP was critical to bringing about China's economic development. They certainly did not share Gorbachev's belief that the ruling party was an obstacle to development that either had to be radically reformed or removed.[2]

The CCP was also based on a firmer foundation than any of the ruling parties of Eastern Europe. The CCP had come to power as a result of a broad-based revolution. In Eastern Europe, reform efforts were seen, at least by large portions of the population, as pushing back against an alien system that had been imposed and remained supported by the Soviet Union. In China, the relationship with the Soviet Union was fundamentally different. The Sino-Soviet split of the 1960s had unleashed vitriolic rhetoric and expunged direct Soviet influence in China, making the exponential growth of radicalism in the Great Leap Forward and Cultural Revolution genuinely domestic tragedies. The split with the Soviet Union also made Marxism-Leninism more Chinese and less alien (of course, this was a process begun much earlier, particularly in the Rectification Campaign of 1942–1944). The ideological debt to the Bolshevik Revolution was still acknowledged, but the development and practice of Marxism-Leninism-Mao Zedong Thought was rooted in China's own revolutionary experience. In Eastern Europe, the withdrawal of Soviet support for repression led to the Velvet Revolution and the crumbling of socialism, but the demise of the Soviet Union in 1991, just two years after Tiananmen, led not to renewed questioning of socialism—the repression of Tiananmen closed off that alternative—but rather to a renewed emphasis on nationalism. As a neo-conservative manifesto put it in 1991, the legitimacy of the communist revolution was built on the dual pillars of the Bolshevik Revolution and the loess soil of Yan'an (the CCP's base from 1936 to 1947); with the crumbling of the Soviet Union, it was all the more necessary to emphasize the indigenous origins and development of the Chinese Revolution (*China Youth Daily* 1996).

This reemphasis on the Chinese Revolution was almost a necessity of the times. The collapse of socialism in Eastern Europe removed a reference group that had been important for reforms in China because reform measures in Eastern Europe had provided models and legitimacy for China's own reform efforts. The collapse of socialism in Eastern Europe and subsequently in the Soviet Union underscored, as had the demonstrations in Tiananmen Square, the fact that reforms could lead to economic development and greater personal freedom but they could also lead to political collapse. Thus, Deng Xiaoping warned in the immediate aftermath of Tiananmen that there were two types reform: socialist reform that would lead to economic development and capitalist reform that would lead to the collapse of socialism (Deng 1993:302–308).

Thus, in the aftermath of Tiananmen, China was thrown back on self-referencing understandings of socialism (even the most conservative leaders never contemplated looking to Vietnam and North Korea for models of socialism) and nationalism. Much of the cosmopolitanism that had informed thinking about reform in the 1980s was lost or at least could not be articulated publicly. This created something of a hothouse for the further development of nationalistic thinking. Fortunately Chinese leaders did not fall back on prereform notions of running the economy by reliance on central planning, not even conservative elder Chen Yun (陈云) would have favored this, and Deng Xiaoping was still the paramount leader. Nevertheless, the tendency to look to China's indigenous experience was reinforced both by the failure of "shock therapy" to reform the Soviet economy and the "discovery" that Chinese "incremental" reform was successful (Fewsmith 2001:80–83). There was a much greater confidence by the early 1990s that Chinese economists and policy makers could guide the reform process and that Western theories and policy prescriptions (later summed up as the "Washington consensus") were either wrong for China, pernicious, or both.

The Evolution of Elite Politics

The Tiananmen suppression represented a political meltdown on the part of China's party elite—a culmination of disagreements stoked by different ideological approaches and interests, succession politics, and the clash of strong personalities. Political meltdowns are generally a prelude to more thoroughgoing sociopolitical crises, not to a period of stable politics and rapid economic growth. But Tiananmen did nothing to disrupt the party structure, and once power relations and policy directions had been sorted out in Beijing (at the expense of former general secretary Zhao Ziyang's political life and personal freedom), the Party was perfectly capable of restoring order throughout the country and implementing the policies decided in Beijing. Moreover, Tiananmen did not affect the core position of Deng Xiaoping (though his political prestige was certainly weakened by Tiananmen). Not only did Deng survive as the paramount leader of China, but those who might have thrown the polity off balance had they lived longer than Deng died in the early 1990s—ideologue Hu Qiaomu in 1992, party elder and former president Li Xiannian (李先念) also in 1992, and conservative economic policy specialist Chen Yun in 1995. The actuarial tables thus gave Deng's designated successor, Jiang Zemin (江泽民), a chance to establish his authority in Beijing under Deng's tutelage.

Deng's final interventions in politics set the political and policy directions decisively. In January 1992, Deng travelled to the Shenzhen Special Economic Zone in Guangdong province to state unequivocally that anything that developed the "productive forces" (the economy) of socialism was ipso facto socialist and to tell his leftist adversaries that if they did not support reform (Deng's definition of reform) they must "step down" (Deng 1993:370–383). Deng was able to impose his views on the party by engineering the retirement of several influential conservatives at the Fourteenth Party Congress in September 1992, having the congress strongly endorse his views of reform and then, shortly after the close of the congress, purging top military officials who had not accepted the leadership of Jiang Zemin (Fewsmith 2001:64–68). If we think of the stabilization, some would say institutionalization, of elite politics in the 1990s and the first decade of the new century, the irony is that it was brought about by distinctly noninstitutional means—Deng's Xiaoping's forceful intervention and the careful balancing of interests in the party.

The leaders who succeeded the revolutionary generation—Jiang Zemin and, after 2002, Hu Jintao (胡锦涛)—were clearly not as strong as their predecessors. They lacked the accomplishments, prestige, personal networks, and decisive personalities of the previous generation; they simply could not "strike the table" (pai banzi, 拍板子) and make decisions the way Deng could. In a highly authoritarian polity, weaker leadership could lead to infighting and paralysis or perhaps to democratization as leading officials give in to societal pressures. So far, this has not proved to be the case; there have been trends toward further centralization as the government in Beijing has become wealthier, as the Chinese economy has performed well, and as the center has fought against decentralizing tendencies in the provinces.

The general political stability under Jiang Zemin and Hu Jintao is also attributable to the growing routinization of Chinese politics. Membership in the Central Committee is decided by position rather than by a single leader appointing cronies. For instance, all provincial party secretaries and governors, heads of military regions, and a number of other positions are routinely promoted to the Central Committee. This does not eliminate the promotion of political protégés, but it does keep a check on such behavior—at a minimum, a political leader has to plan some years ahead to be able to put a young protégé in a position from which he or she can be further promoted.

Stability in politics has also been promoted by China's system of revolving leadership change. Unlike democratic systems in which the whole administration turns over with the election of a new president, China replaces leaders over time. Thus, roughly half of the membership of the Central Committee turns over every five years. Because the previous general secretary of the party will have considerable influence over the composition of the Central Committee and makeup of the all important Politburo Standing Committee, a new general secretary needs years to be able to consolidate his position—indeed, just in time to give way to a new general secretary. It is a system that both promotes cronyism and, at least so far, has prevented cronyism from becoming dominant (Fewsmith 2010a:149–164).

It is, however, too early to say that China's political system has become institutionalized. Weaker leadership perhaps promotes a tendency to consult widely in the interest of building consensus and spreading responsibility, but it also reinforces cronyism or factional politics. This tendency exists at least in part because the criteria by which one gets promoted to the highest levels (general secretary, premier, Politburo Standing Committee, and Politburo) become blurrier over time. For the revolutionary generation, political office could be distributed more or less according to accomplishments in the revolution, but doing so becomes more difficult when the revolutionary generation passes away. Deng was able to delay this leadership uncertainty by designating not just one but two successors, Jiang Zemin and Hu Jintao. This personnel arrangement has provided two decades of relative political stability, but as the CCP heads toward the Eighteenth Party Congress, scheduled for 2012, it appears as if it is becoming more difficult to decide who should be promoted to high office. How does one compare, in the absence of voting, the accomplishments of, for example, Wang Yang (汪洋), the party secretary in Guangdong, against the record of Bo Xilai (薄熙) in Chongqing, against the achievements of Yu Zhengsheng (俞正声) in Shanghai and Zhang Gaoli (张高丽) in Tianjin? The difficulty of such comparisons appears to be fueling greater factionalism and more public "campaigning." It is difficult to say how far such tendencies will go, but these trends suggest that the political arrangements that have prevailed in the 20 years since Tiananmen may not be as stable as they have appeared.

When viewed from the perspective of two decades after the event, the combination of the Tiananmen suppression, on the one hand, and the collapse of socialism in Eastern Europe and the breakup of the Soviet Union, on the other, marked an end to the deep ideological and personal divides of the 1980s and made clear to the party elite that destructive political struggles could result in the collapse of the CCP. This perspective renewed the focus of the party on economic development, which the party has pursued with single-minded devotion and singular success ever since. But this focus on economic development came at the expense of the discussions on political reform that had drawn so much attention in the 1980s. However, a lot of the issues that preoccupied intellectuals in the 1980s continue to be relevant: the personalization of power inevitable in a hierarchical, single-party system; corruption; the weakness of institutions; and the difficulty of sorting out state-society relations. What the crackdown in 1989 did in political terms was to truncate some of the alternatives that were beginning to be explored, such as the separation of party and government, in favor of a re-emphasis on party rule in practice if not in theory. Twenty years later it is evident that single-party rule can promote economic growth, but it is far from clear that it can successfully tackle the issues that were already evident in the 1980s. Looking at local politics suggests why.

The Contradictions of Local Government

One impact of Tiananmen was that political reform at the central level was simply not possible, at least for the foreseeable future, so reformers began to look more earnestly at the grassroots level. After the National People's Congress (NPC) Standing Committee, despite dissension, reaffirmed the Organic Law for Villagers' Committees, village elections began to be held throughout the country. As villages became experienced in the holding of elections and villagers began to perceive them as meaningful (at least in some areas), nominations of candidates for at least some villages became more open. Jilin province pioneered the practice of "sea elections" (*hai xuan* 海选) in which anyone could be nominated.

The spread of village elections opened up the possibility of another route to democratic reform. If village governance were democratized, reformers hoped, then, over time, elections might be gradually extended upward to townships, counties, and eventually to the highest levels. There were, however, at least three obstacles to this path. First, in China's constitutional system, villages are conceived of as "self-governing." There are, of course, party branches in villages and the party secretary is in charge of running the village, but village cadres are not part of the formal bureaucracy (that is to say, they are not "civil servants," *gongwuyuan*, 公务员) and are paid out of village funds. So there is an important political gap separating villages from townships, the lowest level of official bureaucracy. Thus, there was no necessary logic, except perhaps psychological pressure, by which elections at the village level would pressure higher levels to democratize.

Second, in a significant number of villages, elections created political tensions between elected village heads and appointed party secretaries. Village heads, claiming a popular mandate, frequently defied the leadership of the party, and party secretaries sometimes would refuse to give the seals of office to elected village chiefs. In one widely publicized instance, 57 village chiefs in Shandong province resigned from office collectively, publicizing the failure of party secretaries to allow them to take office (Cui 2001). This political conflict led the party to look for ways to prevent dissension and to appeal to popular opinion. One way the party has done so has been to encourage party secretaries to run as village heads—a method that ensures the party secretary has some level of support in the village and unifies the two positions in one person (a system known as "one shoulder pole," *yi jian tiao*, 一件条). This system is now used in about half of all villages in China.

Finally, township officials generally opposed the spread of democratic elections at the village level. Township officials are evaluated (by county officials) on how well they have performed the tasks set out for them by the next highest level. Such tasks normally revolve around tax collection (before the agricultural tax was eliminated), economic development, and social stability. Democratic elections could affect the fulfillment of all three. Village heads could side with villagers in refusing to pay taxes or at least the amount demanded by higher levels. They might have different ideas about how to develop the local economy, and thus they might not perform satisfactorily the tasks assigned for them by township leaders. Disputes with village party secretaries and the defiance of tax burdens could lead to social disturbances or petition movements that would make township leaders appear to be ineffective. Thus, township authorities generally had an interest in manipulating elections in the villages below them to ensure that the "right" people were nominated and elected. The political logic of local government was generally for higher levels to suppress democratic tendencies at lower levels rather than for village elections to stimulate democratic demands at higher levels.

Although there is no necessary logic that pushes elections from the village level up to the township level, there have been numerous elections—mostly, but not exclusively, within the party at the township level. Underscoring the disconnect between the lack of democratic demands and the emergence of these semicompetitive elections is the fact that not one of them was the result of popular demand from below (Lai 2009:84). On the contrary, the motive for elections at the township level is rooted in the need of local cadres to resolve social tensions. In less developed areas such as Sichuan province, which has been the locale of most township elections, tensions between local cadres and citizens have risen as tax revenues have fallen, either because of the 1994 tax reform that centralized much revenue or because of the abolition of agricultural taxes in the first decade of this century, or both.

With shrinking resources, it became increasingly difficult for local cadres to secure the revenue necessary to build the local economy. Local cadres inevitably did whatever they could to raise revenue, which often resulted in tense relations between them and the local population. In such situations, innovative township party secretaries have been willing to experiment with limited, semicompetitive elections. Such elections expand the number of participants in voting from a small number around the party secretary to perhaps 200 or 300. At the same time, nominations are opened up to a wider group of aspirants (nominations can be through self-recommendation, joint recommendation of 10 or more party members, or by work unit). For a party secretary facing tense social relations and needing to develop the economy, finding ways to expand the talent pool can be a good option. The party secretary earns a reputation as being an innovative and a successful manager of complex situations and thus improves his or her chances of being promoted. Meanwhile, a new cadre entering the situation is likely to find social tensions reduced and thus will have little incentive to continue to pursue democratic reforms. While there is a logic to government innovation at the township level, there is little or no logic to maintaining or expanding local democracy. On the contrary, in the absence of institutionalized procedures, reform tends to backtrack (Fewsmith 2010b).

This tendency to backtrack is not something that occurs independently at the local level but exists because local politics are embedded in a hierarchical system, and it has been in the interests of the central party-state to periodically reinforce the rules of that hierarchy. Perhaps the best-known instance of this behavior is the reaction to the Buyun town (步云镇) election in Sichuan. In 1998, confronted by the sort of social discontent previously discussed, local authorities decided to hold an election for township officials. Although there were limits on nominations and campaigning, the electorate was extended to include all eligible voters. After the election (which the party candidate won), central authorities determined that Buyun procedures had violated the constitution (Zha 1999). Although the central authorities did not prohibit all elections, they did force them back within much narrower confines.

These strictures were later tested in Pingchang county (平昌县) in north-ern Sichuan in 2004 and 2005. At that time, the county extended "public rec-ommendation, direct elections" (*gongtui zhixuan,* 公推直选) to one-third of its townships. Under Pingchang's method, township party secretaries were nominated in meetings that included all party members of the township and representatives of the masses, with the proviso that nonparty representatives could not exceed 30 percent of the number of party members. After nomina-tions and "campaign" speeches, all party members would vote. This greatly extended the franchise, not to the extent adopted in Buyun township in 1998 but well beyond the usual inner party elections adopted in other townships in Sichuan (Fewsmith 2008). Although the Pingchang experiment appeared highly successful at first, soon there were conflicts between officials in charge of the experiment and party cadres who had been dismissed from office when the county had merged townships and villages the year before the end-of-term elections (which served to ratify the new arrangements). Eventually these disputes reached higher levels, which criticized Pingchang county officials for having violated the principle of the "party controls the cadres" (*dang guan ganbu,* 党管干部). The result was that many of the reforms made previously were reversed, and strictures on the scope of democracy, even of the sort previ-ously outlined, were confirmed.[3]

Although it had seemed possible that village elections and the spread of township elections would at least give the old Leninist principle that the party controls the cadres a new and expanded meaning, any movement in that direc-tion seems to have been slowed or halted. This is perhaps a natural tendency in a hierarchical party, but it is one that has been reinforced by the threats seeming to emanate from the "color revolutions" in Georgia, the Ukraine, Tajikistan, and Kyrgyzstan. Such political movements strengthened the fears of Chinese leaders that any expansion of democratic processes could get out of control (from their point of view), and such concerns have reinforced the hierarchical principle that the party controls the cadres. As belief in any sort of overarching ideology continues to decline, however, the tendency has been to reinforce personal ties and, accordingly, to heighten corruption.

The Ledger

Two decades after Tiananmen, China has been remarkably successful in pre-serving political stability. Authoritarian regimes have a difficult time both with passing power on from a commanding leader, such as Deng Xiaoping, and with transferring power in general. Nevertheless, Jiang Zemin took over from Deng, despite Jiang's inexperience at the central level and his absence of military experience, and Hu Jintao took over from Jiang Zemin in 2002. Although these transitions were not as smooth as sometimes depicted, they were generally successful. Deng Xiaoping had a lot to do with this, designating both Jiang and Hu, and thus avoiding the sort of inner-party contention that seemed likely to develop in the absence of Deng's strong hand. Whether or not political succession has really been institutionalized, as some commentators suggest, Deng provided China with two decades of political stability. China has changed dramatically in those two decades, but the possibility of renewed political conflict seems palpable as the shadow of Deng fades and the Eighteenth Party Congress begins to loom large.

Political contention, in the absence of electoral rules, breeds factionalism. The CCP has always had strong prohibitions against factionalism even as personal networks appear critical for attaining and maintaining power. As different contenders for power seem increasingly similar in terms of their qualifications, tendencies toward factionalism and coalition building may increase. Such tendencies, of course, also breed corruption and cynicism. Cynicism can be a demobilizing force but can turn into its opposite in critical moments; the mobilization of students in the spring of 1989 was one such moment.

Similarly, the reliance on the cadre evaluation system to preserve hierarchy and select lower-level cadres for promotion inevitably engenders the personalization of power. When one looks at the articulation of cadre selection rules in the 1990s and beyond, there is a clear sense that the central party organization would like to constrain the power of the party secretary at lower levels but simultaneously demands that the principle of the party controlling the cadres continues to be implemented. To date, the idea of the party controlling the cadres has prevailed, so power continues to be personalized. The personalization of power, of course, means that competing principles, whether "inner-Party democracy" or "rule by law," cannot be established (Minzer 2009). The personalization of power means that corruption, including the purchase and sale of office, flourishes. Worse still is the tendency for corrupt officials to ally themselves with criminal elements.[4]

The result is a political system that, on the one hand, breeds resistance because the personalization of power inevitably leads to the abuse of power and, on the other hand, has been remarkably successful at defusing challenges to power either through compromise, coercion, or some combination thereof. Although there are clear pressures within the system to defuse tension by expanding mechanisms to enforce accountability—through elections (either inside the party or more broadly), supervision (increasing the role of the People's Congresses), or greater transparency (such as publishing budget figures)—the system as a whole has been quite resistant to any mechanism that would constrain the exercise of power within the party.

Conclusion

Two decades later, a new generation of Chinese citizens has grown up with no direct memory of Tiananmen, and most profess little interest, beyond perhaps idle curiosity, about those events. China's economy has raced ahead, raising living standards at least in the prosperous east coast cities, and propelling China to a global status unimaginable at the time of Tiananmen. It is often said in China that whatever the cost of Tiananmen, it brought about two decades of political stability and economic prosperity.

The costs of repression, however, need to be measured not just in GDP figures but also in distortions introduced in China's political system. One might argue that the CCP would have remained the sole source of political power in China irrespective of the outcome of events in 1989, but it is not difficult to imagine that a peaceful outcome of those events would have led to a more vigorous role for the National People's Congress (China's legislative body), more freedom for the media, greater scope for law, and perhaps a more expansive role for local elections. In short, one could have anticipated more political transparency, public supervision, and accountability.

The repression of Tiananmen, however, made the party vigilant against all sorts of threats to the CCP, real or imagined, and thus reinforced hierarchical control, particularly the cadre evaluation system with its underlying principle that the party controls the cadres. Despite efforts to subject local party secretaries to greater scrutiny and to open up the cadre selection system to at least somewhat wider participation, it seems that little has been done in reality to limit the power of the local party secretary. His or her key role inevitably leads to the personalization of power. With the personalization of power (and the decline of ideological constraint) has come a degree of corruption that was beyond the comprehension of protesting students two decades ago.

The abuse of power at the local level has been the primary cause of the growing number of protests, generally called "mass incidents," China has witnessed in recent years. Such incidents have, to date, been localized affairs in protest of particular wrongs and have not yet generated any broad-based movement, or even understanding, aimed at correcting the political system. By "playing by the rules," such incidents seem to reinforce the system rather than challenge it (Perry 2010). But if we understand mass incidents as a social reflection of abuses that are integral to the political system, then one seems to face the prospect of a never-ending drama of protest and the reinforcement of the political system.

As Chinese increasingly talk about the "Beijing consensus" or "Chinese model" and seem increasingly confident about China's place in the world, it is more than a little ironic that the political system itself, reinforced by the repression two decades ago, is the source of social instability.

Notes

1. Philosophically, solipsism is the idea that one can only understand one's own mind (hence, Réné Descartes's famous declaration, "I think, therefore I am"). The term is extended here to mean a privileged claim to the truth, for example, an ideological proposition that cannot be tested by reference to something external to the ideology itself, such as voting.
2. In his memoir, Zhao Ziyang tells of Deng Xiaoping saying in the early 1980s that the Politburo in the Soviet Union could meet and decide to invade Afghanistan. "Could America manage that?" Deng demanded. "I think the U.S. can't overtake (*gao bu guo*, 搞不过) the Soviet Union" (Zhao 2009:275).
3. Interviews with Chinese researchers.
4. The most recent example is in Chongqing, where party secretary Bo Xilai has carried out a high-profile campaign against organized crime (Fewsmith 2010c).

References

China Youth Daily. 1996. "Realistic Responses and Strategic Options for China after the Soviet Upheaval." Trans. David Kelly. *Chinese Law and Government* 29: 13–31.

Cui Shixin. 2001. "Cunguan weihe yao cizhi. (Why Village Heads Want to Resign.") *Renmin ribao (People's Daily)* March 21, 2001.

Deng, Xiaoping. 1993. "Zai tingqu jingji qingkuang huibao shi de tanhua (Talk When Listening to a Report on Economic Circumstances.)" *Deng Xiaoping wenxuan, disan zhuan (Selected Works of Deng Xiaoping, vol. 3)*. Beijing: Renmin chubanshe.

Eckholm, Erik and Elizabeth Rosenthal. 2001. "China's Leadership Pushes for Unity." *The New York Times* March 9, 2001, p. 1.

Fewsmith, Joseph. 2001. *China since Tiananmen: The Politics of Transition*. Cambridge: Cambridge University Press.

———. 2008. "A New Upsurge in Political Reform? Maybe." *China Leadership Monitor* 24. Available at: http://media.hoover.org/documents/CLM24JF.pdf.

———. 2010a. "The Evolution of Elite Politics." In *China Today, China Tomorrow: Domestic Politics, Economy, and Society*, Joseph Fewsmith, ed., 149–164. Lanham, Md.: Roman & Littlefield.

———. 2010b. "Inner-Party Democracy: Development and Limitations." *China Leadership Monitor* 31. Available at: http://media.hoover.org/sites/default/files/documents/CLM31JF.pdf

———. 2010c. "Bo Xilai Takes on Organized Crime." *China Leadership Monitor* 32. Available at http://www.hoover.org/publications/china-leadership-monitor/3601.

Hu, Qiaomu. 1978. "Act in Accordance with Economic Laws, Step up the Four Modernizations." *Xinhua*, October 5, 1978, trans. FBIS, October 11, 1978, pp. E1–22.

Hu, Yaobang. 1983. "The Radiance of the Great Truth of Marxism Lights Our Way Forward." *Xinhua*, March 13, 1983, trans. FBIS, March 14, 1983, pp. K1–22.

Jowitt, Kenneth. 1975. "Inclusion and Mobilization in European Leninist Regimes." *World Politics* 28(1):69–96.

Lai Hairong. 2009. *Zhongguo nongcun zhengzhi tizhi gaige—Xiangzhen banjingzhengxing xuanju yanjiu. (China's Rural Political Reform—A Study of Township Semi-Competitive Elections)*. Beijing: Zhongyang bianyiju chubanshe.

Levitsky, Steven and Lucan A. Way. 2010. *Competitive Authoritarianism: Hybrid Regimes after the Cold War*. New York: Cambridge University Press.

Li, Lianjiang and Kevin O'Brien. 1999. "The Struggle over Village Elections." In *The Paradox of Post-Mao Reforms*, Merle Goldman and Roderick MacFarquhar, eds., 129–144. Cambridge, Mass.: Harvard University Press.

Li Peng. [1989] 2005. "Top-Secret Fourth Plenary Session Document: Li Peng's Life-Taking Report Lays Blame on Zhao Ziyang." In "Three Interviews with Zhao Ziyang," Mei Qiren, ed., 69–84. *Chinese Law and Government* 38(3).

Liu Guoguang. 2005. "Jingjixue jiaoxue he yanjiu de yixie wenti (On Certain Issues in the Teaching and Research of Economics)." *Jingji yanjiu* 10:4–11.

Minzer, Carl. 2009. "Riots and Cover-Ups: Counterproductive Control of Local Agents in China." *University of Pennsylvania Journal of International Law* 31 (Fall 2009): 53–123.

Perry, Elizabeth J. 2010. "Popular Protest in China: Playing by the Rules," in *China Today, China Tomorrow: Domestic Politics, Economy, and Society*, 11–28, Joseph Fewsmith, ed. Lanham, Md.: Roman & Littlefield.

Tsou, Tang. 1986. "Political Change and Reform: The Middle Path." In *The Cultural Revolution and Post-Mao Reforms: A Historical Perspective*, 219–258. Chicago: University of Chicago Press.

Zha Qingju. 1999. "Minzhu buneng chaoyuen falü. (Democracy Must Not Transcend the Law.)" *Fazhi ribao*, January 19, 1999.

Zhao Ziyang. 2009. *Gaige licheng (The Course of Reform)*. Hong Kong: New Century Media.

PART II

RECASTING STATE-SOCIETY RELATIONS

3

Postsocialist Cleansing in Eastern Europe

Purity and Danger in Transitional Justice

KATHERINE VERDERY

Among the many problems that emerged following the collapse of Eastern Europe's Communist Party regimes was a set of issues that peace activists, lawyers, and students of comparative politics treat under the rubric of *transitional justice*. This term refers broadly to various means by which the successor states to "authoritarian" polities seek to address and overcome their legacy of repression; it has been applied to a wide variety of cases, including South Africa, Rwanda, Argentina, Chile, and states of the formerly Soviet bloc. The issues covered are equally broad: how to create democracy and the rule of law in the wake of "lawless" and undemocratic regimes; how to bring to justice those who perpetrated violations of human rights, whether to punish or grant amnesty to such persons, and how to compensate victims; how to prevent supporters of the former regime from corrupting or destabilizing the new order; how to achieve reconciliation among opposing parties; how to come to terms with pasts that were deeply painful and often unacknowledged; and how to revise the nation's historical narrative accordingly.

The literature on transitional justice concerns transforming authoritarianism toward something better, particularly from a legal point of view. The intent is to change the nature of the polity and state—for post-Soviet cases, diminishing the power of the Communist Party and its elites while institutionalizing new political relations between governing entities and the populace. As an aspect of a new governmentality, transitional justice also concerns new ways of managing social behavior. The irony is, however, that as with transformations of the economy, postsocialist state retrenchment reduced the capacity to institutionalize new forms of governing. Seen as essential to building democracy, transitional justice as a concept and a practice distinguishes the experience of the former Soviet bloc from that of China, where authoritarian government saw no comparable interruption.

This chapter treats only one of these many issues: the problem of banning persons who had occupied important posts in the communist regimes from holding important posts in the new regimes, usually for a specified period of time (at first, five to 15 years). A subset of this was the problem of preventing people who had worked for or collaborated with the secret police from holding important positions. Solutions to both problems affect the composition of postsocialist elites and open possibilities for citizen action unknown in the previous regime. They target two main kinds of people for exclusion from political life: Some were widely known because they held public offices before (e.g., as party officials, prosecutors, or police), whereas others whose work was defined as secret were known by few, if any. Procedures for identifying and dealing with these two types of targets differ correspondingly.

Terminology varies as to whether scholars and/or participants distinguish between the two types. Some refer to both with the term *decommunization*,[1] others with the term *lustration*, though that word is more often reserved for the problem of police collaborators only. In this chapter I will use *departification* for the process of banning former (usually high) party officials from holding important posts (though the term's possible referents are wider than that) and *lustration*— the process I am more interested in—for the problem of dealing with secret police agents and informers (see also Sadurski 2005; Krygier and Czarnota 2006). To refer to them together, I will use *cleansing*, which draws on one of the meanings of *lustration*: purification. As my choice of this term (with its echoes of ethnic cleansing) indicates, I see the relation of cleansing to democratization as complex, though I recognize that sometimes it has had democratizing effects.

Lustration and departification have been crucial ingredients of the larger issues I raised at the beginning—creating a rule of law, delivering justice, and promoting democratic practice in the transition from socialism. If former party officials were allowed to keep running things after 1989, there was no reason to think significant regime changes would happen: Their values and habits of mind, ongoing social relationships, future interests, and institutional locations would prevent it. They would be able to use their networks, which covered most of the principal economic, administrative, and judicial resources, "to exchange political power for economic assets and then use the latter to regain political influence, undermining the integrity of the state and its key organs," as David puts it (2004:789). New leaders, even if they, too, were former communists, realized that the internal and external legitimacy of the new government would be enhanced by at least the appearance of calling the Communist Party to account for its actions. But the literature also reveals major obstacles in the path of these cleansing policies as ways of establishing democracy and the rule of law. Among the thorniest was that, because under the communist system it was legal to obey party orders and collaborate with the secret police, the principles of *nulla poena sine lege* and *tempus regit actum* (so-called nonretroactivity principles) would prohibit prosecuting that behavior after the fact. In Hungary, the Constitutional Court invalidated lustration laws on precisely these grounds, one example of the conundrum of trying to create lawfulness across the divide between socialism and postsocialism.

My goals in this chapter are, first, to survey briefly some of the forms these solutions took in Eastern Europe in the 20 years after 1989, then to offer some open-ended thoughts about the process and the way it has been formulated that depart from the lawyerly and political science concerns informing most of the voluminous literature on the topic. I hope to raise provocative questions about "state-society relations" from an anthropologist's viewpoint, thereby complementing Weller's paper, from a different angle. Weller examines how the Chinese state has gone from "seeing-eye" to "blind-eye" governance, adapting its policies to everyday practices it has learned to tolerate, and he shows how citizens take advantage of the state's resources and its blind eye to pursue their own goals. By contrast, this chapter explores attempts to make the seeing eye of socialism emerge from the shadows by instituting procedures for governmental transparency; I speculate on how new political resources provide opportunities for people to make their way in a postsocialist order, rendering politics more opaque in the process rather than increasing visibility. Both of us reveal a mix of opacity and vision in practices of governance and citizenship, a combination of people who obey the law and others who push its margins, though in my case the actors are more likely to be politicians than the ordinary citizens Weller discusses. Each of us in different ways seeks to add nuance to the global categories of state and society in looking at politics since 1989 and to look beyond laws and institutions for the ways behavior is managed.

Overview of Lustration and Departification, 1990 to circa 2008[2]

We owe the term *lustration* (*lustrace*) to Czechoslovakia, which framed an early cleansing law in 1990 and 1991. A term with a complex derivation, *lustrace* was used by the Czechoslovak secret police (StB) to mean "to review or examine" (and not, as is often claimed, "purification by sacrifice").[3] Czechoslovakia and Germany provided the model for other countries of the region, even though the absorption of East Germany into a unified German state made it an unsuitable model for the others. Only in Germany was there a radical separation between those who legislated the screening, West Germans, and those who were screened, East Germans (Sadurski 2005:233). Everywhere else, screeners and screened were intermingled, with consequences for the forms and pace of cleansing practices. Moreover, Germany devoted extraordinary resources to using the enormous Stasi archive to ferret out collaborators, allocating to the task a staff of more than 3,000 employees and a budget exceeding 200 million Deutsche Mark (the entire defense budget of Lithuania). Crucial in the German case was longstanding criticism of West Germany for not having pursued a sufficiently stringent denazification policy after World War II; this made the German government after 1989 eager to show it could do better this time and contributed to the relatively harsh solution adopted (Sadurski 2005:233). Moreover, Larson suggests, because each German state had long accused the other of not having fully repudiated the Nazis, going after the Stasi was a way for West Germany to "socialize" the East into the kind of purification it considered itself to have undergone already.[4] I will first summarize the form of cleansing that emerged in Czechoslovakia, the originator of lustration, and then more briefly characterize other instances.

In Czechoslovakia, strong public pressure to eliminate communist officials from the new polity led all parties but the Communist Party to purge from their rosters for the June 1990 elections any candidate with a secret police record.[5] A cleansing law narrowly passed Parliament in October 1991, despite criticism from both President Václav Havel and assembly head Alexander Dubček. It disqualified persons from specific forms of employment on the basis of two lengthy lists: One specified the positions held or activities engaged in during the socialist period that after 1989 would prevent a person from holding positions on the other list, containing posts for which any applicant must pass the lustration test. The first list contained officials extending downward to relatively low positions in the Communist Party and state administration at the district and even township levels; the StB, intelligence, and security apparatuses; and anyone collaborating with those organizations. Persons on that list were to be excluded from positions on the second list for five years (thus, to 1996), later extended to 2000, and then extended indefinitely. The second list contained jobs in civil service, intelligence, and the judiciary; managerial positions in the media and press, national bank, and state enterprises; higher ranks in administration, police, army, and universities, as well as the Academy of Sciences—but not, significantly, parliamentary or other positions contested in the elections. For all the posts on the list, one had to pass the lustration test. This meant receiving from the Ministry of the Interior a certificate stating that one did not appear in the files as a collaborator—therefore, one was "lustration negative." Although the law did not cover elected office, nearly all parties required their candidates to present a negative certificate in order to run for elected positions.

According to Sadurski (2005:236–237), there were a number of motives for this swift and punitive law. The Czechoslovak regime had been among the harshest in Eastern Europe, and its secret police had heavily infiltrated all social groups. The party had all along required loyalty not to the Czechoslovak state but to the party alone; in 1989 its leaders had ordered the police to do anything possible to destabilize the opposition. Moreover, some 90 percent of the StB files had been destroyed or hidden. These facts appeared to justify seeing the StB as a real and present danger to the state and lustration as necessary to preserve its safety and democratic prospects. In addition, the Czechoslovak regime's collapse was not "negotiated," like those in Poland and Hungary, but represented a near-revolutionary break, after which the remnant Communist Party was a weak force in Parliament (in contrast with, for example, Romania). Cleansing would make room for a new elite uncorrupted by ties to the communist past, and the communists were too weak to prevent it.

This law and its early results led to immediate challenges; these went to a Review Commission created in 1992, which proved unable to keep up with the complaints about false lustration "positives." Problems with how to define *collaborator,* among other things, led to a challenge before the Constitutional Court, which made some changes but otherwise upheld the law. A crucial difficulty was that prior destruction of numerous files meant that for many people the only proofs of collaboration were the registration card the StB had filled out for its collaborators, with no further behavioral evidence (e.g., informers' reports, signed statements). The main people with extensive StB files were likely to be dissidents, whom the StB might have approached for collaboration or interrogated at length and then created files on, even if those approached had refused to cooperate (ibid.:334); their mere presence in the files made them lustration positive. A number of celebrated Czech and Slovak cases served to reveal the dark face of lustration, particularly its inability to separate victims from perpetrators (see Wechsler 1992; Priban 2007:333–337). Between 1991 and 2001, the ministry issued 402,270 certificates (Priban 2007:315). Polls conducted in 2000, when the law was extended, showed that only one-third of the population favored it (ibid.:316). This relative lack of interest on the part of the public contrasted with ongoing activity in Parliament, where communist deputies in 2003 proposed killing the law but failed: It had proved too useful in political infighting to be dispensed with.

East German cleansing, which was legislated in the August 1990 unification treaty, conformed with that in Czechoslovakia by assigning collective guilt to groups of perpetrators—all officials of certain kinds, all secret police collaborators—and made them ineligible for certain kinds of employment. Although from a social point of view Germany's cleansing was retributive (to sanction behavior that occurred under the communist regime), from the legal point of view, as in Czechoslovakia, the cleansing laws concerned labor issues—a person's qualifications for holding public office. The clash between these two understandings was the source of much frustration (Wilke 2007:349). The main target of cleansing efforts was the civil service in general, but special attention went to members and collaborators of the Stasi. Although the unification treaty did not provide for variation in the vetting process, its actual implementation varied widely across sectors, states, and administrative departments. Some institutions (courts, universities) tended to use more stringent procedures across the board, while others (such as town administrations) differentiated their practices according to an employee's level of responsibility (Wilke 2007:391).

As in the Czechoslovak case, there was heated debate about the definition of collaboration, with the fundamental difference that because citizens across eastern Germany occupied Stasi headquarters early on, far more of the Stasi archive survived the regime change than in any other country.[6] That archive thus provided a detailed database for assessing collaboration. In addition, Germans had access to their files so as to vindicate themselves, as Czechs and Slovaks did not until much later. The purge of Stasi collaborators proved unexpectedly difficult because surveillance was so pervasive (with an estimated 91,000 full-time employees and another 174,000 collaborators,[7] there was about one Stasi contact per 35 adults). In contrast to Czechoslovakia, implementation of the law provided for more extensive proofs, allowed more room for nuance, regarded human weakness with some dispassion, and made exceptions for valuable people who had shown one way or another that they were trustworthy and had rejected the communist system. Still, as a result of vetting and shrinking budgets, by 1996 some 60,000 to 100,000 people had been dismissed for their Stasi connections (Bruce 2009:29). In a study of four institutions, between 25 percent and 45 percent of people found to be Stasi collaborators had to leave (Wilke 2007:391).

The Czech[8] and German cases are generally regarded as the harshest cleansing measures in Eastern Europe, in terms of both the laws passed and their implementation; they excluded former party officials and secret police collaborators from a broad range of posts for 15 years in Germany and indefinitely in the Czech Republic. Other countries instituted cleansing measures at various times thereafter, targeting various groups with various sanctions.[9] Sometimes parliaments passed cleansing laws that their constitutional courts then tossed out or modified, or subsequent parliaments altered laws passed earlier. In contrast to such countries as Czechoslovakia and Germany that banned the accused from office (referred to as punitive lustration), others such as Poland, Romania, Lithuania, and Estonia merely required them to acknowledge past collaboration (informative lustration), after which their political careers might continue. Some countries eventually gave access to people wanting to read their own secret police files (East Germany, Romania, and Hungary), while others allowed more restricted access (the Czech Republic, Poland, and Bulgaria); some (Albania, Serbia) did not open their police files at all.

In Poland, lustration laws were passed in 1992 and 1997; the latter and subsequent versions criminalized not the fact of collaboration but lying about it, making the Polish lustration process much less harsh than the Czech one (Czarnota 2007:245). Poland's constitutional court challenged its procedures multiple times; as of 2011, though, modified lustration was still in process. Bulgaria's laws, first passed in 1992, were likewise invalidated by its constitutional court; it remained with the provisions of a 1997 law, which required members of parliament and senior government officials (but not the president or constitutional court judges) to declare their collaboration with the secret police or risk being "outed," yet they could keep their jobs; the range of posts affected was narrow. Albania passed a stringent law in 1993, which the constitutional court soon invalidated, and a second one in 1995, largely unimplemented, which expired in 2001; a new law was passed in 2009, with immediate court challenges. Slovakia inherited the early cleansing practices of its predecessor state but did not at first enforce them; under the conservative-neoliberal government of 2002 to 2006, it revived a limited vetting procedure, partly in view of EU accession. In Romania, lustration started late: Legislation passed in 1999 provided access to secret police files and a procedure (implemented with numerous shortcomings) for vetting public officials; a 2006 lustration law was rejected as unconstitutional in 2008; and the sequence was repeated not only in May–June 2010, but again in February –March 2012. The Baltic countries differed from others in Eastern Europe because, after independence, most secret police files were withdrawn when the KGB that had produced them departed, but modified lustration was variously legislated in all three, largely through citizenship and electoral laws that emphasized self-declaration. Hungary took a distinctive middle course, which Halmai and Scheppele define as "living well is the best revenge" (1997). There, strong demands for lustration produced lustration laws in 1994 and 1996 as well as subsequent amendments, provisions of which the constitutional court repeatedly invalidated on the argument that even those who have violated the principles of a law-governed state must be assured the same rights as others. Sanctions were initially weak, but the return of a Fidesz government (2010) made the law harsher.

On the little-to-no-cleansing side are Slovenia, where the few initiatives launched came to naught; Croatia, where Parliament twice failed to pass a law; and Serbia, which passed a very limited (and unenforced) measure in 2003 strictly concerning human rights violations. Macedonia did not manage to pass a measure until 2008, and it was soon challenged in court. According to a 2005 report by the Center for Democracy and Reconciliation in Southeast Europe (Hatschikjan, Reljić, and Šebek 2005), in the former Yugoslavia this form of cleansing basically did not take place, despite the passage of some relevant laws; energies went instead into *ethnic* cleansing.[11] Likewise in the former Soviet Union: aside from the Baltic countries, cleansing was almost nonexistent, notwithstanding some attempts to get laws passed. In Moldova and Ukraine, lustration bills were proposed—unsuccessfully—in 2004 and 2005; in other former Soviet republics such as Belarus, Armenia, Azerbaijan, and the Central Asian states, none was seriously entertained.[12]

What generalizations, if any, can we make about the kinds of cleansing measures reviewed here? I will advance three from my review of this literature. They concern the difficulty of comparatively assessing whose measures were harsher, the role of constitutional courts, and explanations for the variation in outcomes.

First, although Kaminski and Nalepa (2006) distinguish between cleansing practices that were "harsh" versus "mild," such designations are somewhat problematic. The provisions of the law are one thing, its implementation another. Solutions that on paper seem quite harsh, such as the Albanian law, might be implemented laxly. In Lithuania, for example, laws were initially strict because of widespread concern about the country's independence, given that its secret police was the KGB—now servant of a different state. Subsequently, however, the lustration process languished—perhaps because the political elites were overwhelmingly former communists (Clark and Pranevičiūte 2008). Laws or parts of them might be blocked by constitutional courts or presidential vetoes, such as those that eliminated departification provisions from lustration bills in Bulgaria and Albania. Moreover, laws varied as to which positions disqualified one or required vetting, but the sanctions applied did not covary: A law might affect positions far down the party hierarchy yet do no more than make collaborators' names public, rather than actually exclude them from their posts. The zeal of prosecutions depended heavily on what party was in power and what influence it had over the judiciary, constitutional court, Ministry of the Interior, or postcommunist security organizations.

For these and other reasons, it is difficult to make general comparative judgments about the severity of cleansing provisions. Stan (2009:262) arrays countries into four groups according to whether they: 1) adopted early and vigorous lustration, granted file access, and instituted court proceedings (Germany, the Czech Republic, the Baltics; see Clark and Pranevičiūte 2008); 2) employed less radical or later measures (Hungary and Poland); 3) adopted weak or partial measures (Bulgaria and Romania); or 4) went with some version of "forgive and forget" (Slovakia, Slovenia, Albania, and the former Soviet Union other than the Baltic states). Even this grouping, however, seems subject to further nuance, as Slovak politicians reversed their "forgiving" stance between 2001 and 2006.

Second, Kaminski and Nalepa point to the constitutional courts, which were pivotal in reducing the severity of whatever cleansing practices were legislated. They argue that the former communists who negotiated the transfer of power were determined to create as strong a judiciary as possible in the new system, gambling that it would take longer to replace the communist judicial elites than to turn over members of Parliament. Outgoing communist leaders in Czechoslovakia, Hungary, and Bulgaria, for example, insisted on establishing a constitutional court, hoping to slow down the transitional process and to construct institutions that would save them from retroactive justice (2006:391–392). This insight would encourage us to look case by case for the specific institutional sites (particularly constitutional courts) at which members of the communist nomenklatura were retained or managed to exert continued influence over the passage and implementation of cleansing laws. A separate question is whether or not this was a bad thing: The result of their influence may well have been to prevent witch hunts that could have seriously damaged the prospects for democratic politics.

Third, concerning explanations for the variety of cleansing practices, a number of theories have been advanced, focusing especially on the nature of the experience under communism and the path out of it, whether through the overthrow of the party or through negotiations between it and the opposition (see summary in Stan 2009:262–267). The most compelling ideas, in my view, concern the nature of the political field after 1989 and the timing of elections (see, e.g., Horne and Levi 2004; Williams, Fowler, and Szczerbiak 2005; Stan 2009). Williams, Fowler, and Szczerbiak conclude their comparison of the Czech, Hungarian, and Polish cases by stating, "The story of lustration, therefore, is one of post-communist political competition and legislative coalition-building" (2005:39). Likewise Łoś contends: "The lustration debate is…a terrain of a ruthless power struggle" (1995:119). Some of the stakes were, of course, cleansing's implications for who would remain in the labor force; in several countries, including Czechoslovakia and Germany, the law was part of the labor code, not the criminal code (Kaminski and Nalepa 2006:385). The East German case showed this particularly clearly: Collaborators were banned for 15 years from any public-sector job. Rosenberg attributes this to the surfeit of public employees that unification produced, whom lustration helped to winnow down (1996:325, 327).

Whatever its initial motivations on the part of various groups, then, cleansing was largely the creature of the anticommunist forces and entered into political conflict as such. Where post- or cryptocommunist parties dominated the scene, cleansing laws mostly failed or fell into abeyance; when anticommunist opposition parties emerged or reemerged, so did cleansing. Nalepa, however,

introduces a vital qualification: Wherever the secret police had deeply penetrated the political opposition to communism, this opposition might delay
passing lustration laws even if it held the balance of power, because such laws
would compromise its own politicians at least as much as the former communists (2009:12–16). Similarly, former communists in power might initiate lustration laws (usually weak ones) in order to prevent the passage of harsher laws,
and a compromised opposition would accept that (ibid.:20–22). Her examples
are Poland and Hungary. The fact that former communists knew how compromised the political opposition had been—knew, that is, how many secret
police skeletons were in the opposition's closet—gave them the upper hand in
determining the fate of this basically anticommunist policy.

To emphasize this sort of Realpolitik is not to deny "the genuine needs for
justice, truth, and atonement" to which such laws responded (Stan 2009:4),
but only to underscore the thoroughgoing politicization of the means devised
for addressing those needs. Bugaric reports that the upsurge in lustration legislation in Poland in 2007 resulted from the new right-wing government's assault
on the network of communist and new business elites the brothers Kaczynski
saw as their main enemies (2008:193), and something similar might be said
of Fidesz's intensified lustration in Hungary after 2010. Even where cleansing began as a means of righting historical wrongs, it quickly became a potent
means of political conflict—one that former communists could wield as well as
anyone else. Austin and Ellison's (2008) analysis of lustration in Albania exemplifies this scenario. More Albanians were tried under the lustration law than
elsewhere, they write, but not to punish the crimes of communism: Rather, the
trials demobilized the opposition and exacted personal vengeance.

Overall, my survey of the literature convinces me that cleansing practices
were politically productive. Although it is uncertain whether they accom-
plished much by way of rendering historical justice or "coming to terms with
the past," they provided an idiom that proved useful for a variety of groups
across the political spectrum in a variety of circumstances, and I believe
they will continue to do so. They mobilized resonant symbols that affected
the bounding of political arenas. The symbolic effects of declaring that secret
police collaborators were unwelcome in postsocialist governments helped
to define the political landscape, in that persons with such pasts—whether
actively identified or not—were stigmatized for some time because of their
collaboration. Given the questionable evidentiary value of information from
the secret police files, the declarations had often unfortunate performative
effects: Simply publishing lists launched the stigma, implicating persons as
presumed guilty until proved innocent, rather than the reverse. As Teitel puts
it, "The purge begins with the list" (2000:171). The political productivity of
cleansing practices lends ongoing continuity to something we can call Eastern

Europe despite the incorporation of various Eastern European countries into the EU. Cleansing was a collective product: The idea of it and practices associated with it ricocheted throughout the bloc, unifying a postcommunist political field with certain distinctive properties.

Seeing such practices as generalizable political weapons helps to account for otherwise puzzling facts, such as that debates about cleansing kept returning to the political arena even when public sentiment for it had waned (Horne and Levi 2004:26) and long after the end of the former regimes or after initial legislation had lapsed (Stan 2009:248). Not even EU membership staunched interest in cleansing: As late as 2006, after Poland's EU accession, Polish politicians resuscitated public shaming of secret police collaborators; Czechs revisited the practice in 2007. Horne draws from this the conclusion that the aims of late lustration policies differ from those of early ones, expanding their size, scope, duration, and transparency measures so as to "enhance citizen trust in the new regime, thereby promoting good governance and democratic consolidation" (2007:6–8). I confess to a more jaundiced interpretation: Whatever its moral motivations, cleansing is good business, politically.

In the following sections I will expand on this possibility and take up some more general questions concerning cleansing practices. Given my disciplinary formation, I feel uncomfortable addressing some of the serious matters other scholars have asked about cleansing practices: Have 20 years of them promoted democracy or not? Would amnesty have been preferable? Did they enhance or endanger trust in government? For whom have the practices fostered a useful coming to terms with the past and for whom have they not?[12] Instead, I see 20 years in which certain forms and technologies considered to promote democracy and the rule of law were domesticated in sometimes "undemocratic" ways by groups in the various societies they were brought into, the result being in many cases to void the initial impulse for them even as the practices served other, perhaps unanticipated tendencies. I would rather ask questions such as, What directions is cleansing likely to take, and what broad tendencies might it be participating in? What light does cleansing shed on our own practices? How can we think about the effects of socialism on the form they took?

Coming to Terms with the Past, or Caught in Its Toils? The Past in the Present

Thinking about Purification

A number of observers have commented that cleansing shows some similarities with communist-era practices, suggesting that the region is trapped by its communist past even in the methods used to try to overcome it. Teitel writes, for example, "the post-1989 purges are just the most recent in a line of purges. Even in its mild form, lustration evokes the dreaded lists of the totalitarian regimes" (2000:173). Adam Michnik, too, observed, "This philosophy of de-communizing was drawing directly on the Bolshevik principle according to which so-called representatives of the bourgeois order and the Tsarist regime would be deprived of citizens' rights" (cited in Killingsworth 2010:88), and he noted similarities between various forms of anticommunism in Poland and the antifascism of the Comintern and post-1945 socialism. Although given how lethal the purges of communism were, we must be careful to avoid too facile comparisons. I wish to explore the parallels between the communist and postcommunist cleansings. My inspiration comes from two anthropologists, Serguei Oushakine and Jane Schneider.

In his discussion of Soviet *samizdat*, Oushakine argues that, contrary to standard models of resistance in which Soviet dissidence is situated outside the discursive field of power, dissidence was situated firmly within this field, being constituted by the authoritative discourse and partially reproducing it (albeit from a different location), thus limiting dissidents' impact on Soviet society (2001:204). I find Oushakine's argument provocative for thinking about lustration, which was simi-larly formed from resistance to a particular regime whose logic nonetheless set its agenda even after the regime itself disappeared.[13] To pursue the parallel, we should closely inspect important features of the discursive field of socialism, espe-cially in the Czechoslovak case that launched the lustration idea. We would want to note the deeply dichotomous universe of Czechoslovakia's Charter 77 dissi-dents, some of whom emphasized sacrifice and moral capital that set them off from the political capital of party members (see Eyal 2000). Ripened—like inter-war communist parties themselves—in prison cells and marginal social locations after 1968, the Czechoslovak opposition differed from similar groups in Hungary and especially Poland in being smaller and more heavily persecuted, and in devel-oping not alternative socialisms with a human face (they had already tried that) but an explicitly antiregime strategy of "living in truth" and "antipolitics." The idea was to create parallel structures to compensate for the failings of the official ones, providing a parallel polis to materialize the dissidents' sense of mission and moral commitment (ibid.:68). But this antipolitics strategy may have unwittingly trapped its authors in the terms of the regime agenda that they strove mimetically to reject. I believe the cleansing policies that emerged in Czechoslovakia after 1989 show precisely that. The experience at their heart, including the strategy of antipolitics practiced in several countries, was nonetheless a general one. This fact, plus Czech dissidents' deep moralizing of the us-them distinction so ubiquitous in the region, enabled lustration's logic to spread rapidly from its Czechoslovak birthplace, translated into multiple vernaculars.

A second approach to the socialist-parallels problem makes use of Mary Douglas's famed *Purity and Danger*, which would see in the purges of both the 1950s and the 1990s a process of labeling certain people the political equivalent of "matter out of place"—sources of pollution to the body politic—and ejecting them from it. A technique of expulsion, rather than one of (re)incorporation and reconciliation (as in South Africa or Peru), governed both regime-building moments, and both involved a kind of ritual sacrifice to purify the body politic. Jane Schneider's brilliant analysis of the link between Prohibition in the United States and the expansion of the Sicilian mafia on US soil (2009) transforms Douglas's structural opposition between purity and danger into a dialectical process. The quest for purity, she argues, in the form of legislating Prohibition, had the effect of creating greater danger, as the thing prohibited spread through efforts to eradicate it. Banned pollutants proliferate. This insight seems apt for the process of lustration, with its attempts to purify the postsocialist body politic of the "pollutants" of the previous regime.

How and why might this purification process create new dangers? One fairly obvious possibility comes from something common to both communism and lustration: the denunciation. Lustration cases often begin when someone denounces another for having been a collaborator. Practices that invite collaborators to come forth on their own avoid this, but the potential for denunciation is always there.[14] Consider this article from February 13, 2009, in the online publication "AllBusiness, a D & B Company," titled "Czech CSSD's Mrstina has dubious lustration certificate" and citing a story in the Czech newspaper *Mlada fronta Dnes (MfD)*:

> Miloslav Mrstina, a significant Czech Social Democrat (CSSD) whose suspicious business deals surfaced recently, has a dubious lustration certificate confirming that he did not cooperate with the Communist secret police StB under the previous regime....Mrstina's suspicious past [includes a 5.2 million-crown state subsidy the CSSD ministers provided him] in 2006 to finance the reconstruction of his hotel in Nachod, east Bohemia, which, however, he later ran as a brothel....In addition, CSSD colleagues gave Mrstina a lucrative post of a member of the supervisory board of the state-owned oil company Cepro, *MfD* wrote. The CSSD leadership protested [the story] and said it is considering lodging a criminal complaint against an unknown perpetrator.[15]

According to Williams, the incident was likely part of a power struggle within local branches of the CSSD and does not appear to participate in a widespread trend.[16] Nonetheless, it is striking that *lustration* is the idiom selected, and that a lustration-negative Czech remains vulnerable to competitors' accusations that he had his certificate falsified—a possibility enhanced by the revelation in 1998 of a black market in fake certificates (Williams 2003:21). Here, the effects of lustration have strayed far from its democracy-protecting roots and are available to business competitors, alternative aspirants to elite status, and— who knows?—possibly even rivals in love. A charge of collaboration makes a person visible, no matter whether the outcome is negative or positive, and this visibility clings to the person like a diagnosis of HIV. One never knows when it will become virulent and in what forms.

Examples such as this suggest to me that lustration has moved out from politics into the wider society and is fulfilling its purificatory functions in unanticipated ways. No longer working to cleanse politics of potentially disloyal or blackmailable public officials, it is available for broader competition. Something like this is what anthropologist Saygun Gökarıksel has been finding in Poland.[17] Anyone can be accused of secret police collaboration, whether directly, anonymously, publicly, or in private (though without evidence the accusation would not stick). The means can be more or less overt, and they can involve subtle pressures. Gökarıksel gives the example of a university professor whose name is mentioned in a newspaper article, with an insinuation that he collaborated. The professor might decide not to respond because the accusation is groundless, but then his dean invites him for a drink and turns the conversation to his past, in something like these terms. "We're wondering what you'll do about this rumor. Our university wants to maintain its reputation for integrity, and we can always find other faculty willing to prove their character." The professor is now obliged to submit to the verification procedure, which can entail a great deal of time, uncertainty, and anguish. If the verification report comes back lustration positive, then he can challenge that finding, but to do so is not easy: It poses major legal problems, because a person accused may not be able to see his file unless he decides to go to court. Only then is he allowed to go into a special room, by himself (that is, without a lawyer), and look at the file (which might be hundreds of pages long), but he is not allowed to take notes. Poland's law justifies this on the grounds that the person could well be a perpetrator, not a victim, and the files contain state secrets. On the basis of this exposure to his file he must construct his defense. But what if he cannot locate evidence to exculpate himself? What if no file on him can be found—does this mean he is clean or, rather, that he is powerful enough to make it disappear? It is precisely because of this legal nightmare that the Helsinki Committee on Human Rights has become involved in challenges to Poland's (and other countries') lustration procedures as violations of due process. Even if the professor brings suit and is vindicated, the stigma of his having been rendered visible in this way can cling permanently to him and his family.

Lustration, in other words, has set loose a possibility reminiscent of the denunciation of earlier communist times (though perhaps with less devastating consequences). Its effects are no longer limited to the public sphere or to qualification for high office. Like the denunciation, it brings the instruments of state power and surveillance directly into the hands of any citizen, creating a state-subject relation different from the one we generally imagine as the basis of democratic citizenship.[18] The analogy suggests to us something about the new forms of state power being constituted in the post–September 11 "neoliberal" world, with its injunction "if you see something, say something" and other incitements to make the citizen part of the surveillance apparatus. Have communist practices shown us the image of our own future, which postcommunist incitements to denounce are reinforcing? Is the purity sought by lustration pushing dangerous pollution outward through ramifying denunciations? Writer Milan Kundera, filmmaker István Szabó, and others targeted by charges of collaboration would surely say yes.[20] We need much more ethnography to explore these potential forms of the past in the present.

Thinking about Historical Truth

My final point concerning lustration's implications is an open-ended question about truth. One of the most powerful discourses around lustration and access to secret police files concerned getting at the historical truth, revealing hidden secrets, making the guilty accountable, and enabling society to come to terms with the past. Maria Łoś, commenting on the lustration debates in Poland, finds in them competing notions of truth: "For some participants in the debate, the main goal of lustration is to uncover 'the truth.' For others, 'the truth' is a false construct that hides the complexity of many subjective truths. [In] the latter view,...lustration is perceived as an attempt to recentralize and renationalize 'truth'" (1995:155–156). In brief, she raises the clash between modernist and postmodern conceptions of truth, attributing the former to lustration and the latter to its opponents. Thus, lustration's effects include promoting a form of truth that is absolutist, sure of itself, over a more relativizing, skeptical notion of truth.

This absolutist, modernist variant was the regime of truth characteristic of socialism as well, and of the secret police files that were its signature product. The guiding question behind surveillance was, Who is this person *really*? and the underlying assumption was the modernist one that surfaces give only appearances, with truth hidden below. The secret police aimed to unmask internal enemies, uncover their truth; the secret police archives are its repository, a monument to communism's knowledge of its population. As I have learned from researching the secret police (Securitate) archive in Romania, one characteristic of its knowledge is its preoccupation with socialities, with attachments among people (see Verdery 2012). The most crucial form of secret knowledge concerned people's networks: Knowing these would reveal a person's truth. Because the Securitate understood that power flows in social relationships, officers sought to colonize attachments, disrupt them, and forge new ones. They knew that people's sociality is dangerous and that breaking up their networks by introducing collaborators and false friends was essential to containing this danger.

Like being under surveillance, collaboration, too, was a networked phenomenon, not an individual one. Many people became collaborators because they had friends and families whom they wanted to protect or whose suspect actions had implicated them—that is, they became collaborators because they were socially embedded. They were targeted for recruitment for the same reason: Documents from the Securitate archives instruct that the best people to recruit as informers are those who have the largest possibilities for contact and movement—that is, those who are well connected (Banu 2008:12). Informers reported not just on individuals but on social networks. Moreover, the police rarely acted on information from a single informant but triangulated multiple sources, making it difficult to attribute responsibility for the arrest of a dissident, for example, to any single informer.

People in socialist Romania were not autonomous individuals then, but were constituted as persons by having social relations with others. Secret police work was successful precisely to the extent that persons under socialism were not individuals. This is why international pressure to individualize lustration—from the belief that the rule of law works only when collaborators are treated as individuals, not as members of a category (collaborators)—seems to me misguided: It distorts the historical reality of collaboration. Among the reasons behind such international pressure is that it is much easier to punish individual than collective responsibility, but the effect of international organizations' individualizing accountability is to impose notions of truth seeking that do not fit the crime. It is precisely because of these network properties that cleansing was instituted in the first place: to disrupt the networks of party officials, police agents, and informers and thus diminish their effective opposition to exiting socialism. Because lustration laws were formulated to require demonstration of the collaborator's intent, it is impossible to formulate a lustration law that would simultaneously satisfy the rule of law based on individual responsibility and yet reflect the context of informing for the communist secret police.[21]

The problems with using secret police files as truth are legion—the "signing bonuses" that motivated agents to extend the web of informers (such as a television for every three signatures; Wechsler 1992:80) and that encouraged them to manufacture collaborators; the fact that because the secret police could recruit informers among party members only with the permission of their local party organization, their fabrications would come disproportionately from the very group most likely to be pushing for lustration laws after 1989—the former political opposition; and so on. I will not continue in this vein, since numerous other observers have noted the difficulties with using secret police files as repositories of historical truth, few as eloquently as Adam Michnik: "It seems that things are becoming absurd if secret police colonels are to give out morality certificates" (Michnik and Havel 1993:23).

Thus, the laudable effort to manage the social behavior of former regime supporters so as to make them democrats falls victim—differently in different Eastern European countries—to the inevitable politicking that accompanied the end of the old regime. The contrast with China, however, is stark: There, with minimal state retrenchment, no laws seek to hold the regime's agents accountable. It is China's party leaders alone, rather than the multiple kinds of actors populating the field of politics in Eastern Europe, who determine the extent to which China's authoritarianism is mitigated. Instead of the possibilities for politicking opened by lustration, we find in China depoliticized subjects hoping their survival strategies will not awaken the state's "blind" eye.

Acknowledgments

I am very grateful to Benjamin Frommer, Gail Kligman, Sally Merry, Susan Woodward, and the participants at the "1989: Twenty Years After" conference at the University of California, Irvine, for helpful conversations concerning this chapter, and especially to Saygun Gökarıksel, Marek Kaminski, Jonathan Larson, and Kieran Williams for their extensive written comments.

Notes

1. Thanks to Jonathan Larson for suggesting this term. See Borneman 1997:26–27 for a discussion of the problems with "decommunization."
2. Different sources I have consulted have different cut-off dates according to when they were published, and I have not been able to bring my account up to the minute for each case. Moreover, most of these countries continued to revisit these policies, so a statement that was accurate in 2009 might no longer be so in 2012.
3. Williams, Fowler, and Szczerbiak state that Slavophone archivists have long used the term simply to refer to the compilation of an inventory or register. To lustrate someone was to check whether his name appeared in a database. The term was more widely adopted *not* because, as is commonly alleged, of its etymological association with ancient Roman rites of purification, but because politicians and the public heard it used by bureaucrats during battles for control of Czechoslovak files in early 1990" (2005:40 n.8). According to David (2003:388), the StB used it in requesting confirmation from their statistical department as to whether they had in their records information on a particular person. An alternative history comes from Bertschi (1994:436), who says the term was used by the police in verifying whether communist cadres

were loyal to the party and removing them if not. In this meaning of "to vet," Benjamin Frommer (personal communication) finds the term in documents from the 1960s, for example in investigations of police officers but also, more interestingly, during the Nazi occupation, when *perlustrace* of Jews' documents to determine their validity was a frequent police activity. He thus suggests that the StB's later use of *lustrace* may have originated in *perlustrace*, which was "normal foreigner police jargon" before the war.

4. Personal communication.
5. Sources for this discussion include: Wechsler 1992; Łoś 1995; Williams 2003; David 2003, 2004; Sadurski 2005; Kaminski and Nalepa 2006; Priban 2007; Nalepa 2009; Larson 2013.
6. The Stasi archive is vastly larger than those of other, more populous Eastern European countries. Reinke estimates it at 180 kilometers of paper records, 1 million photos, 150,000 audiotapes, 4,000 videocassettes, plus 5,000 sacks of shredded paper (Bruce [2009: 17] says 17,200 sacks), and 7 million file cards on individuals (1997:106n.28). Compare this with the reported 35 kilometers of Romania's Securitate—another very active police force.
7. Figures from Glaeser (2011:2, 149).
8. Although technically speaking the initial legislation was Czechoslovak, not just Czech, I use the latter designation because throughout the 1990s the provisions of lustration were applied so much less stringently in Slovakia.
9. In order of the appearance of their first formal lustration measures, we have East Germany (1990 Unification Treaty), Czechoslovakia (1991), Lithuania (1991), Bulgaria (1992), Albania (1993/1995), Hungary (1994/1996), Latvia (1994), Estonia (1995), Poland (1997—a preliminary lustration attempt in 1992 having been invalidated by the constitutional court), and Romania (2006, with a law on access to secret police files in 1999). See, inter alia, Kaminski and Nalepa 2006; Stan 2009.
10. Thanks to Susan Woodward for suggesting this connection.
11. Kaminski and Nalepa (2006:403–405) offer a summary of the laws and outcomes for a number of countries.
12. For one judicious attempt to address some of these questions, see David 2003.
13. The parallel with post–World War II purges of Nazi collaborators is perhaps not inapt, for there, too, we were dealing with a preeminently "purgative" regime, albeit in forms different from those of communist parties; the reaction was similarly violent purges of collaborators. I realize that there were major differences, most significantly the much shorter time period of Nazi collaboration than was true of communism.
14. Kieran Williams proposes another way of linking lustration to danger, seeing it as a means of securitizing democracy, that is, making democracy a question of security and surrounding it with a sense of danger and anxiety (Williams 2003:2).
15. See http://www.allbusiness.com/government/elections-politics-politics-political-parties/12125211-1.html, accessed October 10, 2009. Standard Czech diacritics absent in the original.
16. Williams, personal communication.
17. My thanks to Mr. Gökarıksel for an illuminating conversation on this question.
18. Recall, however, the denunciations of the McCarthy period.
19. See István Rév's fascinating discussion of these issues (2008).
20. I owe this summary to an anonymous reviewer.

References

Austin, Robert C., and Jonathan Ellison. 2008. "Post-Communist Transitional Justice in Albania." *East European Politics and Societies* 22(2):373–401.
Banu, Florian. 2008. "Rețeaua informativă a Securității în anii '50: constituire, structură, eficiență.'" *Caietele CNSAS* 1(2):7–38.

Bertschi, C. Charles 1994. "Lustration and the Transition to Democracy: The Cases of Poland and Bulgaria." *East European Quarterly* 28(4):435–451.

Borneman, John. 1997. *Settling Accounts: Violence, Justice, and Accountability in Postsocialist Europe*. Princeton, N.J.: Princeton University Press.

Bruce, Gary. 2009. "East Germany." In *Transitional Justice in Eastern Europe and the Former Soviet Union: Reckoning with the Communist Past*, edited by Lavinia Stan, ed., 15–36. London, U.K.: Routledge.

Bugaric, Bojan. 2008. "Populism, Liberal Democracy, and the Rule of Law in Central and Eastern Europe." *Communist and Post-Communist Studies* 41:191–203.

Clark, Terry D., and Jovita Pranevičiūte. 2008. "Perspectives on Communist Successor Parties: The Case of Lithuania." *Communist and Post-Communist Studies* 41(4):443–464.

Czarnota, Adam. 2007. "The Politics of the Lustration Law in Poland, 1989–2006." In *Justice as Prevention: Vetting Public Employees in Transitional Societies*, Alexander Meyer-Rieckh and Pablo de Greiff, eds. 222–258. New York: SSRC.

David, Roman. 2003. "Lustration Laws in Action: The Motives and Evaluation of the Lustration Policy in the Czech Republic and Poland." *Law and Social Inquiry* 28(2):387–439.

———. 2004. "Transitional Injustice? Criteria for Conformity of Lustration to the Right to Political Expression." *Europe-Asia Studies* 56(6):789–812.

Eyal, Gil. 2000. "Anti-Politics and the Spirit of Capitalism: Dissidents, Monetarists and the Czech Transition to Capitalism." *Theory and Society* 29(1):49–92.

Glaeser, Andreas. 2011. *Political Epistemics: The Secret Police, the Opposition, and the End of East German Socialism*. Chicago: University of Chicago Press.

Halmai, Gabor, and Kim Lane Scheppele. 1997. "Living Well Is the Best Revenge: The Hungarian Approach to Judging the Past." In *Transitional Justice and the Rule of Law in New Democracies*, A.J. McAdams, ed., 155–185. Notre Dame, Ind.: University of Notre Dame Press.

Hatschikjan, Magarditsch, Dušand Reljić, and Nenad Šebek. 2005. *Disclosing Hidden History: Lustration in the Western Balkans*. Thessaloniki: Center for Democracy and Reconciliation in Southeast Europe.

Horne, Cynthia. 2007. "Late Lustration in Poland and Romania: Better Late than Never?" Paper presented at the annual meeting of the American Political Science Association, Chicago, Ill.

Horne, Cynthia, and Margaret Levi. 2004. "Does Lustration Promote Trustworthy Governance? An Exploration of the Experience of Central and Eastern Europe." In *Building a Trustworthy State in Post-Socialist Transition*, edited by János Kornai and Susan Rose-Ackerman, eds., 52–74. New York: Palgrave.

Kaminski, Marek M., and Monika Nalepa. 2006. "Judging Transitional Justice: A New Criterion For Evaluating Truth Revelation Procedures." *Journal of Conflict Resolution* 50:383–408.

Killingsworth, Matt. 2010. "Lustration and Legitimacy." *Global Society* 24(1):71–90.

Krygier, Martin, and Adam Czarnota. 2006. "After Postcommunism: The Next Phase." *Annual Review of Law and Social Science* 2:299–340.

Larson, Jonathan. 2013. *Critical Thinking in Slovakia after Socialism*. Rochester, N.Y.: University of Rochester Press.

Łoś, Maria. 1995. "Lustration and Truth Claims: Unfinished Revolutions in Central Europe." *Law & Social Inquiry* 20(1):117–161.

Michnik, Adam, and Václav Havel. 1993. "Justice or Revenge." *Journal of Democracy* 4:20–27.

Nalepa, Monika. 2009. *Skeletons in the Closet: Transitional Justice in Post-Communist Europe*. Cambridge, U.K.: Cambridge University Press.

Oushakine, Serguei. 2001. "The Terrifying Mimicry of Samizdat." *Public Culture* 13(2):191–214.

Priban, Jiri. 2007. "Oppressors and Their Victims: The Czech Lustration Law and the Rule of Law." In *Justice as Prevention: Vetting Public Employees in Transitional Societies*, edited by Alexander Meyer-Rieckh and Pablo de Greiff, eds., 308–347. New York: SSRC.

Reinke, Herbert. 1997. "Policing Politics in Germany from Weimar to the Stasi." In *The Policing of Politics in the Twentieth Century: Historical Perspectives*, Mark Mazower, ed., 71–106. Providence, R.I.: Berghahn.

Rév, István. 2008. "The Man in the White Coat." *Past for the Eyes: East European Representations of Communism in Cinema and Museums after 1989*, Oksana Sarkisova and Péter Apor, eds., 1–55. Budapest and New York: Central European University Press.

Rosenberg, Tina. 1996. *The Haunted Land: Facing Europe's Ghosts after Communism*. New York: Vintage Books.

Sadurski, Wojciech. 2005. *Rights before Courts: A Study of Constitutional Courts in Postcommunist States of Central and Eastern Europe*. Dordrecht, Netherlands: Springer.

Schneider, Jane. 2009. "Purity and the Production of Danger: American Empire and Organized Crime Formation." Paper presented at the seminar "Anthropology Today for Tomorrow." Graduate Center of the City University of New York, October 2, 2009.

Stan, Lavinia, ed. 2009. *Transitional Justice in Eastern Europe and the Former Soviet Union: Reckoning with the Communist Past*. London: Routledge.

Teitel, Ruti G. 2000. *Transitional Justice*. Oxford, U.K.: Oxford University Press.

Verdery, Katherine. 2012. "Secrets and Truths: Knowledge Practices of the Romanian Secret Police." The 2010 Oskar Halecki Lecture. Leipzig: Leipziger Universitätsverlag.

Wechsler, Lawrence. 1992. "The Velvet Purge: The Trials of Jan Kavan." *The New Yorker* October 19, p. 66ff.

Wilke, Christiane. 2007. "The Shield, the Sword, and the Party: Vetting the East German Public Sector." In *Justice as Prevention: Vetting Public Employees in Transitional Societies*, Alexander Meyer-Rieckh and Pablo de Greiff, eds., 348–400. New York: SSRC.

Williams, Kieran. 2003. "Lustration as the Securitization of Democracy in Czechoslovakia and the Czech Republic." *Journal of Communist Studies and Transition Politics* 19(4):1–24.

Williams, Kieran, Brigid Fowler, and Aleks Szczerbiak. 2005. "Explaining Lustration in Eastern Europe: A 'Post-Communist Politics' Approach." *Democratization* 12(1):22–43.

4

Responsive Authoritarianism and Blind-Eye Governance in China

ROBERT P. WELLER

This chapter focuses on two broad areas of life—religion and environmental awareness—that shed light on Chinese forms of governance that have been evolving especially in the years since 1989. China is of course the one major communist state that weathered the challenges of 1989 with its political structure fundamentally intact. Nevertheless, its actual forms of governance have changed enormously since the height of Mao Zedong's totalizing project in the Cultural Revolution. The underlying vision of how state and society should relate to each other has been transformed. Looking at religion and environmental groups allows me to concentrate on those aspects of informal politics that loom large in people's daily lives, even if they do not appear clearly in official documents and pronouncements. In particular, I argue that the more open forms of state-society relations that have been developing for several decades represent new forms of responsive authoritarianism and what I will call blind-eye governance—a "don't ask, don't tell" attitude toward many social forms that lie outside the law but are nevertheless mostly tolerated.

Any state needs some kind of mechanism to receive and respond to feedback from the broader society. China's mass starvation after the Great Leap Forward was the result, in part, of just such a failure of feedback. Elections, of course, are the most powerful way of doing this in a democratic society, although there are also many others (a free press, the courts, protests). A state like China, however, where elections on any significant scale are not used, must instead develop other techniques of responsive authoritarianism. China since the Cultural Revolution has looked seriously at the models of other authoritarian states that were longlasting and economically successful, especially such Asian polities as Singapore, Malaysia, and Taiwan or Korea in the four decades before they democratized. The many mechanisms China has developed to solve the problem of feedback include petitions and letters to government offices, limited demonstrations, some use of lawsuits, the rise of nongovernmental organizations (NGOs), and many more informal techniques.

Other scholars have also discussed ways in which China's authoritarian structures may prove resilient and robust over the course of decades (Shi 1997; Nathan 2003). Nearly all of that work, however, concentrates entirely on purely political mechanisms. Here I will examine instead mechanisms that are not strictly political but that exist at the boundaries between state and society. Much religion in China falls outside the state framework, including tens of millions of people in unregistered Protestant "house churches" and probably hundreds of millions who take part in at least occasional local temple or household rituals. In much the same way, many environmental NGOs evade or manipulate the state registration system, and environmental protests take place outside the law.

I will look especially at the peculiar but important technique of governing with a blind eye, or as the Chinese metaphor goes, with one eye open and one eye closed (*zhengyizhiyan, bi yizhiyan,* 睁一只眼, 闭一只眼). This refers to cases in which people act outside the law, but their actions are clearly visible to local officials and there is a mutual understanding that the officials will avert their gaze and the local people will not force those officials to look by flaunting their wrongdoing. Many of the cases I will discuss involving religion or the environment fall into this category.

Finally, I will turn briefly at the end to a comparison with the experience of Eastern Europe, where both religious and environmental issues played a vital role in the events of 1989 in some of the countries. The same was not true in China, and this has much to do with the contrasting institutional histories of these different parts of the communist world. I will also compare the techniques of blind-eye governance with the kinds of seeing-eye governance discussed in some of the Eastern European chapters in this volume, especially Verdery's work on lustration and the secret police. The result of these different histories was, in part, that 1989 in China did not result in a transformation comparable to Eastern Europe but instead was a moment of disequilibrium, after which China returned to much the same path it had already been on since its reforms began a decade earlier.

Local Society and the Invention of "Religion" and "Nature"

Understandings of both religion and the environment were utterly transformed in China in the early part of the twentieth century, including even the invention of key terms for basic concepts that powerfully shape these ideas today, including "religion" (*zongjiao*, 宗教), "nature" (*ziran*, 自然), and even "society" (*shehui*, 社会). Each of these terms took on its modern meaning in Japanese translations of Western thought, which then entered China from Japan. Because this historical legacy has been so important in how religion and environmental activism developed, let me begin with a brief overview of the way these fields have evolved over the past century.

The early twentieth century was the moment when many Chinese elites embraced imported ideas of modernity. They did this with much less anxiety and nativist reaction than we saw in much of the rest of the developing world at that time, especially in colonies such as India or most of Africa. The great symbol of this moment was the May 4th Movement of 1919, in which Chinese intellectuals first moved decisively away from the use of written classical Chinese, with the implied rejection of the entire world of imperial literati culture. "Mr. Science" and "Mr. Democracy" were watchwords for the movement that comfortably embraced many Western liberal values of the time, from social evolutionism to freedom of the press.

The effects of this were especially clear for religious policy. The state cult and all the cosmological underpinnings of the imperial polity had been swept away by the Republican Revolution of 1911. The new constitution embraced much of Western modernity, including an understanding of the necessary separation of church and state. The Chinese form of this separation emulated the radical French version of secularity. (It differed significantly from Germany's solution to the problem, even though German examples were generally more important for the republic's new legal system.)With the partial exception of Christianity (which had relatively few followers but was important to some of the elite), this meant the systematic undercutting of the economic power of religious organizations, often by taking their land. It also entailed defining religion as a separate category of thought for the first time. That is why a novel term for religion, *zongjiao*, came into use at this time where no exactly comparable term had existed before. The new idea of religion took a largely mainstream Protestant form, with an emphasis on belief, sacred canon, voluntary membership, and trained specialists.

By this definition, the local temple and household rituals of the great majority of China's people were not a form of religion at all but fit instead into another new usage entailed by the category of religion: These rituals were superstition (*mixin*, 迷信). Confucianism was also omitted from the list of religions at this time, because its fit with the new definition was shaky. The result was a government that found much local religiosity embarrassing. The state often repressed it, banning rituals and turning temples into schools or government buildings (Nedostup 2008). This attitude continued to characterize the Nationalist

Guomindang (GMD) regime in China (1927–1949) and persisted in doing so even after its move to Taiwan.

The early communists, of course, also accepted this basic understanding that the state should be entirely independent of religion and that religion itself had little to offer in a modern world. Karl Marx's own writings on religion were few, but they suggested that religion was an escape for the emiserated classes and that it would simply fade away as the end of exploitation allowed them to give up its false comforts (Marx [1943] 1983:115). Mao Zedong, however, also planted another seed in 1927, when he described religion as a major tool of exploitation, one of the four thick ropes that bound the Chinese people (Mao [1927] 1971:23-39). This less benign view would come to the fore many decades later, but at the time the GMD and the CCP sounded rather similar notes, all generally unfriendly to religion, with the greatest difference being that the communists worried more about the imperialist connections of Christianity.

The GMD regrouped official religions as social organizations of a kind— one for each of the recognized traditions such as Buddhism and Daoism (with none, of course, for temple worship or Confucianism, neither of which now had a legitimate legal space). The goal was less an active civil society with religious participation than a structure that allowed effective political supervision. In this sense, religious policy matched the kind of corporatist structure that would become increasingly prevalent during GMD rule (especially in Taiwan) and more recently in the PRC.

The other main area I will be discussing here is environmental organization and protest. Of course, there was little directly relevant activity in the early twentieth century (as in most of the world), but the period still brought two changes that would ultimately shape environmental action. First, there was the entry of the idea of NGOs. International NGOs evolved from charitable Christian movements in nineteenth-century Europe and the United States. Pioneer groups such as the Red Cross and the Young Men's Christian Association (YMCA) entered China early. These new social developments promoted a universalist view of humanity and an image of a self-organized society conceived as independent of the state. China needed a word for this new concept too, leading to the adoption of *shehui* ("society") from Japanese translations of Western thought. NGOs were one of the important carriers of the new concept.

Second, the early twentieth century also brought completely new ways of thinking about the environment, including yet another term borrowed from Japanese to translate a Western idea that had no exact Chinese equivalent— *ziran,* "nature" (Weller 2006). Western thinkers of the time did not have a single concept of nature. It was the time of John Muir's efforts to protect an unsullied natural realm as much as it was of the great canals, mines, and railroads that transformed nature for human benefit. The version of this new environmental thinking that resonated most powerfully with China's new elite of the time, however, was not Muir's at all, but instead imagined a separate nature to be controlled. The earlier Chinese view of an intertwined humanity and cosmos (*tien ren he yi,* 天人合一) was left behind in favor of military imagery of conquest and control. As with the new attitudes toward religion, these changes had consequences that shaped much of the century that would follow.

The Rise of a Totalitarian Model

Communism has usually been as enthusiastically dedicated to the project of modernity as any form of market liberalism. It rejected free markets but embraced ideals of mass production, efficiency, rationalization, and bureaucracy. Perhaps for this reason, in areas as diverse as religion and the environment, China had many more continuities across the revolutionary divide of 1949 than we might expect. Religious policy in the 1950s still saw nominal guarantees of the separation of church and state, a broadly corporatist structure for incorporating recognized religions through national associations and an abandonment of Confucianism. The primary difference, as I mentioned, was the generally harsher treatment of Christianity, although still within the same broad system of control. The new government, much like the republic before it, continued to condemn temple and household worship as "feudal superstition." These practices were not yet thoroughly repressed, but temples and lineage halls tended to lose their former functions and become government buildings, just as under the GMD.

Elite concepts of the environment, and especially the idea of bending nature to humanity's economic wants and needs, did not really change at all after 1949. Many of the communist slogans that Judith Shapiro decries in her study of PRC environmental policy in fact began in the republican era and showed up in Taiwanese textbooks of the 1950s as much as in PRC ones (Shapiro 2001). These include such claims as "Man must conquer nature!" that would have been almost unthinkable before the twentieth century. Long-term commitment to some of the same projects, most famously the Three Gorges Dam, also surfaced at the time.

On the other hand, the idea of NGOs (not just environmental ones) as independent voices of society was increasingly undercut and replaced by Soviet-style mass organizations in the 1950s. While this was not totally out of character with the corporatist tendencies of the GMD state, both on the mainland and later in Taiwan, in the PRC they weakened even further the independence of social actors, empowering the state at the expense of society. This trend increased dramatically with the Cultural Revolution, the one period when the state truly embraced something like a totalitarian project.

This period brought systematic attempts to end anything that recollected older Chinese culture and that resembled a society independent of the state. For most religions, this meant a rapid increase in the repression of local temples and religious practitioners throughout the 1960s, to the point that there was almost no public religiosity. More institutionalized religions such as Buddhism, Christianity, or Daoism were reduced to a few tokens. For the environment, the introduced idea of humanity conquering nature continued to dominate, while remnants of earlier views (such as feng shui) were repressed. NGOs were forbidden by the state, and even most of the mass organizations ceased to function as the leaders embraced an image of governance in which society dissolved completely into the state.

Reforms and Beyond

The totalitarian project never succeeded completely in stamping out religion, local social organizations, or even alternate ways of thinking about the environment. We can see this especially clearly for local temple religion (which itself strongly influences both potential civil associations and environmental views). Many villagers hid god statues or other ritual paraphernalia, which might be pulled out of hiding at safe moments. In one Shaanxi village during the Cultural Revolution, for example, people credited the spirit of Norman Bethune (a critical propaganda figure in the Cultural Revolution due to an essay of Mao's) with performing miraculous cures; his spirit was invoked by smoking Yan'an cigarettes, his favorite brand (Chau 2005:47). Jing Jun writes that a female spirit medium had constructed a makeshift shrine at his field site in Gansu as early as 1975 (Jing 1994:4). Some Christian house churches, as we now know, also continued to function throughout this period. Kao Chen-yang, for instance, discusses several areas of Fujian where charismatic Christianity created a foothold and gained significant strength at the height of the Cultural Revolution. The growth during that period, as he explains it, came from a combination of the forced radical privatization of religion and the opportunities this created for the conversion of women (Kao 2009).

After the reforms began, however, China retreated rapidly from the totalitarian project back to a model in which society had some separation from the state. To some extent, this was a direct consequence of the reinvigorated role of the market, which is itself partially independent of the state. The reforms went far beyond the market alone, however, and we can see an enormous range of social changes beginning almost immediately with the start of the reforms in 1979. Local social institutions such as irrigation associations or lineages rose again from the ashes. Not all of this activity had legal support, and thus it always felt the threat of repression was constant. Nevertheless, growth was rapid, and most groups that stayed local and apolitical thrived.

In the realm of religion, there was a quick return of the least institutionalized rural forms, because the small scale offered no threat. This included ancestor worship (and most publicly the annual grave-sweeping ritual) and even spirit mediumship, which the government continued to discourage but would usually overlook locally. Women often took the early lead, again probably because the state found them less worrisome (Dean 1993; Jing 1994). A more public and permanent revival occurred soon afterward, at least in some parts of China, with the construction or reconstruction of local temples, the reopening of churches and monasteries, and the public reappearance of Buddhist, Daoist, and Christian clergy.[1] Kenneth Dean, for example, judges that more than 100 temples were reconstructed in one Fujian county alone during the 1980s (Dean 1993:64, 84, 100, 211). I saw dozens of new earth god temples in remote areas of Guangxi in 1985 and revived, large, local temple festivals have been documented as early as 1978 and 1979 (Chau 2005; Gao 2005).

Almost all of these activities go on outside the legal and regulatory framework and right under the noses of local officials, who choose to look the other way. In one case, for example, a well-known Hong Kong medium in the 1990s made regular trips to the mainland with her followers to construct and consecrate new local temples. Officials knew, of course, but they always arranged to be away on business during the consecration ceremonies.[2] In another case, Gao Bingzhong describes an association that raised money from the townspeople to build a temple to the local dragon deity and also received funds from the government to establish a museum dedicated to "dragon" (i.e., Chinese) culture (Gao 2005). The building carries signs indicating its double identity as both temple and museum. No one is really fooled by such maneuvers, of course, but the diplomatic illusion works for both sides.

Temple festivals in parts of China can now attract up to 100,000 people. There is a great deal of regional variation in this, but local temple worship has been revived strongly at least in some parts of China; it is especially prevalent in the southeast (particularly Fujian) and parts of the northwest (Gansu, Shaanxi). Buddhism's rapid increase (measured in terms of both temples and the few polls taken) has also been regional and has been especially marked in its old strongholds such as the lower Yangzi region.

Christianity has had a spectacular growth rate, especially for Protestantism, often in its more charismatic and evangelical forms. Even the official numbers indicate an enormous growth since 1949, from less than a million to about 16 million. The actual number is unknown but certainly much higher. Many estimate followers in the range of 80 million, or very roughly 5 percent of the population. The most rapid growth has been in the house churches, which have no affiliation with the state-mandated religious organizations and are therefore technically illegal, just like village temples. House churches existed even during the most repressive period of the Cultural Revolution, but the really rapid expansion has occurred after the reforms (Hunter and Chan 1993; Liang 1999).

There has been serious conflict between house churches and official churches in some places and direct repression by the state in others. Although tension continues, especially when churches expand into realms the government considers political, the dominant pattern has increasingly been for the state to turn a blind eye to house churches as the reforms have continued. In many cases, these churches are large, clearly marked, and can attract up to several hundred worshipers at a time. There is no doubt that authorities are well aware of them. The eye is not always blind, however. In some parts of China, especially the provinces around the Huai River valley, repression has outweighed diplomatic tolerance. The regional variation between blind-eye governance and big-stick governance has not yet been well explained when it comes to the practice of Christianity, but it seems to involve a combination of the particular forms of Christianity that have thrived and particular traditions of cadre attitudes that have hardened over time. House churches in the Huai River area, for example, tend to have relatively more charismatic leadership, more rural and less literate followers, and to be subject to more severe repression than elsewhere.

The environment and NGOs involve dynamics that are quite different from religion in many ways, but like religion, they illustrate the rapid increase in personal and social space since the reforms began. They also show a similar pattern of corporatist control of some activity, accompanied by still more blind-eye governance. China's legal structure governing the activities of NGOs first developed in the mid-1980s. The model imagined an explicitly corporatist relation between state and society: One organization had a monopoly on representing each social sector or issue (such as the environment), with strong political controls on registration. The environmental niche was filled by a group registered with the Environmental Protection Bureau (later the State Environmental Protection Agency), and it was largely the creation of that office.

Other groups thus had to register more creatively. Global Village Beijing, like many other groups that were NGOs in intention but found their niche already filled by state-affiliated groups, simply registered as a for-profit company. This was a far easier process, largely without the political litmus tests that mark registration in the nonprofit sector. Still others registered as NGOs but with government bodies that differed greatly from the intention of the rules, usually because they were in an inappropriate sector. For example, Friends of Nature, the earliest of the more independent groups (founded in 1994) registered under the Academy of Chinese Culture within the Chinese Academy of Social Sciences. We see these approaches being adopted across the entire NGO sector (Unger and Chan 2008).

Religious groups get involved in this too. They are not allowed to pursue nonreligious functions such as poverty relief or emergency aid, but they typically do so anyway by registering an apparently secular and independent NGO under the name of lay followers. One prominent example is the Ren Ai Charity Foundation, founded in 2006. The careful wording on its website describes the group as "guided by" the Venerable Xuecheng, who is a vice chairman of the officially sanctioned Buddhist Association, a member of the Standing Committee of the Eleventh People's Political Consultative Congress, and generally influential at a very high political level ("Profile of the Ren Ai Charity Foundation"). When I asked one of the monks at his base temple, Longquan Monastery in Beijing, how this was possible, the monk explained that on paper the foundation had no ties to the monastery nor any of its monks, including Xuecheng.[3] Instead, a group of lay followers had registered the foundation with the Civil Affairs Bureau. Their name refers to broad Confucian values of benevolence and love rather than to anything specifically Buddhist. The monk said that the civil affairs officials simply assumed it was a nonreligious group. However, this seems unlikely, given the national prominence of Xuecheng. Even if the connection were somehow unclear at the moment of registration, it is certainly clear now—not just openly stated on the website of the monastery but well known to anyone looking at the philanthropic sector. It is another example of the state choosing to accept a convenient fiction by ignoring inconvenient details.

Both the religious and environmental sectors thus include a minority of groups that are officially incorporated by the state with its legal blessings. Both, however, also have extremely large penumbras of groups that push the margins of the law (registration under an inappropriate state agency, a village temple calling itself a museum) or are simply extralegal. It is highly likely that no government officials are fooled at all by these evasions in either sector. Instead, it is a case of politics with a wink and a nudge, blind-eye governance (Deng 2010). [4] Note how different this is from the basic ideology of lustration in Eastern Europe, as discussed in chapter 3 in this book. Lustration attempts to bring all the dark recesses into the light, while this kind of diplomatic illusion instead accepts that some behavior may enhance governance even if it takes place in the shade.

Modes of Repression

Such techniques rely, from the state's point of view, on the threat of enforce-
ment of the letter of the law at any moment. Like any standing threat, the effectiveness of this one depends on actually carrying the threat out from time to
time. We have seen this, for example, in the attempts at large-scale repression
of house churches in parts of Anhui and Henan. Some urban house churches
have also recently been in the news due to acts of repression, although they
differ significantly from the Anhui and Henan model in general theological
approach—more like mainstream American Protestants than the charisma and
Pentecostalism that tend to characterize the rural churches in central China.

NGOs are no different. While there has been enormous growth since the
reforms created a space for them, there have also been periods that saw the
massive deregistration of thousands of NGOs; environmental groups were no
exception. These periods always followed important political crises, especially
the Tiananmen demonstrations of 1989 and the Falun Gong demonstrations
of 1999. In each case, problems in another sector (public protest, religion) led
to a broad period of repression, when the tension inherent in the idea of NGOs
led to a temporary reversal of policy. Even though massive numbers of NGOs
lost their registrations during these periods, the fundamental idea of having a
space for them did not change, and each time growth picked up again unabated
after the period of repression.

More frequently, a single group may be harassed, pushing it back away
from some line of political tolerance that the government feels has been
encroached on. This is almost identical to what happens in the religious sector. Even occasional and arbitrary repression accomplishes the major goals of
this form of governance—it minimizes potential threats by creating powerful
self-censorship and keeping the scale of organization small. These modes of
repression that accompany blind-eye governance serve, above all, to encourage self-censorship. Each act of repression clarifies exactly where the line falls
between extralegal acts that will be tolerated and those that will be crushed.
It also warns every other group that it is officials, not citizens, who draw that
line and redraw it at will. Repressive acts tell all social groups—from temples
and churches to environmental protestors and NGOs—that they need to keep
themselves on the safe side of the line.

Beyond State and Society

Influences from outside China complicate state-society relations for both religion and environment. The direct effects may be most obvious through the role

of foreign missionaries. Missionaries have come to China from many parts of the world—South Korea as a site of origin has been just as important as the United States or Hong Kong. Many of these people come as English teachers (more blind-eye governance, since it is illegal to propagate religion among minors). Yet China already had significant pockets of Christianity, going back more than a century in some Protestant cases, and more than 400 years for some Catholic villages. Foreigners were an important source of funds and Bibles immediately after 1979, but it also seems clear that China's Christian community is expanding primarily through its own internal dynamic and that the situation would probably not be very different if there were no missionaries. For Islam, foreign funding has also been important in mosque construction in the western part of the country, but again the internal dynamics seem far more important.

The indirect effects of globalization on religion, however, are much clearer than the role of propagation. The greatest of these is simply the flood of new information and experience, not just new media such as the Internet or cell phone messaging and not just the new openness to outside sources of information through old media but the entire world that comes with the expansion of consumption in a market-driven economy—the multiplicity of products, images, and ultimately alternative self-conceptions that the marketplace encourages. This has shaken many of the sureties of the Maoist period and helped drive new searches for values and selves. For some, this search takes religious form, for others it is social contribution through NGOs.

In the world of popular religion, the most important effects of outside contact came from the Chinese global ecumene, realized through visits from Hong Kong, Southeast Asia, and Taiwan. The influence of the Taiwanese may have been the greatest, partly because they could not visit at all until the late 1980s when they flooded in, and partly because the level of local religiosity in Taiwan was so high that there was a major drive to visit mother temples on the mainland. The religious effects, though limited largely to Fujian, the origin of the ancestors of most Taiwanese families, were powerful. The hope of investment by Taiwanese entrepreneurs or of large payments for social contributions such as education or medical care encouraged local cadres again to turn a blind eye to the revival of massive local temple rituals that these visits encouraged.

More generally, China has also felt some influence from the broad growth of a humanistic and philanthropic Buddhism (again with a strong base in Taiwan). These groups do not usually directly conduct their own activities in China but instead serve as an indirect source of influence on both religious groups and NGOs there. The most obvious examples are Taiwan's Buddhist Compassion Relief Tzu-chi Foundation and the Buddha Light Mountain association, each of which provides public charity, education, and emergency relief. Both are widely known and emulated (on smaller scales) in China. With Islam as well, especially in the northwest, Muslims have been thinking hard about the new global waves of rationalizing and modernizing their faith (sometimes in the name of a return to fundamentals).

For NGOs, the situation is complex. The NGO forum that accompanied the 4th UN Conference on Women in Beijing in 1995 had a powerful effect despite the state's enormous discomfort with the event when it occurred. For the NGO sector, 1995 was thus probably a more significant date than 1989, although hosting the forum was possible only in the broader context of the reforms. There was increasing official talk after 1995 about the positive role that NGOs could serve, which meshed with official statements at the time about needing a smaller state and a bigger society. In addition, many Chinese associations greatly welcomed the infusions of cash that foreign connections could bring, and many foreign NGOs and governments sought to promote the activities and capacities of Chinese NGOs. Environmental groups have been no exception, with foreign NGOs acting both directly under their own auspices and indirectly by funding Chinese groups. On the other hand and not so different from the situation of Christians, NGOs with strong foreign ties could be damaged in the eyes of both the government and local supporters by appearing insufficiently nationalist.

If there were no direct ties to foreigners for either religion or NGOs, the current situation might not be radically different. Still, global influences have been absolutely vital in less direct ways. The expansion of the market has been crucial in creating a niche for new moralities, supplied by both NGOs and the various religions. The retreat of the state from a totalitarian project has created a space in which even extralegal groups (again in both religion and environmental and other NGOs) have been able to thrive through blind-eye governance. Recent globalization has thus been most influential in spreading ideas about social organization (such as NGOs) and about alternatives to an older socialist concept of self (through religion, among other things), rather than through a direct organization of NGOs or religious groups by foreign parties.

1989

The ability of Chinese temples or environmental groups to affect national movements such as those of 1989 differed greatly from what happened in Eastern Europe. In religion, for example, China simply had no equivalent to the churches of Poland or East Germany. The old state cult had collapsed with the fall of the last emperor in 1911, and it had no existence apart from that extinct state. Confucianism, if we want to call it a religion at all, had been badly discredited through the entire twentieth century and is only now beginning to find some respectability again. In 1989 it had no institutional base of support at all. As for the rest, none of the important Chinese religious traditions had been closely tied to the state for almost a millennium. At the national level, the late imperial and republican states had exerted some control over them, but no religion had ever occupied a position in the nationalist imagination comparable to the position of the churches in many Eastern European countries.

This long history of a relative lack of institutional religious strength at the national level, and religion's relative absence from the way the Chinese nation imagined itself, continued under the PRC. Its religious strategy had successfully created two levels of religion: At the national level the five official, corporatist religious organizations were quite tame, while at the local level temples and house churches thrived but had little potential to expand their activities. Such local religious groups had strong incentives to stay out of politics. Finally, again unlike some of the other communist countries, most members of China's elite were profoundly irreligious as a result of both their own traditions and the twentieth century's powerful secularization there. Thus quite unlike some of the Eastern European cases, religious groups were virtually invisible in China's Tiananmen and related demonstrations.[5]

For NGOs, including environmental groups, China already had a robust development by 1989, but the state's corporatist strategy was relatively successful in reducing their independence. In many ways, they had a bimodal structure similar to religion. National-level groups were controlled and obedient. Such associations had much more freedom of action below the radar, but only if they remained small, local, and apolitical. No independent social organizations on a large scale were possible. There was thus nothing comparable to Solidarity in Poland or to the environmental movement in Czechoslovakia. Instead, the primary building blocks of social mobilization in China in 1989 remained, ironically enough, the socialist work units (including the universities, for students). In big cities where the Tiananmen movement centered, these units were at the time still primarily state owned.

Thus none of the new social forms that had been developing so quickly since the reforms began in 1979 had an important institutional presence in the Tiananmen demonstrations of 1989. This is not really an argument for the success of the Maoist project in breaking down independent social groups and merging everything into the state as just the opposite had been happening for a decade. Instead, we can attribute the quiescence of these groups to the success of a new image of state-society relations—an authoritarian corporatism that brought large organizations under the careful wing of the state. Local groups—from NGOs registered as businesses to temples—could be governed with a blind eye, and could be controlled through occasional repression, either to draw clearly whatever political line these groups could not cross or simply to remind people that it is the state that determines the rules.

This strategy, to some extent, reflected the experience of nondemocratic economic successes in the region. Malaysia and especially Singapore loomed large as models for successful governance. Even Taiwan, which democratized in 1987, was a model. After all, while Western scholars tend to see Taiwan's transformations as a case of inevitable democratization, the island's experience also shows that an authoritarian one-party state can deliver rapid economic growth in a relatively quiet political climate for many decades on end.

The blind-eye techniques of governance, as well as the loosely corporatist vision of state-society relations that China and some other Asian regimes developed, appear to contrast significantly with our image of more fully centralized and domineering state structures in the Soviet-dominated world. In this image, which included China before the reform period, state and society tended to merge into each other, at least in principle. The eye of the state was not blind but saw and illuminated all, as in the Cultural Revolution trope of Chairman Mao as the sun rising in the East. Nor was this simply a propaganda stance, because the state made clear to all that it was watching. One of the first things I was told while living in China early in the reform period was how to identify members of the Public Security apparatus by their shoes; they were not really hiding because it is useful to have people know they are watched. As Verdery in particular shows elsewhere in this volume, the secret police were an important aspect of the seeing-eye state throughout Eastern Europe. It is difficult to know how the current situation of surveillance in China compares to China of an earlier time or to communist Eastern Europe. Certainly the secret police remain important, but they seem to have a much smaller visibility in daily life than they once did. Rather than monitoring every moment of every life, they give the impression instead of clamping down only on actions that cross some line between subversion and tolerability.

If this is correct, then it helps explain why religious and environmental groups were so much less visible in China in 1989. The seeing-eye state may be able to avoid the tensions associated with allowing some forms of societal self-governance (including all the blind-eye forms), but any unrest will also be directed straight at the central state. There is no other target. Postreform China, on the other hand, loosened the central image of the state as the one that both sees all and cares for all. By opening space for a semi-independent social sector, it allowed people's attention to focus in many different directions—toward gods (or God) and local communities or toward polluters and local farmers, for instance.

In the end, the events of 1989 in China were little more than a blip in the development of the new forms of postreform governance. The repression that followed after June 4 led to many NGOs losing their registration and to harsher conditions for a good number of religious groups. None of this lasted long, however, and both kinds of organizations soon resumed their growth. Much the same happened again after the Falun Gong demonstrations a decade later, with a period of repression leading to renewed growth for many organizations.

The Legacies of 1989 in China

The long-term consequences of the events of 1989 pale compared to what happened in other communist countries at the time. Rather than leading to fundamental political or economic shifts, 1989 in China brought a temporary retrenchment but ultimately saw a return to the trends that had already been developing for a decade: an economic turn away from central planning toward market incentives and a political system that retained a commitment to one party rule under an authoritarian structure and a relatively corporatist ideal—but not practice—of the relation between state and society. If anything, watching the events that unfolded after 1989 in Russia and its former allies reinforced China's commitment not to emulate its neighbors at all, to continue moving ahead with gradual economic reform but not to budge on the political front.

That commitment, however, helped lead to a number of innovations in governance intended to consolidate rule in a very different way from the Maoist era. One of the key issues was to find mechanisms to create a responsive authoritarianism—to solve the problem of how to get feedback from the people without subjecting the state to the risks of open elections. These techniques include allowing letters and petitions to the state, granting some access to legal recourse, giving the media more investigative freedom, and even allowing localized demonstrations (Shi 1997; Nathan 2003; Weller 2008).

One side effect of this informal face of rule has been the increase in what I have called blind-eye governance—the combination of a willingness to look the other way most of the time plus an ability to maintain control through occasional repression. This is evident in many sectors in China today, including religion and NGOs. Most of China's rapid religious growth over the last several decades has taken place in this legal gray zone, including the expansion of the presence of Christianity and local temple worship. This same point applies even to Buddhism, although Buddhist groups in China in general have tended to be more cautious. The recently opened Lingshan Buddhist Palace in Wuxi, for example, is a large and spectacularly sumptuous Buddhist compound that houses a community of monks and hosts international Buddhist meetings. Nowhere, however, does it refer to itself as a Buddhist temple or even a religious organization; it is instead a commercial joint enterprise with the Wuxi metropolitan government's tourism office.

The world of environmental and other NGOs is similarly complex in its relations to the state, which range from the obedient corporatist organizations well within both the letter and the spirit of Chinese law to a wide range of false registrations. No one is actually being fooled by most of these techniques, but they do at least allow local officials to claim they were unaware of the existence of these organizations if there is pressure from above. Blind-eye governance contributes indirectly but importantly to responsive authoritarianism by allowing a certain amount of societal self-organization, which can then remove some burdens from the state such as buffering family and community members from economic and health disasters (as religion often does), delivering needed social services such as old age care or emergency relief (as both religious groups and NGOs do), or monitoring such difficult issues as the environment. One of the legacies of both 1979 (the start of the reform era) and 1989 for China has been the continuous move away from the totalitarian model of governance and toward an authoritarian and corporatist model that assumes a social world separate from the state. Blind-eye governance may have been an unintended consequence of that legacy, but it is nevertheless an important contributor to the process.

Notes

1. I ignore Islam here, due to a combination of space and knowledge limitations, even though it is an important part of the story.
2. Liu Tik-sang, personal communication.
3. The interview took place in July 2009.
4. Deng argues that there are hidden rules governing these decisions, although he actually documents only one such case and cites many cases in which local officials seem to be improvising instead; he calls implementation of these hidden rules "unintentional in some cases" (192).
5. It is worth noting, however, that the student-led protests in Tiananmen were preceded by large-scale demonstrations by Islamic minorities against the book *Sexual Customs*, which was widely considered insulting to Islam and whose author was dubbed China's Salman Rushdie (Gladney 1994). There does not seem to have been any coordination, however, with the student-led protests, even though some of the important student leaders were also members of Islamic minorities.

References

Chau, Adam Yuet. 2005. *Miraculous Response: Doing Popular Religion in Contemporary China*. Palo Alto, Calif.: Stanford University Press.

Dean, Kenneth. 1993. *Taoist Ritual and Popular Cults of Southeast China*. Princeton, N.J.: Princeton University Press.

Deng, Guosheng. 2010. "The Hidden Rules Governing China's Unregistered NGOs: Management and Consequences." *The China Review* 10(1):183–206.

Gao, Bingzhong. 2005. "An Ethnography of a Building Both as Museum and Temple: On the Double-Naming Method as an Art of Politics." Paper presented at the annual meeting of the American Anthropological Association, December Washington, D.C., 2005.

Gladney, Dru. 1994. "Salman Rushdie in China: Religion, Ethnicity, and State Definition in China." In *Asian Visions of Authority: Religion and the Modern States of East and Southeast Asia*, Charles F. Keyes, Laurel Kendall, and Helen Hardacre, eds., 255–278. Honolulu: University of Hawaii Press.

Hunter, Alan and Kim-Kwong Chan. 1993. *Protestantism in Contemporary China*. Cambridge, U.K.: Cambridge University Press.

Jing, Jun. 1994. "Female Autonomy and Female Shamans in Northwest China." Paper presented at the annual meeting of the American Anthropological Association, Atlanta, 1994.

Kao, Chen-yang. 2009. "The Cultural Revolution and the Emergence of Pentecostal-Style Protestantism in China." *Journal of Contemporary Religion* 24(22):171–188.

Liang, Jialin 梁家麟. 1999. *Gaigekaifanghou de zhongguo nongcun jiaohui* 改革开放后的中国农村教会 *(Chinese Village Churches after the Reforms)*. Hong Kong: JiandaoShenxueyuan.

Mao, Zedong. [1927] 1971. "Report on an Investigation of the Peasant Movement in Hunan." In *Selected Readings from the Works of Mao Tsetung*, 23–39. Beijing: Foreign Languages Press.

Marx, Karl. [1943] 1983. "Critique of Hegel's Philosophy of Right." *The Portable Karl Marx*, Eugene Kamenka, ed., 87–91. New York: Penguin.

Nathan, Andrew J. 2003. "Authoritarian Resilience: China's Changing of the Guard." *Journal of Democracy* 14(1):6–17.

Nedostup, Rebecca. 2008. "Ritual Competition and the Modernizing Nation-State." In *Chinese Religiosities: Afflictions of Modernity and State Formation*, Mayfair Mei-hui Yang, ed., 87–112. Berkeley: University of California Press.

"Profile of the Ren Ai Charity Foundation." 2009. http://longquanzs.org/eng/articlecontent.php?id=194.

Shapiro, Judith. 2001. *Mao's War against Nature: Politics and the Environment in Revolutionary China*. New York: Cambridge University Press.

Shi, Tianjian. 1997. *Political Participation in Beijing*. Cambridge, Mass.: Harvard University Press.

Unger, Jonathan and Anita Chan. 2008. "Associations in a Bind:The Emergence of Political Corporatism." In *Associations and the Chinese State*, Jonathan Unger, ed., 48–68. Armonk, N.Y.: M. E. Sharpe.

Weller, Robert P. 2006. *Discovering Nature:Globalization and Environmental Culture in China and Taiwan*. Cambridge, U.K.: Cambridge University Press.

———. 2008. "Responsive Authoritarianism." In *Political Change in China: Comparisons with Taiwan*, edited by Bruce Gilley and Larry Diamond, eds., 117–133. Boulder, Colo.: Lynne Rienner.

PART III

REFORMING ECONOMIC SYSTEMS

5

Notes on the Geopolitical Economy of Post–State Socialism

JÓZSEF BÖRÖCZ

The overall transformation of the external linkage structures of the economies of the erstwhile Soviet bloc was a crucial aspect of the disintegration of the state socialist "system" in eastern Europe and northern Eurasia.[1] The collapse of the Soviet bloc occurred in the context, and was in some important ways the historic culmination, of the most outstanding historical achievement of the neoliberal hegemony that so thoroughly penetrated the economic and political dimensions of suprastate relations for the preceding decades.[2]

After the collapse of the state socialist system of controls over cross-border flows of people, capital, commodities, and ideas in 1989-90, the relative proximity of the states of eastern Europe to western Europe and their pre–state socialist histories of insertion in the European circuits of capital made these societies particularly easy and obvious targets for foreign direct investment, especially from western Europe. Given the magnitude of intra-European inequalities in capitalization, the resulting property transformations in eastern Europe—which constituted relatively small outlays for western European capital—resulted in foreign direct investment of enormous domestic economic significance for the target societies, creating textbook examples of foreign investment dependence. In those parts of the former Soviet bloc that had had less significant and more tentative histories of exposure to west European circuits of capital—such as the successor states of the former USSR—the privatization of the state's assets had more of a domestic-oligarchic character, setting those societies apart from east-central Europe from the onset of the transformation.

The post-state-socialist transformation took the form of a geopolitical "game" largely overdetermined by the mostly voluntary, sometimes forced, importation of governmentality from the EU and the iron embrace of the world's mightiest military-strategic alliance, the North Atlantic Treaty

Organization (NATO)—with the two forces offering an opportunity no east-central European state could refuse. Again, except for the Baltic states, which steadfastly stuck to the east European pattern of geopolitical reorientation, most of the more distant successor states of the erstwhile USSR had recognizably different outcomes, marked by the creation of the Commonwealth of Independent States, the Shanghai Organization, and a number of local conflicts that erupted with great fervor, especially in the Caucasus.

It would be hard to overestimate the significance of global forces in institutional change in eastern Europe (Böröcz 2001). Important recent work has made great steps toward developing a nuanced understanding of how the local institutionalization of such global forces has taken place in east-central Europe, focusing either on the EU (see, for example, Jacoby 2001, 2004; Bohle and Husz 2005), on various organizationally concrete forces of multinational capital (see, for example, Bohle and Greskovits 2006; Bandelj 2008, 2009; Drahokoupil 2009), or both (Vliegenthart and Horn 2007) as nodes transmitting global transformative effects to the societies of the former state socialist bloc, especially in eastern Europe. It is unfortunate that work in the same vein on the rest of the vast, and no less complex, former Soviet "space" is much sparser, if not entirely absent.

Framework and Trajectories

In this chapter, I focus on two important dimensions of the consequences of 1989 as a major transformation in the ways in which the erstwhile socialist states have been integrated into the capitalist world economy. In contrast to the well-nigh exclusive focus of the literature on the impact of economic performance on per capita rates—a feature I have criticized in detail elsewhere[3]— I open up the analysis of over-time trajectories to incorporate an additional dimension: Besides relative wealth (i.e., per capita rates of performance), I also observe changes in relative global economic weight (share in the gross world product).[4] By including a dimension (relative global weight) that is geopolitical[5] par excellence, I hope to be able to shed light on important patterns that remain hidden if observed exclusively through the "rates" lens.[6]

My analysis extends to all societies that underwent a post-state-socialist transformation since the late 1980s, including not only east-central and south-eastern Europe, but also the former Soviet area. I examine these cases against the backdrop of the increasingly diverse capitalist world economy as a whole, highlighting some relevant comparative angles. The empirical material comes from a data set initially published by the Organization for Economic Co-operation and Development (OECD) as an online supplement to a magisterial compilation of *longue-durée*[7]estimates of economic performance[8] by British economic historian Angus Maddison (2006a, 2006b). For the years from 2002 to 2008, the OECD data set has been updated posthumously on Maddison's online historical data archive (Maddison 2010).

Let us place the societies of the world in a two-dimensional space (Figure 5.1 offers a visual aid for this conceptual exercise.)[9] The vertical (*y*) axis represents per capita economic performance (computed, in order to make over-time comparison—the purpose of this exercise—visually feasible, as percentage of the world mean per capita GDP in any given year). In figure 5.1, I have subdivided the *y* axis into three categories and labeled them, respectively, "rich," "medium," and "poor." As my empirical analyses refer to the twentieth century—a period after the spatial completion of the capitalist world-economy as a global system in the last decades of the nineteenth century—it is historically justified to use the familiar, Wallersteinian trichotomy of "core," "semiperiphery," and "periphery." In this analysis, I define the semiperiphery, arbitrarily, as societies that have between 50 percent and 200 percent of the world mean per capita GDP in the given year.

The horizontal dimension (axis *x*) marks what I have called[10] external economic weight, expressed as the share of a unit (here, a state or a group of states) in the total gross world product. I have also subdivided this dimension, just like the *y* axis, into three categories, and labeled them, respectively, as "lightweight," "middleweight," and "heavyweight," with the one- and ten-percent marks serving as cutoff points among the three.

The three-by-three categorization created in this way allows the analysis to separate nine characteristic combinations of two geopolitical-economic factors, ranging from poor (or peripheral) lightweight ("PL" in the bottom-left corner of the graph) to rich (or core) heavyweight ("RH," in the opposite corner).

Figure 5.2 contains some of the principal directions of possible movement within this trajectory space. It marks vertical movement as up- and downward mobility and changes in horizontal position as extensive growth and extensive

	lightweight	middleweight	heavyweight
rich	RL	RM	RH
medium	ML	MM	MH
poor	PL	PM	PH

Figure 5.1 Trajectory Space: Static View

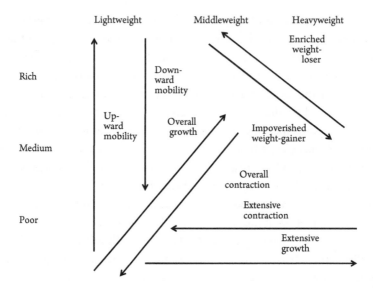

Figure 5.2 Trajectory Space: Dynamic View

contraction. A successful state would cover a diagonal trajectory, crossing the rectangle from the bottom left to the top right corner, or from the poor lightweight to the rich heavyweight position; I label this "overall growth" and its disastrous opposite as "overall contraction." Finally, I call diagonal movement from the rich lightweight toward the poor heavyweight location "impoverished weight gainer" and its opposite "enriched weight loser."

With this preparation, we are now ready for an overview of the trajectories of the formerly state socialist societies. Let us start with two composite pictures. The two of them together will allow us to visualize the trajectories of the Soviet bloc during the state socialist period.

Figure 5.3 indicates the trajectory of the Council for Mutual Economic Assistance (CMEA)—the Soviet bloc's economic integration system[11]—along with the multiple predecessors of the EU and a few important, additional states[12] in the two-dimensional trajectory space of the geopolitical economy of the global system between 1950 and 1989. CMEA begins the period at almost exactly in the middle of the semiperiphery (around 102 percent of the world mean GDP per capita), accounting for approximately 13 percent of the gross world product. The CMEA experiences a period of modest upward mobility, reaching the historic peak of its performance in per capita terms with 127 percent in 1961. CMEA's relative global weight does not increase in proportion to its wealth; it reaches its apex, with 14.38 percent of the gross world product, in 1964. Since then, the history of the socialist suprastate unit of economic integration has been a downward slide: CMEA slid to 91 percent of the world mean GDP per capita and 10.42 percent of the gross world product by 1989.

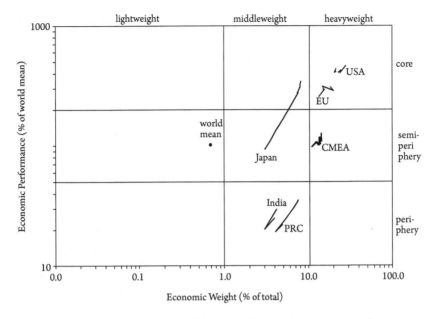

Figure 5.3 Trajectories of the Council for Mutual Economic Assistance, the European Union, and Some Large States: Gross Domestic Product per Capita as Percentage of World Mean and Gross Domestic Product as Percentage of Gross World Product, 1950 to 2008. Source: Computed from Maddison 2001. Note: Labels indicate earliest datapoint.

Four basic observations bear mentioning. First, treated as an aggregate of its member states, CMEA had been a resolutely heavyweight, semiperipheral phenomenon throughout its history, and it was the only such entity on the global map of systems of economic integration.

Second, during its history the CMEA did not experience a radical change of position. Even though in 1989 the CMEA occupied an overall less advantageous global position than in 1950, its decline in GDP per capita, relative to the world average, was moderate at worst, and the less than 4 percent weight loss experienced over the second half of its existence was, while noticeable and likely a cause for concern for those in charge, certainly not a catastrophic collapse.

More important, third, as a comparison to the curves representing the soaring two-dimensional growth pattern of Japan, on the one hand, and the two-dimensional contraction and modest rebound of India and China, on the other, will reveal, the CMEA's curve shows a relatively moderate amount of change, portraying the CMEA as a large, semiperipheral, suprastate organization with little, gradual movement in either direction.[13]

Fourth, as compared to the EU—the only economic integration throughout this period that occupied a core heavyweight position—the CMEA was

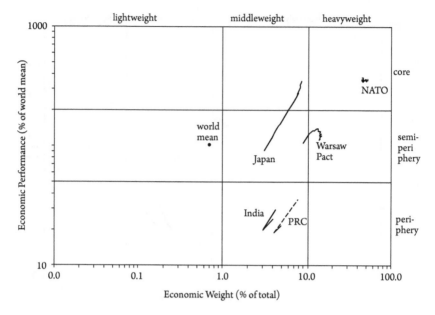

Figure 5.4 Trajectories of the Warsaw Pact, NATO, and Some Large States: Gross Domestic Product per Capita as Percentage of World Mean and Gross Domestic Product as Percentage of Gross World Product, 1950 to 2008. Source: Computed from Maddison 2001. Note: Labels indicate earliest datapoint.

never on par with it in terms of wealth, and it almost matched the EU's global economic weight (it had a global economic weight of about 1 percent less than the EU) only up to 1960. A major difference between the CMEA and the EU has been the latter's history of enlargements,[14] resulting, in turn, in significant weight gains. As a result, the gap between the CMEA and the EU kept widening so that, by the time of the CMEA's dissolution in 1990, the EU's proportion of the gross world product was almost double that of its state socialist counterpart.

We can obtain another angle on the global position of the socialist bloc by comparing, as Figure 5.4 does, the trajectory of the Warsaw Pact (computed as a composite of its member states) to its counterparts worldwide.[15] This picture tells a strikingly different story.

Starting from a point just slightly above (at 114 percent) the world mean GDP per capita and commanding 13.4 percent of the world product, the Warsaw Pact climbed to 141.4 percent of the world average by 1975, while hovering around 13 to 14 percent of the gross world product throughout the same period. The Warsaw Pact's loss of global economic weight begins around 1971. By 1991—the year of its dissolution—the Warsaw Pact's overall contraction had put it at a mere 8.8 percent of the gross world product, having fallen back to around the world mean GDP per capita. By contrast, its main Cold War adversary, NATO, never had less than 44 percent of the gross world product and was never poorer than three and a half times the world average GDP per capita during the same period. In the year of the dissolution of the Warsaw Pact, NATO states represented 44.4 percent of the gross world product and 377 percent of the world average GDP per capita.

The Warsaw Pact was a bloc firmly anchored, like the CMEA, in the semi-periphery. However, as it becomes obvious when we compare the curve for the CMEA (in figure 5.3) to that depicting the Warsaw Pact (in figure 5.4), the two had radically dissimilar trajectories. Specifically, the inverted *U* of the Warsaw Pact diverges from CMEA's curve in two ways. First, the Warsaw Pact started an overall contraction sometime around the mid-1970s, causing a precipitous drop in its global economic weight—a decline the CMEA never experienced.

The second, and geopolitically crucial, difference has to do with the structure of the global adversaries against which the CMEA and the Warsaw Pact were to be compared. The EU comprised a just slightly higher percentage of the gross world product than the CMEA until 1960, and even by 1990, after numerous steps of expansion, the EU's total global economic weight was barely twice the weight of the CMEA. In contrast, the global economic weight of NATO was around 3.3 to 3.6 times greater than that of the Warsaw Pact between 1958 and 1976. By 1980, this ratio increased to 3.71, passing the mark of 4 in 1985. By 1991, NATO represented almost exactly five times greater a share in the gross world product than the Warsaw Pact. As the main purpose of the Warsaw Pact was to a large extent maintenance of the Soviet bloc as an intricate system of political dependencies, this strikes me as a powerful piece of indirect geopolitical-economic evidence that goes a long way in explaining Mikhail Gorbachev's decision to dismantle the bloc as such.

Against this history of "system-competition," we can then examine the trajectories of individual socialist states,[16] starting with the period of 1950 to 1989 (portrayed in figure 5.5). The trajectories contained in the CMEA and Warsaw Pact graphs were composed of a varied set of state-by-state experiences. This variation calls into question a number of widely held assumptions concerning the degree to which the Soviet bloc should be considered a monolith.

One typical trajectory is that of the USSR, the largest state of the Soviet bloc. Its curve depicts a history consisting of three phases. The first is marked by overall growth—an upswing in both dimensions—lasting from 1950 to the mid-1970s, when the USSR went from 135 percent to around 150 percent of the world average GDP per capita and managed to push its own global share from 9.5 percent to 10 percent in the post-Sputnik years of 1958 to 1961. This is followed, second, by a period of stagnation in terms of GDP per capita, and, third, the erosion of global weight so that the USSR's share in the gross world product fell below 9 percent by 1979 only to drop below 8 percent by 1987. By

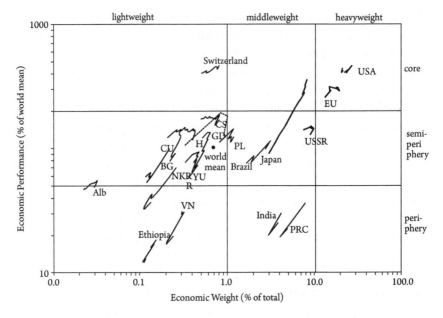

Figure 5.5 Trajectories of the States of the Socialist Bloc and Some Other States: Gross Domestic Product per Capita as Percentage of World Mean and Gross Domestic Product as Percentage of Gross World Product, 1955 to 1991. Source: Computed from Maddison 2001. Note: Labels indicate earliest datapoint.

1989, the USSR stood at 138 percent of the world mean GDP per capita, with a mere 7.7 percent share in the gross world product.

The German Democratic Republic's (GDR) dashed line resembles the inverted *U* of the Soviet pattern in an exaggerated form. East Germany experienced impressive overall expansion until 1972 when, with more than 190 percent of the world mean GDP per capita, it arrived at the doorstep of the core of the world economy. From 1954 to 1963, the GDR contributed approximately 1 percent to the gross world product. In 1972—its peak in per capita terms—the GDR still registered a .87 percent share in the world product, only to experience a precipitous decline, along both dimensions, from the mid-1970s until the late 1980s, so that, by the time of the fall of the Berlin Wall in 1989, the East German economy accounted for no more than .31 percent of the gross world product while, in per capita terms, it had fallen back to the world average, approximately 30 percent below its earliest available post–World War II figure (132.4 percent in 1950). The decline of its state socialist economy put the GDR in a global position worse than the one it had occupied after World War II (when it was of course part of defeated Nazi Germany).

During its state socialist period, the trajectory of Poland also replicated the Soviet pattern, reaching its apex in terms of global economic weight around

1958, with 1.4 percent of the gross world product while peaking, in per capita terms, with 141 percent of the world average GDP per capita in 1975. By 1989, Poland had fallen back to 110 percent of the world mean and to .81 percent of the gross world product. Albania, too, shows the same pattern, only at a much lower level, peaking in terms of GDP per capita at 55 percent of the world mean in 1975, followed by a precipitous decline into the periphery well before 1989.

An inverted *J* pattern—a variant of the inverted *U* where the decline is shorter and less severe than the preceding upswing—can be observed with respect to a larger group of states, all of them in eastern-central Europe. Bulgaria, Romania, Yugoslavia, Hungary, and Czechoslovakia each experienced longer and more radical upswings than the USSR and the GDR, followed by declines in global economic weight and, to a lesser extent, in per capita terms. The reduction in global economic weight is, in all of these cases, more persistent and of greater magnitude than the loss of position in terms of per capita incomes.

A different pattern involves what could be referred to as the "Third World" socialist states: the PRC, Cuba, North Korea, and Vietnam. Vietnam and North Korea endured major wars, Cuba was under a US economic embargo for more than a generation, and the PRC underwent the Cultural Revolution, not to mention its involvement in several regional wars during this period. Despite the radically different histories, the four curves appear to form a shared pattern: precipitous declines followed by a "rebound" that takes them back, almost exactly along the same lines, but to nowhere near the position from which they started. The emerging trajectory of the "Third World" socialist states is, notably, by and large the opposite of the predominant pattern for the states of eastern Europe and northern Eurasia.

Two marked regularities with regard to the states of eastern Europe and northern Eurasia are observable during the socialist period. First, and most strikingly contradicting standard neoliberal critiques, if not dismissals, of state socialism as an inherently unfeasible economic system, its onset did not result in measurable initial drops in economic performance in a vast majority of the cases. To the contrary, the early period of state socialism is marked by measurable, significant improvements both in per capita terms and in the dimension of global economic weight. Three things are in common among the cases that show this pattern: 1) they are a geographically contiguous bloc of predominantly semiperipheral states; 2) the cases are closely associated with the USSR, forming a geopolitical network clique (the Soviet bloc) manifested not only in coordinated international behavior but also in such organizational forms as the CMEA and the Warsaw Pact; and 3) their improvements unfold during peace time. (The widely used metaphor of the "Cold War" is, hence, somewhat misleading here.)

Second, as table 5.1 indicates, the economic woes and the erosion of the global position of the Soviet bloc states began well before their transformation to capitalism between 1989 and 1991. Two periods stand out: the oil shock years of the mid-1970s (also marking the first wave of indebtedness for the economies of east-central Europe) and the mid-1980s (the time of the second wave of debt obligations, largely aimed at refinancing the first wave).

Figure 5.6 is the first in a series of graphs depicting the trajectories of the former socialist states since 1989.[17] The overwhelming pattern in the figures, focusing on the eastern-central European members of the Soviet bloc, is clear. A series of italicized Vs—a trajectory composed of two phases—becomes evident: a period of overall contraction (marking a drop in global position in terms of both the world mean GDP per capita and shares in the gross world product), followed by a rebound of sorts. Whether the second, upswing phase brings the curve back to the level of relative wealth at which the transformation began varies among the states in the region: Albania (Alb), Bulgaria (BG), *Czechoslovakia* (*CS*), and Hungary (H) had, finally, by 2008, reached their starting positions of 1990. *Yugoslavia* (*YU*) and Romania (R) are far behind even that modest growth.

Poland (PL) stands apart from its fellow eastern European former state socialist economies as a case unto itself. Here, the initial post–regime-change contraction is short, followed by a near-perfectly vertical climb, placing Poland at about 50 percent higher in terms of world mean per capita GDP than its starting position in 1990.

Meanwhile, loss of global economic weight is a pattern that applies uniformly to all postsocialist states, even if the losses of weight due to the dissolution of

Table 5.1 **Beginning of the Downturn in Terms of Per Capita Gross Domestic Product in the States of the Soviet Bloc (expressed as percentage of the world average)**

State	Year
Albania	1973
Bulgaria	1985
Czechoslovakia	1985
German Democratic Republic	1973
Hungary	1985
Poland	1977
Romania	1973
Yugoslavia	1987
Union of Soviet Socialist Republics	1987

Source: Computed from Maddison 2010.

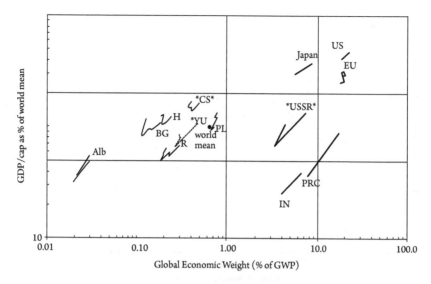

Figure 5.6 Trajectories of the East-Central European States of the Former Socialist Bloc and Some Other States: Gross Domestic Product per Capita as Percentage of World Mean and Gross Domestic Product as Percentage of Gross World Product, 1990 to 2008. Source: Computed from Maddison 2010. Note: Labels indicate earliest datapoint.

the former federal states of the *USSR*, *Yugoslavia*, and *Czechoslovakia* are accounted for. While there is considerable variation in terms of relative wealth, the geopolitical dimension of economic performance shows a near-uniform pattern of contraction; only the degree of the contraction shows some mild variation.

Figure 5.7 reviews the same period, focusing on the successor states of freshly dissolved *Czechoslovakia* (*CS*) and *Yugoslavia* (*YU*).[18] Again, the patterns are strikingly similar, with three outliers; Slovenia (SL), Bosnia-Herzegovina (BiH), and Slovakia (SK) had reached, by 2008, the already quite reduced levels of per capita GDP with which they started the era of their independent statehood in 1990 and 1991. The effect of wars can be observed in the magnitude of the collapse in the cases of Croatia (CRO), Macedonia (FYROM), and Serbia-Montenegro (SM). Of the two successor states of the former *Czechoslovakia*, only smaller and poorer Slovakia has surpassed its initial wealth in global per capita terms by a minuscule percentage. The trajectory of the Czech Republic (CZ) shows an involuted pattern just below the threshold of the core of the world economy. Slovenia (SL) seems to have entered the core sometime in the closing years of the twentieth century, while Serbia-Montenegro, Bosnia-Herzegovina, and the Former Yugoslav Republic of Macedonia, slid into periphery status for various amounts of time during the two decades that elapsed after the collapse of the Socialist Federal Republic of *Yugoslavia*.

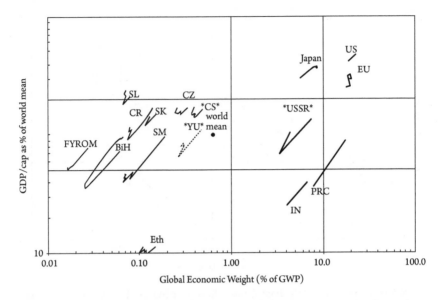

Figure 5.7 Trajectories of the Successor States of the Former Czechoslovakia and Yugoslavia and Some Other States: Gross Domestic Product per Capita as Percentage of World Mean and Gross Domestic Product as Percentage of Gross World Product, 1990 to 2008. Source: Computed from Maddison 2010. Note: Labels indicate earliest datapoint.

There is a fascinating political message concerning secession in the last graph. To the extent that at the heart of the political calculus leading to demands for secession was the idea of taking a certain loss of global weight in exchange for a better world-system position in terms of national income, and an expectation on the part of the relatively wealthier federal states that they would grow in per capita terms faster than the fellow republics they would leave behind, that expectation was met in only one case: Slovenia. Neither the Czech Republic nor Croatia—the two additional wealthier secessionist republics whose political elites may well have had a similar set of expectations—have experienced any major increase in their global position in per capita terms. As for war as a means of state building, in aggregate, the successor states of the former Yugoslavia dropped from 121 percent to approximately 65 percent of the world mean GDP per capita in four years (1989–1993) and barely managed to return to the world average by 2008. The two successor states of the former Yugoslavia that have managed to improve on their initial position are Slovenia—that was by and large saved from the ravages of civil war—and Bosnia-Herzegovina, whose postwar recovery since 1996 has occurred in a period during which the former Yugoslav republic was a de facto protectorate with sharply reduced sovereignty.

As for global economic weight, each of the successors of the federal states of east-central Europe commanded—just like their intact neighbors—less global economic weight in 2008 than they did at the point of the dissolution of the states from which they seceded. Their total loss of global weight (a drop from Yugoslavia's .48 percent of the gross world product to an average of .06 percent for the successor states of Yugoslavia and a reduction from Czechoslovakia's .49 percent to an average of .20 percent for its two successor states) has, thus, two causal components: 1) the carving up of the federal states and 2) their further, *sui generis* post-state-socialist decline afterward.

Figure 5.8 shifts the focus to the post-Soviet context. The dissolution of the USSR produced 15 post-Soviet republics. The figure portrays the trajectories of those three successor states of the USSR—Estonia (EE), Latvia (LA), and Lithuania (LI)—that in 2004 became members of the EU. All three show essentially the same trajectory, one that is also by and large the same as the one for the societies of eastern-central Europe: a steep initial overall decline followed by an upswing. Estonia's and Latvia's upswing vaulted them above their starting positions (although the Latvian case shows only one year, 2007, when its per capita GDP stood at a point higher than in 1991) by 2008. Lithuania's curve also replicates the *J*- pattern associated with eastern-central and southeastern European polities.

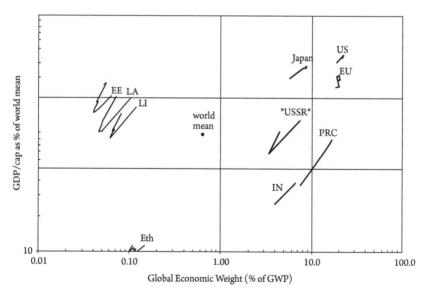

Figure 5.8 Trajectories of the European Union Member Republics of the Former USSR and Some Other States: Gross Domestic Product per Capita as Percentage of World Mean and Gross Domestic Product as Percentage percent of Gross World Product, 1990 to 2008. Source: Computed from Maddison 2010. Note: Labels indicate earliest datapoint.

In terms of global economic weight, all three post-Soviet EU member states conform to the by now all too familiar single pattern of contraction followed by a shorter and less powerful expansion.

As is discernible from Figure 5.9, even the largest and most powerful of the successor states of the USSR, Russia (Rus), has considerably less global economic weight than the USSR at its weakest. More striking, Maddison's estimates suggest that most of the USSR's non-EU-bound successor states— a vast majority of the former USSR's population—underwent a reduction in terms of both per capita income and global economic weight after the end of the USSR that approaches the catastrophic. Again, eight *J* patterns emerge, with only four *V*s: Armenia's (Arm), Azerbaijan's (Aze), Belarus's (Bel), and Kazakhstan's (Kaz) global position in terms of the per capita GDP of 2008 exceeds their standing in 1991.

The post-1991, post-Soviet world produced such new entrants to the global periphery as Ukraine (with its GDP per capita sinking to 43.9 percent of the world average in 1999), Belarus, Azerbaijan, Tajikistan (Taj), Georgia (Geo), Moldova (Mol), Kyrgyzstan (Kyr), and Turkmenistan (Tur), listed in decreasing order of global economic weight. Of those, Kyrgyzstan, Moldova, and Tajikistan did not, until 2008, re-emerge from the periphery. Particularly severe is the case of Tajikistan, whose per capita GDP stood, in 2008, at 20.2

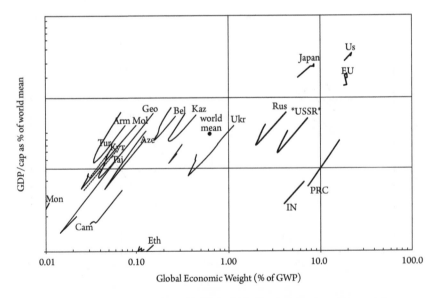

Figure 5.9 Trajectories of the Non–European Union Member Republics of the Former USSR and Some Other States: Gross Domestic Product per Capita as Percentage of World Mean and Gross Domestic Product as Percentage of Gross World Product, 1990 to 2008. Source: Computed from Maddison 2010. Note: Labels indicate earliest datapoint.

percent of the world average, almost half of India's percentage and barely above Bangladesh's.

The first years of the transformation were, clearly, disastrous for most post-Soviet societies. Armenia, Kyrgyzstan, and Turkmenistan saw their per capita GDPs cut by approximately half. Even more catastrophic was the transformation in Azerbaijan (dropping from 90 percent to 34 percent of the world mean), Moldova (120 percent to 36 percent), Ukraine (117 percent to 45 percent), Georgia (148 percent to 41 percent), and Tajikistan (59 percent to 14 percent). Making matters truly calamitous is the fact that those drops occurred suddenly, within just four to eight years after the dissolution of the USSR.

The aggregate of the successors of the former USSR sank from 7.7 percent to 3.3 percent of the gross world product between 1989 and 1998. The *USSR*'s 15 successor states combined registered a drop from 133 percent to 67 percent of the world mean GDP per capita between 1990 and 1998. At its dissolution, the USSR contributed a much reduced 7.3 percent of the world economy; by 2008, its 15 successor states had an unweighted average global economic weight of .29 percent.

A loss of half or more of a state's world-system position in terms of GDP per capita over a four- to 10-year period is unprecedented in peacetime. It is also important to note that the earliest point of comparison in the numbers previously quoted (from 1990 or 1991) is already, without exception, a point by which approximately five to 15 years of economic stagnation or contraction had already taken place.

No less significant for an adequate understanding of the global trajectories of the societies of the postsocialist context is the issue of global economic weight. In 1989, the most powerful state of northern Eurasia was the USSR, already reduced to 7.7 percent of the gross world product from the 9.5 percent to 10 percent it had during much of the state socialist period, followed by Poland (.81 percent), and Czechoslovakia (.513 percent). In 2008—the most successful year for the three largest postsocialist economies in the two decades following 1989—the region's economic powerhouse, the Russian Federation, registered a mere 2.51 percent of the gross world product, followed by Poland (.77 percent) and Ukraine (.45 percent). Thus it is obvious that the states of the former Soviet bloc became severely marginalized in terms of their ability to exert influence on the global economy and project their geopolitical power onto the outside world.

The global geopolitical-economic weight of northern Eurasia as a whole has been considerably reduced, not only compared to the peak of the state socialist period but also to the already diminished global economic weights that prevailed at the end of state socialism. Of the 27 states on which this chapter focuses, only two—Russia and Poland—displayed economic weight greater than the world mean in 2008, and all except Russia were, at that point, light-weight powers in global terms.

Implications

The implications of this overall reduction in the global sway of the states of the region, especially in the context of the recently ever more spellbinding increase of the global geopolitical-economic weight, and the resulting return to global prominence of a number of large Asian economies, especially China and India, are far reaching. The overall contraction of the former Soviet Bloc not only posed a stark counterpoint to the spectacular rise of parts of east and south Asia, it also served a closely related, crucial geopolitical function. For, given the zero-sum technique of computing percentage shares of gross world product, *ceteris paribus*, the increases in the global economic weight of the PRC and India would have to entail parallel reductions somewhere—likely, at least to some extent, in the global economic weights of other polities that are large and powerful actors in global geopolitics today.

The total magnitude of the losses of east-central and southeastern European and northern Eurasian former socialist states during the 1990s—approximately 5 percent of the gross world product—more than matched the then still relatively modest gains made by China and India (altogether 4.43 percent) during the same period. The precipitous contraction of the global economic weight of the former Soviet bloc thus provided a geopolitical buffer that absorbed China's and India's gains and postponed what appears to be an inevitable geopolitical conflict between the rise of the two Asian giants and the current heavyweights of the capitalist world economy. However, this post-Soviet buffering process was a distinctly short-term phenomenon; for, during the first decade of the twenty-first century, the combined gains of China and India grew by more than 8 percent, while the former Soviet bloc stopped contracting and even registered a modest 1 percent overall growth. China's and India's percentage increases will have to be, therefore, absorbed by geopolitical locations other than the former Soviet bloc and through geopolitical means other than the collapse of state socialism, which is of course an unrepeatable historical event.

A second corollary reflects the fact that the collapse of the imperial power of the USSR and the dissolution of the region's federal states redrew the map of power relations in the region itself. What was in 1989 a group of nine socialist states is now 27 smaller, in some cases much smaller, capitalist states, a transformation that one would expect to increase the complexity of international relations exponentially, even if one had no knowledge of the historical tensions that exist among various sets of these states. This is particularly relevant to the issue of the relationship between the states of east-central Europe and the Baltic region, on the one hand, and Russia, on the other. Membership of some, but by far not all, of the postsocialist states in the EU and NATO further complicates the new global geopolitics as it applies to the former Soviet Bloc.

Meanwhile, the possibility of at least one new kind of inequality has appeared, one that involves the processes of state formation on the ruins of what used to be the socialist federal states. This transformation is specific to the post-state-socialist history of the region, owing to the fact that, while some states have been carved up into several successors—and each of these successors marshal, by definition, considerably less global power than their former federal state—other states did not undergo such a process of dissolution. Having avoided this round of dissolutions and its corollary, the drastic reduction in global economic weight, such states as Poland, Hungary, Romania, and Bulgaria have found themselves in somewhat more powerful positions vis-à-vis their subdivided neighbors. From a geopolitical perspective it is crucial to note that each of these four states exists in a context in which at least some, if not, as in the case of Poland, all of its neighbors have undergone radical changes in their global economic weight in the aftermath of state socialism.

The uncomplicated modernizationist expectations that the post-state-socialist states would rapidly catch up with the rest of Europe were simply wrong. This, by itself, comes hardly as a surprise to global analysts.

What is most striking about the post-1989 transformation is the uniformity with which the global economic positions of a vast majority of the region's states collapsed, along basically a single precipitous pattern, followed by a somewhat feebler rebound. It appears that, ironically, the state socialist period showed much more variation among members of the Soviet bloc than post–state socialism. Whether they are predominantly western Christian, eastern Orthodox, or Muslim, whether their governments pursue policies that are neoliberal, embedded neoliberal, or neocorporatist (Bohle and Greskovits 2007), whether they are poorer or richer, small, medium-sized or large, whether they privatized their assets primarily to foreign multinationals or domestic oligarchs, whether their current economy depends on exports of machine products, agricultural goods, or energy and raw materials, each lost global positions, to a significant degree, along both of the dimensions previously surveyed. At best, some could boast only of having regained their already reduced positions of 1990 in GDP per capita terms; others have not succeeded in making even that dubious achievement. Even more striking, none among the 27 postsocialist states surveyed here had by 2009 recuperated its already significantly reduced global economic weight of 1989.

As for the exceptions, a much more thorough investigation would be required to find a model specifying the concrete mechanisms that produced them. This is not something I could attempt in this chapter in a systematic manner.

As for Poland, the clear outlier case in terms of per capita GDP, the one thing that set it apart from most former eastern-central European members of the socialist bloc is that approximately half of its foreign debt—approximately $33 billion (Farnsworth 1994), primarily that part which was owed to foreign governments—was forgiven in 1991 (Callaghy 2004). All other postsocialist states of east-central Europe have been duly paying their debts ever since, and the only form of debt relief available to them is turning privatization revenues to debt repayment, a process that ends up coming close to the debt-equity swap schemes that ravaged a number of Latin American economies in the late 1980s. But this is, clearly, neither a well-worked out, nor a logically sufficient, explanation for Poland's exception. Further weakening the power of this argument as a monocausal explanation, Russia was subject to no fewer than five (Callaghy 2004) similar acts of debt forgiveness during the nineties (1993, 1994, 1995, 1996, and 1999). Yet its per capita GDP shows no upswing similar to that of Poland. Slovenia, on the other hand, also had a discernible net increase in its global position in per capita terms, despite the absence of a debt writeoff.

It is possible to argue that what Maddison's data capture is the first phase of a pattern in which more robust economic change will happen in a later, second phase. A number of considerations prompt me to be skeptical about this reading. First, the only argument I am familiar with that would propose such a development in a systematic fashion suggests that concerted efforts by a developmental state, requiring serious retooling for national development as a large-scale sociopolitical project, might produce a dynamic whereby initial contraction is followed by sustained growth.

The first problem is that there is no discernable evidence of such a developmental state anywhere in the vast postsocialist space that stretches from the Elbe to the Pacific Ocean. Time is a second problem with this argument: It is difficult to claim that retooling the economy by the developmental state would take two decades in a context, like that in the former Soviet bloc, in which a fully literate, well-trained and disciplined labor force is abundantly available and in which a fairly well-organized and coherent economic infrastructure exists, characteristic of semiperipheral economies specializing in export-oriented industrial strategies of growth. In addition, there is no known history of a developmental state that operated under the following set of external conditions: a globally hegemonic neoliberal ideology, high levels of foreign direct investment, and the relinquishment of sovereignty to two meddlesome suprastate public authorities, the EU and NATO.

Meanwhile, the cases of China (see So 2009) and Vietnam seem to serve as powerful examples of socialist developmental states that operate with a considerable degree of global success. If anything, as Barry Naughton's incisive study—chapter 6 of this volume—confirms for China, the differentiation of property ownership (into central-state and local-state-owned, as well as party-owned patterns) and the expansion of nonprivate forms of ownership suggest the reassertion and solidification of the predominantly state socialist character of profit making.

Another optimistic reading could argue that the losses of position the data depict are merely "transformation costs," an idea patterned after the notion of transaction costs. János Kornai argued this position in 1994, introducing the term *transformational recession*. The problem with this interpretation centers on magnitudes. Losses of more than half of the GDP per capita rates and even greater proportions of global economic weight—too large even for periods of war, famines, or natural catastrophies—appear much more significant than diminutions that could be ascribed merely to passing difficulties of adjustment or "transformation costs." If we accept the notion of transformation cost, we need, at a minimum, some additional factors that will help explain the enormity of the losses.

For lack of any convincing argument suggesting that the drastic setbacks outlined in this chapter are short-term and transitory steps toward a brighter future, I am forced to conclude, at least tentatively, that the reductions in global economic performance previously described are the parameters of a new status quo. What the extreme right-wing forces of the region will do with this state of affairs is an open-ended question.

As arresting as the catastrophic drops in per capita GDP is the drastic and generally uniform reduction in the global economic weight of the former socialist states. Economic crises before 1989, the dissolution of the federal states, and the reduction in shares in world product after 1989 have all lessened the ability of these states to exert sovereign influence on the world outside their borders, thus diminishing their ability to be independent geopolitical actors. All other things equal, this trend increases the relative power of all other, already powerful actors in the space of geopolitical power in which the former socialist states operate and makes it more likely that the postsocialist states, especially the smallest ones, will undergo significant pressures to experience increased levels of external political and economic dependency on more powerful public authorities, especially those in their geostrategic proximity.

Notes

The first version of this chapter was prepared for presentation at the 1989 Anniversary Conference, organized by Nina Bandelj and Dorothy Solinger, at the University of California at Irvine, November 6–8, 2009.

Data used in this study have been accessed electronically through Rutgers University's Alexander Library. The original, conference version of this paper was prepared while I benefited from two residential fellowships: one at Collegium Budapest/Institute for Advanced Studies, the other at the Jawaharlal Nehru Institute of Advanced Study at the Jawaharlal Nehru University, New Delhi, India, and it received its final touches while I held fellowships at the Zentrum für Höhere Studien and the Geisteswissenschaftliches Zentrum für die Geschichte und Kultur Osteuropas, both at the University of Leipzig, Germany. Financial support from Collegium Budapest, JNIAS, and the University of Leipzig are gratefully acknowledged. I am truly grateful to Mahua Sarkar for her encouragement, comments, and criticisms.

1. In order to avoid the Cold War-inflected convention of reifying these geographical areas as internally homogenous, externally distinct "regions," I do not capitalize the adjectives that point at them. By "northern Eurasia," I refer to the successor states of the former USSR; "eastern Europe" includes the reminder of former state socialist societies in Europe.
2. Of the many, valuable approaches to understanding the history of neoliberal hegemony, let me quote here the most relevant one, which puts it squarely in the center of an analytical framework developed in the context of the suprastate project of the European Union: van Apeldoorn et al., 2003, especially pp. 37–39.
3. See Böröcz 2010, especially the chapter titled "Global Economic Weight in the Longue-Durée: Nemesis of West European Geopolitics."
4. No doubt, there is a large number of important dimensions along which this transformation could and should be analyzed, so that these two represent—in my mind, very important, but still—a partial subset of the relevant "angles."
5. By geopolitics, I mean simply the ways in which organizations project their power into the world outside their borders.
6. For more on the implications of this two-dimensional view of the global trajectories of states, see Böröcz 2010, especially the chapter titled "Global Economic Weight in the Longue-Durée: Nemesis of West European Geopolitics."
7. Maddison's data set provides estimates for economic performance and population for more than 2,000 years of world history.
8. Geary-Khamis USD. For more detail on the estimation procedure, see Maddison 2006a, 2006b.
9. This section, explaining the logic of the presentation of the empirical data, follows closely the way in which the technique is introduced in Böröcz 2010. For more detail, please consult the chapter titled "Global Economic Weight in the Longue-Durée: Nemesis of West European Geopolitics."
10. Ibid.
11. Maddison's data set does not provide estimates for CMEA, the EU, the Warsaw Pact or NATO; these figures were produced by summing up the global economic weight (measured as percentage share in the gross world product) of their member states and by computing the unweighted mean of their per capita GDP (expressed as percentages of the world average). The CMEA figures have been computed by summing up the estimates for Bulgaria, Czechoslovakia, the GDR, Hungary, Poland, Romania, and the USSR for the entire period and adding the scores for Albania (until 1961), Mongolia (from 1962), Cuba (from 1972), and Vietnam (from 1978). Yugoslavia—which never attained full membership status in CMEA—is not included in the estimates.
12. I have omitted from this figure, as well as all subsequent figures representing "real-life" data, most of the world's more than 200 states. This was necessary because their inclusion would make some parts of the graph, especially the peripheral-lightweight and semiperipheral-lightweight cells so cluttered that it would be impossible to discern the patterns I seek to focus on here. It is important, therefore, to keep in mind that, were this a fully inclusive graph, most of the world's states would be found in the left bottom and left middle cells.
13. The divergence between the trajectories of the CEMA and the PRC clearly outline China's specific geopolitical status in contrast to the rest of the state socialist world. Its

differentia specifica is the absence of what I have described earlier as dual dependency. Instead, socialist China has occupied what Barry Naughton accurately describes in chapter 6 of this volume as a room for maneuver between the USSR and the United States, without any major degree of dependence on either.

14. For a more detailed analysis of the global geopolitics behind the EU's strategy of growth, see Böröcz 2010.

15. The temporal cutoff points (1955 to 1991) are slightly different than in figure 5.3, reflecting the establishment and dissolution of the Warsaw Pact. The Warsaw Pact figures have been obtained by adding the scores for Bulgaria, Czechoslovakia, Hungary, Poland, Romania, and the USSR.

16. For reference, I have included in this and all subsequent graphs the trajectories of Switzerland, Brazil, and Ethiopia as representatives of characteristic trajectories within the core, the semiperiphery, and the periphery.

17. Figure 5.6 shows the federal states of the socialist bloc—dissolved during the period observed here—as if they had remained intact, for example, as composites of their successor states. To signal this fact, the labels referring to the composite numbers of the now defunct, former federal socialist states are marked with asterisks, such as *CS* (for erstwhile Czechoslovakia), *YU* (for former Yugoslavia) and *USSR* for what used to be the Soviet Union.

18. The starting dates for the lines in this graph vary slightly, owing to differences in the times when the successor states were established.

19. See Kornai 1994. The main factors he outlines (and calls "causes") are descriptively accurate, empirical features of the transformation: "(1) the shift from a sellers' to a buyers' market, (2) the transformation of the real structure of the economy, (3) the disturbances in the coordination mechanisms, (4) the macroeconomic consequences of the hardening of financial discipline, and (5) the backwardness of the financial system" (39). How they qualify as causal explanations in a truly comparative-historical sense is left, lamentably, to the reader to decide.

References

Bandelj, Nina. 2008. *From Communists to Foreign Capitalists: The Social Foundations of Foreign Direct Investment in Postsocialist Europe*. Princeton, N.J.: Princeton University Press.

———. 2009. "The Global Economy as Instituted Process: The Case of Central and Eastern Europe." *American Sociological Review* 74:129–149.

Bohle, Dorothee and Béla Greskovits. 2006. "Capitalism without Compromise: Strong Business and Weak Labor in Eastern Europe's New Transnational Industries." *Studies in Comparative International Development* 41(1):3–25.

———. 2007. "Neoliberalism, Embedded Neoliberalism and Neocorporatism: Towards Transnational Capitalism in Eastern Europe." *West European Politics* 30(3):443–466.

Bohle, Dorothee and Dóra Husz. 2005. "Whose Europe Is It? Interest Group Action in Accession Negotiations: The Cases of Competition Policy and Labour Migration." *Politique européenne*. 15(1):85–112.

Böröcz, József. 2001. "Change Rules." *American Journal of Sociology* 106(4):1152–1168.

———. 2009. "The 'Rise of China' and the Changing World Income Distribution." In *China and the Transformation of Global Capitalism*, Ho-fung Hung, ed., 86–108. Baltimore, Md.: The Johns Hopkins University Press.

———. 2010. *The European Union and Global Social Change: A Critical Geopolitical-Economic Analysis*. London: Routledge.

Callaghy, Thomas M. "Innovation in the Sovereign Debt Regime: From the Paris Club to Enhanced HIPC and Beyond." *Working Paper*. Washington, D.C.: The World Bank Operations Evaluation Department, 54. Available: http://lnweb90.worldbank.org/oed/

oeddoclib.nsf/DocUNIDView %20ForJavaSearch/4BC77E9BEC2CAAFC85256E4A
00536A04/$file/hipc_wp_sovereign_debt.pdf Accessed: April 18, 2010.

Drahokoupil, Jan. 2009. *Globalization and the State in Central and Eastern Europe: The Politics of Foreign Direct Investment.* London: Routledge.

Farnsworth, Clyde H. 1994. "Egypt's 'Reward': Forgiven Debt." *The New York Times,* April 9, 1994. Available: http://www.nytimes.com/1991/04/10/business/egypt-s-reward-forgiven-debt.html?pagewanted=1 Accessed: April 18, 2010.

Jacoby, Wade. 2001. "Tutors and Pupils: International Organizations, Central European Elites, and Western Models." *Governance, An International Journal of Policy and Administration* 14(2):169–200.

_____. 2004. *The Enlargement of NATO and the European Union: Ordering from the Menu in Central Europe.* Cambridge, U.K.: Cambridge University Press.

Kornai, János. 1994. "Transformational Recession: The Main Causes." *Journal of Comparative Economics* 19:39–63.

Maddison, Angus. 2006a. *The World Economy: A Millennial Perspective.* Paris: OECD.

_____. 2006b. *The World Economy: Historical Statistics.* Paris: OECD.

_____. 2010. "Statistics on World Population, GDP and Per Capita GDP, 1–2008 AD. Horizontal File." Available: http://www.ggdc.net/maddison/Historical_Statistics/horizontal-file_02–2010.xls Accessed: April 18, 2010.

So, Alvin. 2009. "Rethinking the Chinese Economic Miracle." In *China and the Transformation of Global Capitalism,* Ho-fung Hung, ed., 50–63. Baltimore, Md.: The Johns Hopkins University Press.

van Apeldoorn, Bastian, Henk Overneek, and Magnus Ryner. 2003. "Theories of European Integration: A Critique." In *A Ruined Fortress? Neoliberal Hegemony and Transformation in Europe,* Alan W. Cafruny and Magnus Ryner, eds., 17–46. Oxford, U.K.: Rowman and Littlefield.

Vliegenthart, Arjan and Laura Horn. 2007. "The Role of the EU in the Transformation of Corporate Governance Regulation in Central Eastern Europe—the Case of the Czech Republic." *Competition and Change* 11(2):137–153.

6

The 1989 Watershed in China

How the Dynamics of Economic Transition Changed

BARRY NAUGHTON

The year 1989 in China was marked by the defeat of a group of reformists in the Communist Party leadership and the shattering of hopes of continuing political liberalization that were held by many. In retrospect, it is clear that 1989 also marked the end of one era of cautiously managed economic reform. Economic reform, as such, did not die, but when reforms resumed in earnest around 1992, they took on a new form, more resolute and in some ways harsher. The new reform pattern reinforced state and Communist Party interests, while exposing some social groups to major losses. Income grew dramatically, but inequality increased and economic life became more precarious. The post-1989 model of economic reform was one of concentrated power wielded more effectively and led to a remarkable recovery in the power of the Chinese state.

This chapter addresses the change in China's reform and development model before and after 1989, from a primarily economic standpoint. Both the before and after periods were characterized by gradual marketization and incremental institutional change. Nevertheless, they differed in the priority given to government interests and the willingness to allow specific social groups to bear the costs of marketization. The contrast between the periods should be understood with reference to the international political context, as well as the domestic political framework, within which Chinese reform developed. Before 1989, China had an unusual degree of international space, or room for maneuver. Domestically, by contrast, reformers faced tight political constraints, but they managed to carve out space for reforms by following policies that maximized their own room for maneuver. After 1989, the calculations of policy makers changed dramatically. China frequently felt "crowded" (especially by the United States), but domestically the leaders achieved a new authority to restart economic reform according to a different template. As a result, instead of being a temporary setback for reform, Tiananmen and 1989 ended up permanently altering China's reform trajectory.

Trading Places

For much of the 1980s, China and the Soviet Union seemed to be moving in the same direction. In both countries, market reform was being pursued through tentative measures that cumulatively made their systems more flexible and open but without a clear final objective. Then 1989 came, and the two systems set off in very different directions. In the 20 years since, both countries have pursued the logic of the choices they made in the immediate aftermath of 1989. The result has been a fundamental change in the relative positions of China and the former Soviet bloc countries.

Economically, China and Russia have traded places. As Böröcz notes in chapter 5 of this volume, 1989 was a point of inflection—but not a turning point—in the economic decline of the Soviet Union and the Eastern European economies. Growth in those countries was already slowing, and their economies then shrank dramatically after 1989. China's experience was a mirror image. The economy had already begun to accelerate during the 1980s, and after the 1989 crisis was overcome, growth accelerated further to the "miraculous" levels of the past 20 years. By 1993, the economies of China and Russia were the same size, but they were heading in different directions. Each represented 1.8 percent of the world GDP (measured at exchange rates). Russia, however, was still losing its economic clout, while China was growing at a faster, more sustained pace than ever before. Passing each other in the GDP rankings is a mere curiosity, except that it accurately reflected trends that spanned a 50-year period. In 1960, the Soviet Union was the second-largest economy in the world and, even more emphatically, the second-largest political and military power, while China was essentially irrelevant. In 2010, by contrast, China surpassed Japan to become the second-largest economy in the world and is on its way to becoming the second-largest political and military force as well. Russia, while certainly not irrelevant, languishes far down the ranks of economically and politically important countries and still accounts for less than three percent of the global economy. The year 1989, then, was a pivotal moment in the long-term process through which China and Russia switched places.

Politically, the events of 1989 signify the opposite effect in China of what they marked in the former Soviet republics and Eastern Europe. In 1989 the Chinese reaffirmed the repressive dictatorship that lay at the core of their system, while the Eastern Europeans in 1989 broke definitively with that dictatorship. In Eastern Europe, the initiatives of 1989 led to sustainable democracies and robust civil liberties in most countries of the region. Nineteen eighty-nine was the definitive moment in Eastern Europe and the Soviet Union, the start of the absolute and irreversible collapse of communism. As a result, 1989 is by far the most important date in the history of Eastern and Central Europe in more than a half century. In China, by contrast, 1989 is less important than 1978, when reforms began. Indeed, it is not immediately apparent whether or not 1989 was an important turning point in China. Official Chinese media portray 1989 as an unpleasant but short-term setback, better forgotten, or (as Fewsmith points out in chapter 2 of this volume) as a small price to pay for the subsequent 20 years of stability and growth. This portrayal is not on the surface implausible, but it is mistaken. While 1989 does not have the same epochal significance in China that it has in Eastern Europe and the former Soviet republics, it was nevertheless an important watershed that shaped China's future trajectory in nearly every dimension. Examining the context in which China's earliest reform period developed is the starting point for understanding the 1989 turning point.

Room for Maneuver

For a decade before 1989, China's leaders maneuvered in a policy space carved out by Deng Xiaoping. Defined by the distance between the Soviet Union and the United States, this space allowed Chinese elites to see themselves as more liberal, more pragmatic, and more realistic than Soviet elites, while still maintaining an obvious distance from the United States and its capitalist allies. China was favored by the United States, in that its approach to socialism was seen as being obviously superior to that of the Soviet Union and much less threatening. For the United States, China was both a strategic partner (against the Soviet Union) and the pioneer of a more open variant of socialism that might evolve into a liberal society over time. As a result, the United States was willing to accord favorable policies to China, and the US-China relationship was not viewed by American leaders as controversial. The United States, in turn, was not seen by China as a threat and was plausibly regarded as a protector against a lingering Soviet threat. This alignment of international and domestic policy "spaces" was quite favorable to the evolution of Chinese economy and society in a more liberal direction.

Deng Xiaoping was the most important architect of this policy space. It is a common error to give full credit for China's transformation to Deng Xiaoping solely, but the creation of room for maneuver was the result of his political vision and personal effort. Only Deng Xiaoping had sufficient political capital—due to his experience and multivalent patronage networks—to reorient both international and domestic policy. Deng Xiaoping was not an economic specialist, nor was he particularly self-confident about economic issues. However, he was extremely confident in his judgment about individuals and his mastery of strategic issues. During a two-year period from mid-1977 to mid-1979, Deng reoriented nearly every aspect of Chinese policy around the key area of economic policy. Thus, Deng personally pushed to rehabilitate the education and science and technology sectors, most critically reinstating the fundamentally meritocratic nationwide college entrance examinations in 1977. Deng then aligned China with the United States, permitting China to launch a short, but costly, punitive war against Vietnam without fear of retaliation from the Soviet Union. Although the actual military campaign against Vietnam was not a success, the strategic reassurance that Deng achieved emphatically was. Shortly thereafter, Deng proclaimed that peace was essential for China's development. He then went on to explicitly repudiate a key late Maoist dictum on the inevitability of war and officially declared that peace was the main global trend of the day (Deng 1980, 1985). This strategic reorientation paved the way for the demilitarization of the Chinese economy and the adoption of a strategy of economic reform. Deng thus created a framework for successful economic reforms without contributing much to the specific content of economic reform. Tellingly, the single economic reform most closely associated with Deng was the creation of the Special Economic Zones, which had an important secondary function of signaling to the international community that China's reforms were credible and reliable and which he championed but did not pioneer. In terms of actual economic policies, other leaders made more important direct contributions, but they were working in the space that Deng had opened up.

China's strategic reorientation at the end of the 1970s released resources for the reform process and helped to shape—and ensure the success of—the experimental and tentative reforms. Détente with the United States meant that issues of reform were not entangled with hot-button issues relating to patriotism, nationalism, or regime survival. Reformists envisaged a future China that was richer, more diverse, and more powerful. Reformers possessed both a critique of the economic stagnation caused by Maoism and a program to move toward greater strength and prosperity over the long term. Conservatives could not openly oppose the principle of economic reform, though they did try to obstruct the liberalization process by targeting individual writers and accusing liberals of responsibility for "spiritual pollution." However, before 1989, they were unable to get much traction against the broader reformist agenda.

Although conservatives and liberals struggled against each other throughout the 1980s, they shared a broad agreement about the contours of the political and ideological landscape in which the struggles occurred. The positions advocated by virtually all important intellectual and cultural figures could be located along a continuum that stretched from the orthodox Marxist/Maoist to the liberal democratic. Revealingly, the word *conservative* was universally used during this period to refer to orthodox Marxism or Maoism. Even conservatives acknowledged that China needed reform, to move away from orthodoxy and in the direction of liberalization, though they were emphatic that liberals and democrats wanted to go too far down that road. Yet as the 1980s proceeded, the vague proreform consensus appeared increasingly wobbly. In the crucial year 1989, the student protesters seized rhetorical control of the broadly shared goal of reform—why not go all the way?—and generated wide popular support in Beijing and other parts of China.

It was within this broad international and intellectual space that reformist leaders Hu Yaobang and Zhao Ziyang maneuvered, despite the resistance of an entrenched authoritarian regime. Politically, Hu and Zhao were in fact tightly constrained. They were never the top leaders but middle-aged "successors" who had been given control of the main institutions and policy levers by the Revolutionary Elders, a group of about 10 octogenarians who among themselves held ultimate power. In hindsight, the direct power that Hu and Zhao wielded was rather limited: the elders stood ever ready to reclaim direct control. But this dynamic was obscured for a time in the 1980s by the apparently wide latitude for exploratory policy and political maneuvering that Hu and Zhao had. Each came to office with a commitment to reverse the mistaken policies of the Cultural Revolution. They were, in a sense, hired to reform the system. Moreover, both Zhao and Hu, in their respective realms, crafted strategies of reform that took into account their constrained political conditions. Their approaches were cautious and incremental, of course. More fundamentally, they seized on the openings created by the elders to push reform strategies that released resources for the reform process while minimizing potential social conflicts associated with that process. Zhao, in particular, crafted a distinctive "1980s model" of reform, which is described later.

At the same time, Hu and Zhao each gradually appeared to commit to a more thorough and more profound vision of reform as time went on. For Hu, it was a version of political reform and, for Zhao, a steadily deepening commitment to a market economy. As they grappled with deep-seated problems, Hu and Zhao gradually expanded their conception of the legitimate scope of reform to include a full-market economy and some elements of democracy. As they struggled to resolve immediate problems and challenges, they also kept pushing for more profound solutions. However, the elders, including Deng Xiaoping, had by no means shared in this broad movement toward a more liberal vision, and the position of Hu and Zhao was in the end precarious. Tiananmen brought this contradiction out into the open. The elders became fed up, cleared Tiananmen Square with military force, abandoned their own protégés, and brought the liberalization process to a screeching halt. The changes reflected a contradiction between middle-aged reformers and more conservative elders, as well as a contradiction between the enormous possibilities of reform policy and the tightly constrained political options permitted to China's 1980s reformers. As it happened, precisely when the Chinese domestic process ran into a figurative brick wall at the Tiananmen demonstrations, the external environment was also changing fundamentally. The collapse of the Soviet Union was profoundly shocking to the Chinese leaders and amplified the shock of Tiananmen. When reform re-emerged in the 1990s, it was given an entirely new impetus by these domestic and international events.

Economic Transition before and after 1989

Before 1989, China was pursuing an incremental transition to a market economy under the tutelage of the Communist Party, and the same has been true since 1989. However, there is substantial difference between the two eras. Reform was put on hold for about three years (1989–1991) but then resumed in a much different pattern. (Deng Xiaoping's "southern tour" in early 1992—in which he symbolically reaffirmed economic reform by visiting the Special Economic Zones—is conventionally taken as the kickoff point of renewed reform.) The difference in reform strategy has long been noted by students of the Chinese economy, but they have tended to analyze it narrowly in terms of the choice of an effective reform strategy. From this standpoint, the crucial event is the adoption of a package of reforms in late 1993 and early 1994 (Naughton 2001, 2007; Qian and Wu 2003). These measures launched a period of intense policy reform that lasted through the end of 1999, when Premier Zhu Rongji reached an agreement with the United States on China's accession to the World Trade Organization (WTO). Between 1993 and 1999, reform measures had a coherence that marks an especially clear contrast with those of the 1980s. Each of the periods can be referred to as the "1980s model" and the "1990s model," respectively.

The 1980s model of reform has been characterized as decentralizing, dual track, and making extensive use of particularistic bargains and contracting. The 1990s model of reform, in contrast, focused on recentralizing, stressed market unification, and promoted reforms of ownership and improved regulation. The emphasis in the literature on these policy choices tends to deflect attention from Tiananmen and the events of 1989. But the key policy choices came only a few years after Tiananmen and almost immediately after the political climate shifted to allow a resumption of reforms. How was China able to adopt a coherent, but dramatically different, set of policies so quickly? How did political and other conditions shift in the immediate wake of Tiananmen? Linking the creation of the 1990s model of reform more closely to the impact of 1989 is one means of exploring the answers to these questions.

The Beginnings: Utilizing "Economic Space" to Reform the Economy in the 1980s

In the early stages of economic reform, difficult choices must be taken in order to make some people better off. In the long run, reformers can hope that increased efficiency and economic growth can compensate supporters of reform and solidify reform coalitions, but these gains take time to materialize. At the beginning of economic reform at the end of 1978, crucial economic choices were made that shaped the 1980s. A central role in adopting these choices was played by party elder Chen Yun. Chen was a conservative, but he was also an economics specialist who strongly supported the idea that the economy needed "space." At the core of the initial turn toward reform, in December 1978, was the conviction that the rural economy needed "room to breathe." Development plans needed to be less ambitious and less urgent, so that consumption could recover and families could be reassured that they could keep the fruits of their labors. Agricultural procurement prices were raised, compulsory procurement quotas were reduced, and grain imports dramatically increased. Production was shifted into labor-intensive sectors that increased the supply of consumption goods (Solinger 1991).

Where did the resources come from to increase consumption and support a more "relaxed" growth strategy? Chen Yun took the lead in limiting the overly ambitious 10-Year Plan and Leap Outward promoted by Hua Guofeng. Under Chen Yun's watch, contracts to purchase foreign factories were cancelled, and domestic investment was reduced sharply; space was opened up for greater consumption and for the growth of new organizational forms. This policy called for a three-year readjustment, beginning in January 1979 (intentionally echoing the policy and slogan from 1961–1962, when Chen Yun had presided over the recovery of the economy after the Great Leap Forward disaster). Chen Yun's commitment to this approach to the macroeconomy was so strong that when macroeconomic imbalances re-emerged at the end of 1980, he insisted that China recommence the three-year readjustment period, declaring:

> Some might say, "This will delay us three years." No worry. China's economic construction has already been delayed more than a hundred years, since the Opium War. And besides, it's not really a delay: if we

don't readjust, [economic construction] will end up taking much longer. (Chen Yun 1995: 282 [December 16, 1980])

This became national policy and was sustained throughout the 1980s. Deng Xiaoping did not agree with Chen Yun's position, but he accepted it. Deng had previously supported the grandiose 10-Year Plan, and he continued to support a more rapid investment and growth push. Deng and his protégé and ally Hu Yaobang (nominally the party secretary) pushed to have the target of quadrupling GDP by the year 2000 written into the Report of the 12th Party Congress in 1982. By doing so, he was asserting that the ultimate objective was still to develop into a strong and modern country. But this was a kind of pendant to the moderate macroeconomic policies that were actually being followed in the short term. Deng created space internationally and politically, while Chen created space economically.

Day-to-day management of the economy passed from Chen Yun to Zhao Ziyang, the premier, between 1979 and 1982. Zhao was a next-generation protégé of Deng Xiaoping. Zhao pushed much harder and searched more systematically for institutional innovations than Chen Yun would ever have done. Yet Zhao at first also supported Chen Yun's desire to maintain a relatively relaxed macroeconomic environment. He maneuvered within tight constraints to combine Chen Yun's moderate macroeconomic policy with Deng Xiaoping's open-minded approach to institutional reform.[1] The successful 1980s reform package emerged from Zhao's maneuvering. Chen Yun and other more conservative elders signed off on Zhao's quest, because they were reassured that his vision of economic reform was consistent with relative macroeconomic stability and a cautious approach to the economy. Zhao Ziyang solicited views on reform strategies from outside the government bureaucracy and effectively sidelined the bureaucratic Planning Commission, further reducing the influence of a voice that systematically advocated more investment and faster growth.

This "go slow" policy orientation can be discerned in simple quantitative indicators. Figure 6.1 shows resource outlays for four categories of expenditure that are normally large in a technonationalist, government-dominated, growth-oriented polity. Budgetary defense and scientific research and development (R&D) expenditure were each dramatically reduced during the 1980s from their planned economy highs. Investment in infrastructure was modest—figure 6.1 shows that investment in electricity generation and transport and telecommunications were each at modest levels, around 2 percent of GDP through the 1980s. The figure also shows that these investment levels were low compared to what was later achieved in China. They are also low relative to international best practice: the World Bank has suggested a "rule of thumb"

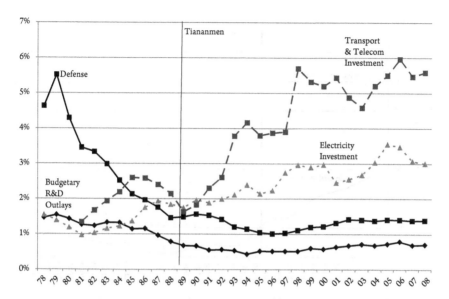

Figure 6.1 Major Public Goods Outlays (Percentage of Gross Domestic Product).
Source: Compiled by author from data in National Bureau of Statistics A and National Bureau of
Statistics B, various years.

that physical infrastructure investment should be at least 6 to 8 percent of
the GDP in order to support sustained rapid economic growth. China in the
1980s was well below this recommended level. This relatively modest investment effort allowed China to maintain a relatively relaxed macroeconomic
environment. The willingness to postpone public goods investment was also
evident at the local level during rural reform, when expenditures for rural education, health care, and irrigation, which had been funded by the collectives,
were allowed to fall. More generally, as figure 6.2 shows, the relative weight of
the government budget as a whole declined dramatically through the 1980s
(although in this case the decline continues into the middle of the 1990s, due
to the time lags involved in creating effective fiscal mechanisms). By releasing its claim on resources, the government opened up space for reform. This
differed from Mikhail Gorbachev's early reform push in the Soviet Union, in
which the urge to accelerate economic growth was predominant.

The Pace of Reform: Bauer-Kornai Cycles

Given the basic caution that conservatives such as Chen Yun imposed on
the reform process, the pace of reform was essentially determined by the
degree of macroeconomic imbalance in any given year. There were dangerous

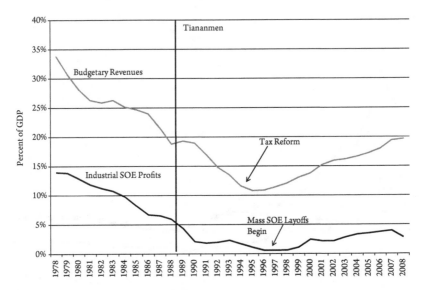

Figure 6.2 Fiscal Revenues and Industrial State-Owned Enterprise Profits. *Source:* Compiled by author from data in National Bureau of Statistics A, tables 7.3 and 13.8.

inflationary episodes in 1980, 1985, and 1988, as shown in figure 6.3 (quarterly data start in 1983, so the 1980 cycle is not shown). Cumulative inflation throughout the entire 1980s was modest, compared with the extreme inflation in the Soviet Union and much of Eastern Europe. Relaxation of price controls in the presence of highly distorted prices inevitably produces inflation, and China's cautious macroeconomic policies can, in this context, be seen to have kept inflation largely under control over the long term.

In the short term, however, inflation was a recurrent and critical problem. A policy-related cycle in the inflation data is evident. Policy decentralizations typically led to surges in investment demand from localities and enterprises, upsetting the macroeconomic stability and leading to inflation. These clearly fit the pattern of so-called Bauer-Kornai cycles, first observed in the context of 1960s Hungarian reforms by Janos Kornai and his colleague Tamas Bauer. Bauer and Kornai found that as reform-induced decentralization spread, macroeconomic imbalances increased, much to the surprise of reformers who had expected a movement away from Stalinist imbalances. The desire to control these imbalances led planners to cut back on reforms, creating cycles that combined macroeconomic and policy elements. The same economic forces were at work in China in the 1980s, but the outcome was different for political reasons. While short-run retrenchments were unavoidable, Zhao Ziyang was eager to resume the reform process as soon as imbalances were under control. The influence of "reformers" like Deng Xiaoping and Hu Yaobang and "conservatives" like Chen Yun waxed and waned along with this macroeconomic cycle (Zhou

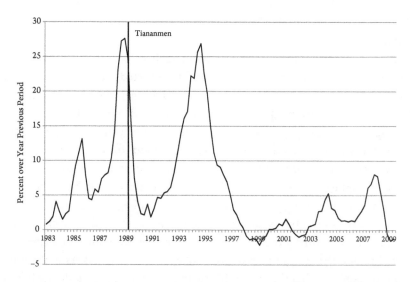

Figure 6.3 Consumer Inflation (1983, Quarter 1, to 2009, Quarter 3). Source: China Monthly Statistics; People's Bank of China website (www.pbc.gov.cn).

1993). With Zhao's hand on most of the policy levers, the reform process kept moving forward. The inflationary cycle of 1988 and 1989 could probably have been mastered as well, but the muddle of Tiananmen, interacting with deadly political infighting, spelled the end of the reformist ascendancy.

Reform without Losers

Given the political realities of fragmented power at the top, combined with a willingness to accommodate the resource needs of economic reform, the policies of the 1980s model were molded into a quite distinctive pattern. Surprisingly, this package of reforms was economically successful and was sustained politically for almost a decade.[2] The resulting pattern of policy has been dubbed "reform without losers" (Lau, Qian and Roland 2001). Reforms in China produced "winners" at various stages: initially farmers, especially those in the economic orbit of large cities; founders of new businesses; and entrepreneurial local officials. The surprising feature of the 1980s was the absence of losers. Few state-owned enterprises (SOE) went bankrupt, even though their profitability eroded steadily. Few workers in state-owned firms lost their jobs. The single most characteristic institution of this period was the dual track, whereby firms continued to fulfill their assigned production plans and buy and sell at planned prices, while also selling above-plan output at market prices. Such a system was a convenient way to grandfather in virtually every SOE with a contract ("plan") customized to its unique conditions and past trajectory.

Most domestic markets were protected against foreign competition, and new foreign-invested enterprises generally exported their output. Budget constraints remained soft, and some productivity gains were deferred, with the result that government revenues steadily eroded. Yet despite these short-comings, the economy grew and became much more flexible; a light-industrial sector developed that could provide consumer goods for China's vast population and eventually for export; a healthy ecology of large, medium, and small firms also appeared. Most important, markets emerged and began to play a crucial role in allocating goods. A market economy began to grow up through the interstices of the bureaucratic economy. China was able to avoid regime collapse because during the 1980s—despite initial economic conditions that were dire enough to lead to potential collapse—policy makers had enough room to maneuver that they were able to find a viable way to gradually rebuild capabilities and shore up their regime.

The Breakdown

The 1980s model of political and economic reform collapsed in 1989. The break-down is easily understandable in terms of the economic and political framework advanced in the previous sections. Politically, one of the reasons reform had been "without losers" was that reformers did not have sufficient political command to impose costs on social groups that could potentially protest and find patrons among the Revolutionary Elders. If reformers caused mass layoffs or the erosion of living standards through sustained inflation, they would lose the backing of the elders without which they could not function. Thus, "reform without losers" was, to a certain extent, the economic policy manifestation of the tightly constrained political power of the reformist camp. Reformers had to proceed with extreme caution.

Though reformers were tightly constrained, they were not paralyzed. After each cyclical pause, reformers began to push forward again. Since there was no compelling national defense or central planner interest that required reforms to be rolled back, reformers were able to maintain the initiative. In this sense, the policy space available to them was adequate. It permitted experimenta-tion and a continuous incremental approach. However, this situation also locked reformers into recurrent Bauer-Kornai cycles: When economic imbal-ances arose in the wake of reforms, the only option was to retreat temporarily. Reformers did not possess the decisive political authority necessary to break out of the cycles by imposing adjustment costs on laggard sectors. They could advance in a pattern of two steps forward, one step back, but only if they successfully managed the complex economic challenges that they faced.

The political crisis at Tiananmen in 1989 was triggered by the inability of Zhao Ziyang to master the inflationary cycle of 1988 and 1989. As inflation peaked in the last quarter of 1988 and contractionary policies designed to reduce inflation caused dislocation and the erosion of real incomes, dissatisfaction spread in urban areas. (For a brief period, the confluence of policies *did* create losers among urban workers.) This dissatisfaction was tapped by the students who rushed into Tiananmen Square to demand proper honors for the recently deceased reformer Hu Yaobang. A commitment to continued liberalization, it seemed, would be sufficient to compensate urban dwellers for the hard economic times they were undergoing. Zhao Ziyang was willing to accommodate the demonstrators' demands, but the Revolutionary Elders were not. The anxiety the elders felt about their political fates made Zhao vulnerable to vicious political attacks. In the wake of Zhao's fall and with the accelerating collapse of the Soviet empire looming in the background, conservatives rolled out a full bill of complaint against Zhao and the reformers. Zhao personally had threatened the stability of the communist regime in pursuit of his own faction, they argued. He had not shown adequate respect for the elders. The result was what Fewsmith, in chapter 2 of this volume, calls a "political meltdown on the part of China's party elite." On the economic front, Zhao found he had lost the support of conservatives such as Chen Yun, because he had failed to master the inflationary cycle of 1988 and 1989. With the reformist camp in disarray, economic conservatives seized full control of economic policy making. They argued that the apparent economic gains from reform were illusory and that the failure to invest in core industries and public infrastructure meant that the economy was on extremely shaky ground. They were wrong, but for the first time, their argument was plausible. Besides, the world was changing, and regime survival was at stake. In response, conservatives tried for three years to roll back economic reforms and get the economy back to basics (CCP 1989; Fewsmith 1997).

The Reform Model after 1989

Economic reform resumed in 1993, ironically in the midst of a burst of decentralization and inflation that constituted the last of China's pure Bauer-Kornai cycles. The policy content of reforms quickly diverged, though, from that of the 1980s model, and the focus of institutional reforms shifted to the effort to usher in tax and corporate reform and to create a regulatory apparatus as well as a level playing field for markets.[3] In addition to the specific institutional content of the reforms, there are two more general characteristics of the 1990s model that should be linked to the change in political economic context after Tiananmen. First was a willingness to expose economic actors to increased competition, which quickly began to impose costs on individuals and social classes, ending the period of reform "without losers." Second was a determination to protect government resources and give priority to state interests.

Removing the Barriers to Marketization: Reform with Losers

After 1993, the Chinese government cautiously but steadily removed the barriers to marketization and let uncompetitive firms and workers fail. This shift in practice is readily apparent in three of the most important economic arenas.

First, publicly owned enterprises were exposed to much more open competition and harder budget constraints on the financing side. Many thousands of state-owned firms closed down permanently. A wave of privatization began in the countryside with the "township and village enterprises" and culminated in the early part of the 2000s with the privatization of many of the smaller SOEs. Over a little more than a decade, traditional SOEs shed 45 million workers, and the overall state enterprise workforce shrank by 33 million workers (once we account for 12 million workers in new government-controlled corporations). Figure 6.4 shows that the workforce of SOEs, including all corporations

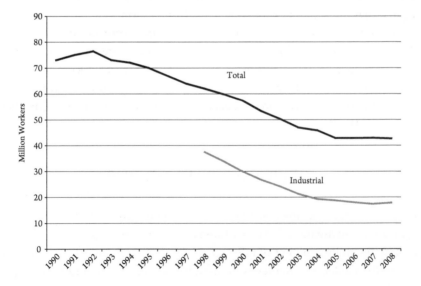

Figure 6.4 Workers in State Enterprises and State-Controlled Companies.
Source: National Bureau of Statistics A, table 4-27 and 2008: 54.

in which the government has a controlling stake, declined from 76 million in 1993 to just under 43 million by year-end 2005, mainly because of retirement and lay-offs.

This massive downsizing of the state sector was associated with a very different kind of management of the Bauer-Kornai cycle that began in 1992 and 1993. Rather than retreat on reform and use administrative measures to rebalance the economy (the 1980s model), Premier Zhu Rongji relied primarily on tight monetary policy and tighter budget constraints to drive a painful but necessary restructuring of the public sector. Painful disinflation was achieved along with a strengthening in the relative position of the state-run banks, which began the long-term and arduous shift to a commercial banking system. Even though the banks ultimately had to write off trillions of RMB in loans to failed SOEs, the process did achieve the twin macroeconomic goals of price stability and a solvent state enterprise sector.

Second, opening to foreign investment and trade culminated in an agreement on WTO accession in 1999 and formal membership in the WTO starting in 2001. WTO membership formalized not only a much greater openness to imports but also a set of ground rules for foreign-invested enterprises to operate and sell freely in the Chinese domestic market.

Third, barriers to rural-to-urban migration were steadily lowered. By the second quarter of 2009, an estimated 150 million rural people were working outside their home counties. Formal and informal discrimination and segmented labor markets still provide some protection for urban workers, but overall labor market competition increased dramatically. Structural transformation of the economy and urbanization both accelerated. These reforms dramatically changed the forces determining income and social outcomes. Low skill and older urban workers were particularly hard hit. They faced new competition from rural migrants, and their job security suddenly evaporated. At the same time, rapid urban growth raised income for highly skilled, younger workers and those with special access to opportunities in the new economy. Overall income inequality increased dramatically, and some groups lost in absolute terms (see chapter 10 of this volume).

Government as the Priority Claimant

While barriers to competition came down, the government took steps to ensure that priority was given to state interests. As figure 6.2 showed, budgetary revenues displayed a remarkable trend reversal after reaching a low point of 10.8 percent of GDP in 1995. After the 1995 turnaround, budgetary revenues climbed as a percentage of GDP each year through 2008, when they reached

20.5 percent of GDP. The expanded tax base following the 1994 tax reform put government on a firm financial footing. The massive downsizing of the state enterprise sector benefited government because most of the loss-making firms were shut down or sold off. Many of the largest and most profitable firms were maintained under government control. The government dubbed this policy "maintaining the large while letting go of the small [zhuada fangxiao]." Generally speaking, though, it was the large firms in natural monopoly or strategic sectors that were retained, while in competitive sectors, the vast majority of firms were privatized or allowed to fail. In monopoly sectors, state ownership was retained, but monopolies were converted into oligopolies, with two or three large state firms competing, while better institutions of corporate governance were put in place. Finally, in 2003, an ownership agency was created to exercise the central government's ownership powers. The State Asset Supervision and Administration Commission (SASAC) assumed ownership of 196 of the largest nonfinancial firms. Following the SASAC's creation, similar agencies were created at the local government level. The SASAC followed an agenda of professionalization, specialization, and the creation of internationally competitive firms that could eventually become "national champions."

This powerful state sector has stabilized and become healthier in recent years. After hitting bottom in 1996–98, state sector profitability climbed strongly during the 2000s (Figure 6.2). More tellingly, after dramatic cuts around the turn of the century, the state sector labor force stabilized after 2005 (Figure 6.4). The Chinese state sector is now composed of about two equal components, one central and one local, reflecting a major structural change. Since the early 1970s, China's state sector had been predominantly local and composed of many medium-sized firms. Soviet-style gigantism was never the pattern of the Chinese state sector, but now most of the local state sector is gone. In its place is a new, Chinese-style capitalism based on private entrepreneurs who maintain tight links with local government officials. The central state sector, on the other hand, has endured. Table 6.1 shows that, between 2002 and 2007, employment in the central state sector increased significantly, even as employment in the local state sector continued to decline.

Explaining the Adoption of the 1990s Model

Why did the dramatic shift occur from the 1980s model of reform to the 1990s model? In the first place, the tightly constrained political power of reformers in the 1980s changed significantly. The post-Tiananmen leadership of Jiang Zemin as party secretary and Zhu Rongji as first vice premier and then premier developed a good working relationship in the area of economic policy.

Table 6.1 **Central State Asset Supervision and Administration Commission (SASAC) Share of State-Enterprise Workers**

	2002	*2007*
All State Enterprise Employees (in millions)	50.3	37.38
of which: Central SASAC	8.6	11.26
Central SASAC Proportion	17.1 %	30.1 %
State Industrial Enterprise Employees (in millions)	24.9	18.544
of which: Central SASAC	5.9	7.713
Central SASAC Proportion	23.7 %	41.6 %
N.B.: All Above-Scale Industrial Employees (in millions)	54.73	78.75
Central SASAC Proportion	10.8 %	9.8 %

Source: Lian Yuming; *SASAC Yearbook*, 2008, pp. 669, 675; NBS-A, 2003, 2008, table 13.1.

More importantly, as Fewsmith describes in chapter 2, the Revolutionary Elders began to die off. Between 1993 and 1997, all of the important elders passed away. As a result, Jiang and Zhu were able to end the fragmentation of power among a large number of powerful veto players. Power at the top passed from the Revolutionary Elders into a more "ordinary" centralized hierarchical communist system, with far more decisive policy making and concentrated power (Naughton 2008; cf. Tsebelis 2002). With power concentrated in the hands of Jiang and Zhu, they were able to push through painful reforms that imposed real costs on important social groups.

At the same time, Jiang and Zhu no longer had the ample policy space that reformers had enjoyed in the 1980s. They could be more decisive, but they no longer had as many choices. Domestically, the decline of budgetary revenues and the evaporation of state enterprise profits meant that continued muddling through was not an option and decisive action was necessary. Internationally, China had few friends after 1989. Changes in the international environment contributed strongly to the particular predicament that confronted the Chinese Communist Party. China was able to ride out the initial wave of revulsion over the Tiananmen massacres and avoid major trade embargoes or international ostracism, but from 1989 onward, the friction between China and the established powers never disappeared. The collapse of the Soviet Union was a profound shock to the Chinese leaders; not only was it unanticipated, it was virtually incomprehensible (Shambaugh 2008). When the coup d'état was attempted against Gorbachev, the Chinese leadership not only welcomed the news, they seemed to experience something like relief. Their basic sense of how elites should behave when their power was threatened seemed to finally have been confirmed; but when the coup disintegrated, this Chinese view collapsed again. Eventually the Chinese developed a complex, even convoluted, critique of the Soviet collapse that tried to knit together many of the criticisms they had made of the Soviet Union through the years. Still, the impression remains that at the core of the critique is their inability to comprehend the behavior of an elite—a Communist Party elite—that failed to take minimal essential steps to ensure its own survival. This sense was shared by other observers, including Richard Nixon (Simes 1999). Ultimately, the Soviet collapse meant that China had to manage a much more thorough reorientation of its domestic policy stance and develop a broader justification for its policy moves. As the shock of the Soviet collapse sank in, Chinese leaders found that all the landmarks that defined their policy space had disappeared. From being the unthreatening variant of communism, China has become the great anachronism, the sole surviving successful country that is still ruled by an authoritarian government, much less a Communist Party. Moreover, the global economy experienced an unexpected event in the 1980s: The United States began to grow slightly more rapidly than the world economy as a whole. Between the early 1980s and about 2000, the US share of the world economy stabilized and even increased slightly. This shift was a sharp contrast to the experience of the world economy in the 1960s and 1970s and ran counter to what economists normally predict (convergence, which implies the catching up of well-positioned follower economies). That shift also ushered in an economic climate far different from the expectations that had prevailed at the end of the 1980s. A common expectation in 1989 was encapsulated in the witticism "the Cold War is over, and Japan and Germany have won." Such a view was, of course, focused on economics and stressed the difference between economic outcomes (seen to favor Japan and Germany) versus ideological outcomes (where American triumphalism reigned). In any case, it did not happen. Japan drifted into its own decade of stagnation, while Germany took on burdens in the transition and reunification process that slowed its growth and diminished its international impact for a decade or more. The world's second, third, and fourth leading strategic powers either collapsed (the Soviet Union) or underwent dramatic slowdown (Japan and Germany). The individual processes seem to have been quite different and domestically driven in each case, but the combined outcome for the three polities was unambiguous: The dominance of the world's leading power, the United States, was bolstered.

The rejuvenation of US hegemony was not something Chinese leaders expected and not something they welcomed. From the Chinese perspective, the failure to move toward multipolarity in the 1990s meant that China could not rely on having international economic space in which to maneuver. On the contrary, Chinese policy makers have since felt constantly crowded by a United

States wary of China's rise. In the security realm, China perceives the United States as clinging to its predominant power. To the Chinese, the United States seems to be steadily focused on a version of its own national interest, an unwelcome antithesis to the policy makers in Gorbachev's and Boris Yeltsin's Russia. This puts greater pressure on China. Since 1989, discourse about security—including economic security—has often been center stage in China, and an acceptable model of economic reform and development has required resources in order to provide for security. These changes frame the shifts in economic strategy that mark the pre- and post-1989 eras.

At the same time, economic and political evolution in China is also being shaped by the manner in which the Communist Party is intertwined with a new business empire. The CCP, like the dominant party in all other communist states, exercises the nomenklatura authority (Fewsmith insightfully discusses this in chapter 2, as the principle that "the party controls the cadres.") Today, the Communist Party remains deeply engaged in the disposition of firms and the appointment of managers. When enterprises established boards of directors as part of the new Company Law, Communist Party committees, as part of their nomenklatura authority, appointed the board members that represented the public owner. This has actually given the Communist Party a more direct stake in state enterprise management than it had before. Of course, this change in the way Communist Party power was exercised changed the party as well. It became more professional, interested in efficiency, and an even more important interest group, furthering its own gains and advocating the public interest as perceived by Communist Party members (see Huang 2008 for a related interpretation).

This evolution of the Communist Party's role can be traced back to 1989. Before 1989, most political reform proposals emphasized redefining and reducing the direct Communist Party role in the economy. This approach was widely rethought after Tiananmen and the collapse of the Soviet Union. Perhaps the most radical suggestion was made in the wide-ranging and provocative 1991 document said to have been written by three young Communist Party insiders, the maverick conservative intellectual He Xin and the two "princelings" Chen Yuan (son of Chen Yun) and Deng Yingtao (son of Deng Liqun) who are also discussed by Fewsmith in chapter 2. Their so-called Princeling Manifesto argued that, just as it was axiomatic that "the Party controls the gun," so it should be accepted that "the Party controls the assets." By giving the Communist Party direct ownership of society's wealth, the question of who was responsible for public assets would be resolved, and the conflicting regulatory and protectionist impulses of varying levels of government would be counterbalanced by a vigorous advocate for asset maximization. Direct party management of the economy would be reinstated, but the party's perspective would become that of the owners of capital ("Theory Group" 1991). Taken literally, this suggestion went nowhere. The CCP never began to accumulate assets in its own name in the way that, for example, the Nationalist Party (Guomindang) did in Taiwan. But in a broader sense, the Princeling Manifesto suggestions pointed the way to the system's future evolution. Today, the Communist Party manages the largest, most concentrated groupings of capital in China, and it perceives many policy issues from the standpoint of the owners of capital.

Conclusion

The political crisis of June 1989 was the catalyst for a shift in the overall pattern of Chinese economic transition. In both political and economic terms, the crisis gave urgency and legitimacy among the ruling elite to a model of concentrated power wielded more effectively. As a result, the next stages of marketization were combined with a stronger role for the state and a regime more capable of mobilizing resources for economic development and national security. Before 1989, China's leaders were willing to subordinate other national interests—and often state interests—in their quest for a viable economic reform model and thus a better economy and society. After Tiananmen, while reformers still pursued a vision of a transformed economy, that vision was linked and often subordinated to strengthened, stabilized, and more effective government power. Inevitably, government power also meant party power, although the nature of the party may perhaps be unrecognizable to one familiar with a Soviet-style party under a socialist economy.

A remarkable fact is that economic policy was primarily successful during both of these contrasting periods. During the first period, Zhao Ziyang maneuvered through a treacherous political environment to loosen the bonds of the planned economy and bring market forces to life. Although he failed politically, he succeeded economically. During the second period, a succession of leaders has maneuvered to strengthen the state and shore up political control while also pushing the economy toward a higher level of economic functioning. In this, they have also been primarily successful. The high point of this model may have come in 2008 and 2009. In response to the global financial crisis, the Chinese government and the Communist Party rapidly implemented a stimulus package that produced the first "green shoots" in the struggling world economy (Naughton 2009). The Chinese Communist Party Central Committee, meeting in conjunction with the State Council, decreed the stimulus and used the hierarchical Communist Party apparatus to convey the urgency of action to the grassroots levels. Within weeks, local governments down to the county level began rolling out "shovel-ready" investment projects that were suddenly eligible for funding. The model of concentrated power, decisively wielded, had economic benefits that rippled through the world economy. Economic success and concentrated political power have allowed China to muscle into a crowded and competitive global economic environment. Whether it will be compatible with the continued evolution and diversification of Chinese society remains to be seen.

Notes

1. This was already the best interpretation of policy dynamics during the 1980s, but it has been strongly confirmed by the publication of Zhao Ziyang's memoirs (2009), especially pp. 91–113.
2. I have addressed in earlier work the detailed components of the 1980s reform policies and tried to explain the basis of their success. These issues are not discussed further in this chapter. Interested readers can consult McMillan and Naughton (1992) and Naughton (1995, 2001, 2007).
3. The specific content of the 1990s reform model is well described in the literature on the choice of reform strategy previously referenced (Naughton 2007; Qian and Wu 2003). Decentralization, particularistic contracting, and the "dual track" were all set aside, and the central plan was discarded at the end of 1993. Tax reforms, corporate reform, banking reform, and opening to foreign trade and investment were pushed through within a few years.

References

CCP. 1989. Chinese Communist Party Central Committee, "Zhonggong zhongyang guanyu jinyibu zhili zhengdun he Shenhua gaige de jueding (zhaiyao). [Abstract of Party Central Decision on Further Rectifying while Deepening Reform]." November 9, 1989. In *Zhongguo Jingji Nianjian 1990*, 16-116. Beijing: Zhongguo Jingji.

Chen Yun. 1995. *Chen Yun Wenxuan [Selected Works of Chen Yun], Vol. 3*. Beijing: Renmin.

Deng Xiaoping. 1980. "The Present Situation," January 16, 1980. *Selected Works of Deng Xiaoping*. Beijing: Xinhua.

———. 1988. *Fundamental Issues in Present-Day China*. Beijing: Foreign Languages Press, 1988.

Fewsmith, Joseph. 1997. "Reaction, Resurgence, and Succession: Chinese Politics Since Tiananmen." In *The Politics of China: Second Edition, The Eras of Mao and Deng*, Roderick MacFarquhar, ed., 472–532. Cambridge and New York: Cambridge University Press.

Huang, Yasheng. 2008. *Capitalism with Chinese Characteristics: Entrepreneurship and the State*. New York: Cambridge University Press.

Kotkin, Stephen. 2009. *Uncivil Society: 1989 and the Implosion of the Communist Establishment*. New York: Modern Library.

Lau, Lawrence J., Yingyi Qian, and Gérard Roland. 2001. "Reform without Losers: An Interpretation of China's Dual-Track Approach to Reforms." *Journal of Political Economy* 108(1):120–143.

Lian Yuming. 2004. "The Total Assets of the 196 Directly Centrally Controlled Enterprises Has Reached 6.9 Trillion." In *Zhongguo Shuzi Baogao 2004 [China Report in Numbers 2004]*, 525–527. Beijing: Zhongguo Shidai Jingji.

McMillan, John and Barry Naughton. 1992. "How to Reform a Planned Economy: Lessons from China." *Oxford Review of Economic Policy* 8:11–30.

Naughton, Barry. 1995. *Growing out of the Plan: Chinese Economic Reform, 1978–1993*. New York: Cambridge University Press.

———. 2001. "Changing Horses in Midstream? The Challenge of Explaining Changing Political Economy Regimes in China." In *China Rising: Implications of Economic and Military Growth in the PRC*, Jaushieh Joseph Wu, ed., 37–65. Taipei: Institute of International Relations, National Chengchi University.

———. 2007. *The Chinese Economy: Transitions and Growth*. Cambridge, Mass.: MIT Press.

———. 2008. "A Political Economy of China's Economic Transition." In *China's Great Economic Transformation*, Loren Brandt and Thomas Rawski, eds., 91–135. New York: Cambridge University Press.

———. 2009. "Understanding the Chinese Stimulus Package." *China Leadership Monitor* 28(Spring). Accessed at http://www.hoover.org/publications/china-leadership-monitor/article/5588

NBS-A. National Bureau of Statistics. *Statistical Yearbook of China*. Beijing: Zhongguo Tongji, Annual.

NBS-B. National Bureau of Statistics. *China Fixed Investment Statistical Yearbook*. Beijing: Zhongguo Tongji, Annual.

Qian, Yingyi and Jinglian Wu. 2003. "When Will China Complete Its Transition to the Market?" In *How Far across the River? Chinese Policy Reform at the Millennium*, Nicholas Hope, Dennis Yang, and Mu Yang Li, eds., 31–64. Palo Alto, Calif.: Stanford University Press.

SASAC Yearbook. Annual. *Zhongguo guoyou zichan jiandu guangli nianjian [China's State-owned Assets Supervision and Administration Yearbook]*. Beijing: Zhongguo Jingji.

Shambaugh, David. 2008. *China's Communist Party: Atrophy and Adaptation*. Washington, D.C.: Woodrow Wilson Center Press.

Simes, Dmitri. 1999. *After the Collapse: Russia Seeks Its Place as a Great Power*. New York: Simon and Schuster.

Solinger, Dorothy J. 1991. *From Lathes to Looms: China's Industrial Policy in Comparative Perspective, 1979–1982*. Stanford: Stanford University Press.

Suraska, Wisla. 1998. *How the Soviet Union Disappeared: An Essay on the Causes of Dissolution*. Durham, N.C.: Duke University Press.

"Theory Group" of *China Youth Daily*. 1991. Zhongguo Qingnianbao Sixiang Lilunbu [Theory Group of *China Youth Daily*]. "Sulian jubianzhihou Zhongguo de xianshi yingdui yu Zhanlue Xuanze [The Practical Challenges and Strategic Choices China Faces in the Wake of the Soviet Collapse]." Processed. September 9, 1991. An edited version of this tract has been translated by David Kelly and published as "Realistic Responses and Strategic Options for China after the Soviet Upheaval." *Chinese Law and Government* 29(March–April 1996):13–31.

Tsebelis, George. 2002. *Veto Players: How Political Institutions Work*. Princeton, N.J.: Princeton University Press.

Zhao Ziyang. 2009. *Prisoner of the State: The Secret Journal of Premier Zhao Ziyang*. New York: Simon and Schuster.

Zhou, Xiaochuan. 1993. "Privatization versus a Minimum Reform Package." *China Economic Review* 4(1):65–74.

PART IV

TRANSFORMING ECONOMIC BEHAVIOR

7

The Rise of Consumer Credit in Postcommunist Czech Republic, Hungary, and Poland

AKOS RONA-TAS

In Central and Eastern Europe, the fall of the Berlin Wall in 1989 and the subsequent transition to a market economy that substantially shrunk the state's role ushered in a period of severe economic hardship. In peacetime, these countries had not seen a recession this deep since the Great Depression. The effect was especially painful as real incomes were falling at the exact time when images and goods of Western consumerism flooded the region. It took almost a decade for these economies to reach the level at which they stood during the last years of communism. As real incomes began to rise, albeit at a slow pace, a new source of purchasing power, consumer credit, appeared and began to expand rapidly (see figure 7.1). The explosion of consumer credit introduced a new form of redistribution in the region and began to reconfigure social relations and social identities, while setting out at the same time to contribute to building a new system of social control.

From the end of the 1980s, consumer credit grew quickly throughout the developed capitalist world. In the member countries of the Organization for Economic Cooperation and Development (OECD), just in the last five years of the last millennium household debt as a ratio of household income rose from 78 percent to 96 percent (Christensen and Mathiasen 2002; Babeau and Sbano 2003). The process, often referred to as the democratization of finance, spawned new types of financial services and expanded credit to new, less affluent segments of the population (Boorstin 1973; Shiller 2003; Greenspan 2005; see also Erturk et al. 2007). An extreme and ultimately disastrous example of this evolution was the subprime mortgage market in the United States that

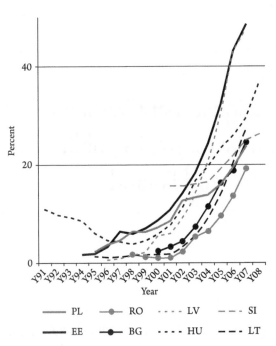

Figure 7.1 Household Debt as the Percentage of the Gross Domestic Product for Postcommunist European Union Member Countriesa. Source: Calculated from EUROSTAT. Note: Eurostat did not have data for the Czech Republic.

brought to a halt two decades of rapid credit expansion. Consumer credit in affluent countries became a crucial pillar of middle-class prosperity (Nocera 1994). As the welfare state retreated to attending to the poorest layers of society and withdrew many of its services from the middle classes (Ferge 1997; Clayton and Pontusson 1998; Starke 2006), societies had to find new forms of redistributing money and wealth so that their consumer economies could still prosper. Middle-class families that now had to pay for services previously provided by the state and whose incomes did not keep up with their rapidly growing expectations needed new ways of accessing homes, vacations, cars, and expensive electronics, as well as education and health care.

Just as with the welfare state, the new consumer credit market is a rationalized system that works by learning about and controlling its clients (Leyshon and Thrift 1999; Marron 2007; Langley 2007, 2008). In both cases, money from some part of the population is reallocated to others, albeit money for consumer credit is not collected by direct or indirect taxes but by deposits, and it is given out not as entitlement but as loans to be paid back with interest. Mass consumer credit, just as welfare, is administered through a bureaucracy that relies on information it gathers about clients it continuously monitors, yet mass consumer credit is distributed not by policy makers but by markets or cartels of lenders, and money is not handed out in dreary welfare offices but in well-maintained, often palatial branches of financial institutions. Both systems supplement their formalized data collection with case workers deployed for certain segments of their clienteles. Both redistribute resources with strings attached (Piven and Cloward 1993). Credit, just as welfare, is a complex bundle of rights and responsibilities, although welfare imposes different obligations than credit does. Both lenders and the welfare state are keen to control the behavior of their clients, although the welfare state has less need but more power to do so. One important difference, however, is that redistribution by credit is only temporary and, unlike welfare, credit decreases demand after a short boost as some of the debtors' purchasing power gets diverted to interest payments.

In the postcommunist world, mass retail credit markets found their footing only in the last years of the last millennium, but once they did, they flourished with gusto. Up until 2008, in Eastern and Central Europe, they grew rapidly, with advertisements for mortgages, car loans, credit cards, and purchase credit beaming from billboards in all the major cities in the postcommunist world, from Sofia to Warsaw, from Moscow to Bratislava. The contrast with the recent past is impressive. Less than a decade ago, banks in postcommunist countries were still complaining that their country's culture was hostile to borrowing and that people were averse to buying on credit. But just a few years later, the same bankers began to worry about overindebtedness (Duenwald et al. 2005; Coricelli et al. 2006; Égert et al. 2006) as people's reluctance to borrow quickly melted.

We will first situate our work in the larger market transition literature. There our main claim is that the transition research has aimed at developing a theory of the transition to a market of producers. As such, this literature has focused exclusively on the supply side of the market and assumed that consumption and its inequalities would be driven solely by incomes earned in production. Because the structure of incentives that optimizes production does not necessarily result in optimal demand, what economic growth really requires is the redistribution of purchasing power; both the welfare state and mass consumer credit markets can fulfill this function although with very different results.

We follow this by identifying the main peculiarities of credit markets. To exist, these markets must solve the problem of information asymmetry and make consumer credit profitable. Then we turn to the history of consumer credit in postcommunist Poland, Hungary, and the Czech Republic. In each country, the initial concentration of retail banking made both tasks difficult to solve. We describe the current state of consumer credit in these countries and explore how lenders solve the problem of information asymmetry in four tiers of the market and how in the process they build a new form of social order.

Market Transition Literature: Supply- versus Demand-Side Approach

For 20 years, the academic debate that focused on the postcommunist transition to a market economy was preoccupied with explaining the way postcommunist economies move from one form of production characterized by state control to another coordinated by the market (Nee 1989; Rona-Tas 1994; Murrell 1995; Szelenyi and Kostello 1996; Cao and Nee 2000). There were ferocious disagreements over the mode and pace of the transition and the proper sequencing of policies; advocates of shock therapy fought pitched battles with adherents to gradualism (Sachs and Lipton 1990; Poznanski 1995). There was conflict over the appropriate role for the state and about how it should privatize enterprises, regulate their activities and tax or subsidize various industries. But there was a remarkable consensus that entrepreneurship—the launching of new and the rebuilding of existing business organizations—was the central problem to be solved (Stark 1996; Kolodko 2000; Djankovic and Murrell 2002). Theorists of the transition operated with a clear supply-side bias. They paid close attention to the creation of new goods and services and trusted that what would be produced would be consumed by people who could afford to buy the output. Creating a market, therefore, meant building its supply side, and the transition to a market economy was thought of as simply aligning supply with existing demand.

In chapter 8, Yasheng Huang addresses the constraints entrepreneurs face in securing financial resources, especially in the Chinese countryside. Following the literature's central concern with production, Huang documents various signs of weakness in the financial institutions that ought to be providing credit for the production of goods and services. He discusses state policies in the context of their influence on the distribution of financial resources among enterprises. Huang's chapter on enterprise (as opposed to consumer) credit engages an important part of the supply side literature on the transition. Wang and Su's chapter evaluating the role of the Chinese state examines its role in redistributing income among households rather than enterprises to buffer increasing inequalities in line with much of the transition literature (Przeworski 1991; Greskovits 1998). However, from their perspective the growing gap between rich and poor is a political and not an economic problem.

There were three good reasons why researchers did not think of demand as an important theoretical challenge that needed the same thought and consideration as production. The first cause was that state socialism left behind a large pent-up demand for consumer goods and as a result the question how former communist citizens decide to become entrepreneurs seemed much more pressing than the problem of how former communist citizens turn into consumers. As Kornai pointed out long ago (1980), socialist economies were supply constrained, while demand seemed infinite. The new economy, according to this reasoning, just had to fill the enormous vacuum inherited from the shortage economies of state socialism, further exacerbated by rapidly rising expectations.

The second reason for overlooking the need to create consumers was that most of these economies, especially those in Central Europe and China, quickly embarked on an export-led growth strategy (Rodrik 1992; Brenton and Gros 1997; Mitra et al. 2010). Producing for consumers in other countries made the need for organizing a viable consumer market at home appear less urgent. Finally, many of the goods and services that were to be produced would be consumed by other producers downstream in the production chain. As these consumers are producers as well, it seemed that they could be subsumed under the supply-side approach of the market transition literature.

The political extension of the supply side approach was that the new social order would be dominated by the new entrepreneurs (Nee 1991) or managers (Eyal et al. 1998), and the ability to produce commodities, control capital, and derive profit from production would organize society and drive social inequalities (Borocz and Rona-Tas 1995; Gerber 2000; King and Szelenyi 2005).

While this scholarly emphasis on production has been justified, researchers' complete neglect of the need to manufacture demand is ironic, because for entrepreneurs who stand at the center of transition research, the main problem to solve has been precisely the creation of markets for their products. Striving to capture a customer base, building market share and finding effective demand for their products are what entrepreneurs mostly do.

Concentrating on how goods and services would be produced does not address directly how those goods and services will be distributed among their consumers. In the transition debate, it was generally assumed that consumption is driven by the money that people earn in their productive pursuits and that money will eventually match up with the commodities produced. Yet, while the incomes derived from production may reflect the productivity of workers, those incomes may not offer a pattern of demand optimal for absorbing what was produced. A highly unequal income distribution may reward those who produce more and encourage even more production, but it shuts out the losers from retail markets as they are unable to afford the products and services offered on the market. This was the big lesson of the Great Depression and led to the creation of the welfare state that redistributes income from the rich to the rest of society, enabling a larger segment of the population to participate in retail markets (Krugman 2009). In short, demand had to be managed independently because the optimal incentive structure of product markets did not deliver the expansive mass markets of consumers in which economies of scale and specialization can flourish and in which there is space for a wide variety of products and services.

In the early years of the transition, Central European economies sought to circumvent internal markets by aggressively targeting foreign ones. Those businesses that could not compete in international markets folded in large numbers. During the first years of the transition, Hungary, the Czech Republic, and Poland lost 15, 12, and 7 percent of their GDP, respectively, and hopes of catching up with "Old Europe" faded (a topic Borocz explores in his chapter in a different context). Poland returned to its 1990 level by 1994, a feat that took the Hungarians eight years and the Czechs ten.[1]

Unemployment, virtually unknown under communism, shot up after 1990, and in Poland has been in the double digits for most years ever since. The job loss in the region was even bigger than unemployment figures suggest, because many people disappeared from the labor force into early retirement (Vanhuysse 2006) or just fell out of the official economy, even as others postponed entering the labor market by extending their time as students (Nesporova 2002). During the first decade of the transition, wages for those lucky enough to keep their jobs did not increase much either as inflation remained high across Central Europe, except for in the Czech Republic.

Moreover, income inequalities grew after 1989 (Heyns 2005), driven by two forces. First, wages and salaries became more unequal as socialist wage regulations were abandoned, markets started to differentiate sharply among workers, and as substantial rent income also became available to a select few. Second, the role of the state in most areas was curtailed, such that its ability to redistribute income through taxation and various public services and insurance schemes declined. With growing income inequalities in Central and Eastern Europe, effective demand for consumer goods began to accumulate in a small segment of the population, while particular demographic and regional and groups were left out.

Thus, one critical case was that entire regions were bypassed by economic growth (Heidenreich 2003). In all three countries, the eastern territories experienced less development than the western parts and the capital cities. Certain age groups fell behind, too: People who were in their late forties in the 1990s and lost their jobs, for instance, were unlikely to find commensurate employment in the new economy. Such people found themselves in dire straits unless they could take early retirement. One more instance is that some ethnic groups, most importantly the Roma, were especially hurt by the transition. With increasing poverty, the retreating welfare state had to refocus its efforts on the destitute, gradually abandoning the working and middle classes (Gracés et al. 2003) that now had to fend for themselves in their struggle to afford the goods and services produced by resourceful postcommunist entrepreneurs and foreign companies eager to exploit the new markets in the region.

The problem of the structure of demand in the domestic consumer market became apparent as soon as export expansion reached its limits when sales abroad slowed down. Once entrepreneurs turned to domestic markets, they realized that the low wages that gave these businesspeople a competitive advantage in world markets created a domestic market in which demand was too narrow.

With the collapse of communism, it seemed the age of the behemoth state withered. Markets were advancing as the new solution to every conceivable distributional problem in society from education to health care, from environmental degradation to poverty. The retail credit market looked like just exactly the kind of institution that the new era needed to take over state functions in the realm of economic redistribution. Mass consumer credit promised a market solution to the problem of narrow consumer demand. The idea here was to repair the malfunction of production markets by yet another market. The consumer credit market, however, was hampered by declining real incomes, high inflation, increasing economic insecurity and rising inequality, the very forces that by sapping consumer demand created the need for credit Moreover, market building encountered other problems specific to consumer credit.

Credit Markets

In order for credit markets to exist, there must be found a means of ensuring that loans are paid back with proper interest, thereby solving the problem of information asymmetry. The problem is that lenders rarely know enough about prospective borrowers' credit-worthiness—their ability and willingness to repay the loan. Borrowers know more about their own resources and motivation, but they are interested in withholding any negative information that makes them appear to pose a risk to the lender and that, consequently, would raise the price of the loan or result in a rejection. The asymmetry caused when the lender knows less than the borrower leads to adverse selection and moral hazard, and, as a result, the price mechanism will not properly regulate credit markets (Jaffe and Russell 1976; Stiglitz and Weiss 1981). Moreover, retail lending is expensive, as it involves small amounts of money and entails relatively large administrative costs. Even mortgage lending is less lucrative than making loans to companies or the government. Retail banks would rather collect deposits from their customers, process their payments for a fee, and lend the savings out as large corporate loans. Consumer loans will not become a priority for banks until competition forces them into that market.

History

Consumer credit has had a peculiar history in postcommunist countries as financial institutions that initially were state agencies developed into market actors that could compete and collaborate to solve the problem of information asymmetry. After 1989, consumer credit started with practically a tabula rasa. Under communism, consumer credit was virtually nonexistent. Unlike state enterprises that could borrow heavily from the state, households lived under hard budget constraints (Kornai 1980). In a system in which wage inequalities were curbed by centralized wage policies, in which various social programs leveled consumption further and in which consumer goods were in short supply anyway, consumer credit remained rudimentary. This was reflected in the simplicity of socialist financial services that were run as a state monopoly. Each country had its own large monobank with specialized branches attending to particular tasks in the financial system. One branch handled foreign trade, another large investment projects, and yet another would attend to residential services. The branches were coordinated by the central bank that was also in charge of the domestic currency and the accounts of state firms. The financial system was strongly controlled by the state, and was subordinated to the needs of central planning.

Banking for individual citizens was managed predominantly by the state savings bank (Kornai 1992). Interest rates on the limited consumer credit that was available from the bank and also from certain large retailers were set centrally, and payments were often deducted from one's pay if the installments were not delivered in time. Because the lenders and the companies where most borrowers worked were state owned, collecting payments involved transferring money by the state from one of its pockets to another.

The creation of a new financial system began in central Europe in the last years of communism. The monobank was broken up, and a two-level system was built with the central bank being the first tier and a large number of commercial banks forming the second. The new commercial banks were born with enormous millstones around their necks. They all had a large amount of bad debt from socialist firms that had been doing poorly even before the collapse but that took an even bigger dive during the transition.

Credit in the First Postcommunist Decade

The Creation of Commercial Banking

In Czechoslovakia, Hungary, and Poland, just as in all former Soviet bloc countries, the postcommunist retail market for financial services began with the dominance of a single giant savings bank, originally the retail arm of the socialist monobank. In socialist Hungary, this bank was Országos Takarékpénztár (National Savings Bank) or OTP. The socialist OTP was not a business but a government agency charged with management functions and entrusted with the educational responsibility of instilling in citizens proper financial habits, including thrift. Similarly, in the Czech lands of communist Czechoslovakia it was Česká spořitelna (Czech Savings Bank) or CS and in the Slovak lands its sister bank, Slovenská sporiteľňa (Slovak Savings Bank) that dominated the retail market. In Poland, Powszechna Kasa Oszczędności (General Savings Bank) or PKO, was in charge of most of retail banking, although there was a second, albeit much smaller bank, Bank Pekao, that played a limited but important role as the foreign currency bank and that, by 1990, developed a network of offices that served a sizable clientele in all the major cities in the country.[2]

In 1989, the three giants, OTP, CS, and PKO, held the vast majority of the residential accounts of their respective countries, which offered them a large amount of information that newcomers did not have. Their customers also became their captives by sheer inertia. People were used to the state savings bank and trusted it because of its size and because of the general belief that the state stood behind it even when it was technically no longer a state institution. Size also meant convenience. Through their large network of branches, the giants could provide easier access than what small upstarts could offer. In all three countries, initial bank reforms tried to eliminate this monopoly, but reducing the immense advantage of the giants turned out to be more difficult than expected.[3]

Finding a foothold next to the national giant was not easy. Between 1995 and 1999, industry concentration measured as the total assets held by the top three banks was 72 percent in the Czech Republic, 57 percent in Poland, and 53 percent in Hungary, where OTP was by far the largest bank, with the second and third ones (K&H and MKB) following at a sizable distance. In the Czech Republic, the top three banks (CS, CSOB, and Komercni) were closer in size and thus held a larger share of the total. The concentration looks more pronounced if we consider retail banking only. Even after two decades of shrinking dominance, in Poland, PKO has a 35 percent share of the retail market, followed by PEKAO with 18 percent, and BZ WBK, with 9 percent, a distant third. In Hungary, OTP has 38 percent of household loans and 44 percent of all deposits, followed by K&H with 10 percent and 14 percent. CS had more than five million customers, very high in a country of ten million where people rarely hold accounts in multiple banks.

This concentration gave rise to a stalemate that exacerbated the adverse macroeconomic conditions. Sitting on top of a large and virtually captive clientele, the giants had little incentive to seriously engage in consumer lending. At the same time, the lack of an existing consumer base made the launching of a retail business difficult for newcomers because they had to lend to strangers off the street rather than to their existing customers. This made the problem of information asymmetry especially severe. Profitability in consumer lending also depends heavily on volume, putting upstarts at further disadvantage. The impasse was resolved slowly by privatization and the entry of foreign-owned banks with deep pockets willing to lose money to gain customers and market share by offering consumer credit.

Privatization of Banking

The privatization of the banking sector happened differently in the three countries, but in the end, each emerged with a banking system owned predominantly by foreign financial institutions. The arrival of foreign banks brought new capital and know-how to consumer credit and forced the postcommunist giants to innovate. For understandable reasons, the giants tried to hold on to their initial advantages as long as they could. They dragged their feet on most measures that required cooperation if that gave their competitors an advantage.

The creation of the institution most important to the solution of the information asymmetry problem, the credit registry, was delayed by the reluctance of OTP, CS, and PKO to share information about their large clientele with other, smaller banks. The duration of this lack of cooperation in the three countries was a direct function of the relative size and strength of the market leader. The Polish giant PKO was the first to abandon its strictly competitive position, partly because its market share was smaller and partly because state ownership put pressure on it to agree to cooperative measures that seemed necessary to the finance ministry that had to consider the health of the entire banking system. CS became largely autonomous from the state due to voucher privatization and was uncooperative until it was acquired by a foreign owner. OTP held out the longest. Like PKO, it managed to avoid being sold to another bank, but at the same time, its chief manager, who originally was appointed by the government as a caretaker, also succeeded in cutting loose from the state as an owner and expanded OTP aggressively, acquiring large banks in Bulgaria, Slovakia, Serbia, and Romania and smaller ones in the former Soviet Union.

Consumer Lending in the New Millennium

Consumer lending grew everywhere in the region beginning around the turn of the millennium (see figures 7.1 and 7.2). The three countries moved in unison, first rising slowly and then growing at an ever-faster pace. By 2008, Hungary

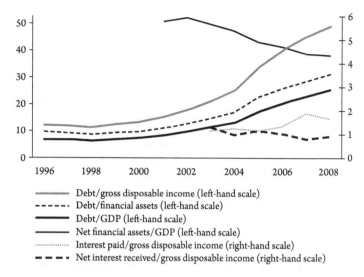

Figure 7.2 The Czech Republic: Ratio of Household Debt to Gross Disposable Income, Financial Assets and Gross Domestic Product: Ratio of Interest Paid and Net Income Received to Households' Gross Disposable Income. Source: Czech National Bank 2009, 29.

had the largest household debt-to-gross domestic product (GDP) ratio, while Poland and the Czech Republic followed close behind. In all three, the expansion in the previous few years was led by housing loans, but other consumer loans—purchase credit, personal and revolving loans—remained an important part of a household's growing debt portfolio (see figures 7.3, 7.4, and 7.5). In Poland and the Czech Republic, the mortgage market grew more slowly, as

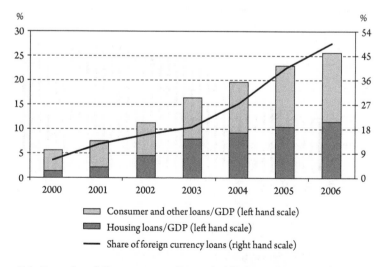

Figure 7.3 Growth and Composition of Household Loans in Hungary (as a percentage of gross domestic product). Sources: Hungarian National Bank 2007.

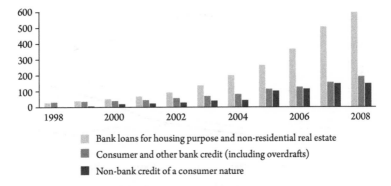

Figure 7.4 The Czech Republic: Bank and Nonbank Credit to Households. Source: Czech National Bank 2009, 29.

housing subsidies were primarily given either through savings support or tax credit (Diamond 2006; Lux 2009). In Hungary, a mortgage boom began in 2000 with a set of policies by the center right government that included interest rate subsidies for mortgages, often with negative real interest. These policies were substantially curtailed by the next, socialist government at the end of 2003, but the boom continued as borrowers discovered foreign exchange denominated loans that carried lower interest rates. Around that time, borrowing in foreign exchange, mostly in the euro, the Swiss franc and the US dollar, became widespread practice in Poland and the rest of the region, except in the Czech Republic and Slovakia (see figure 7.6).

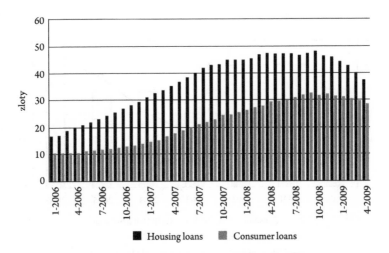

Figure 7.5 Annual Changes in the Value of the Loans to Households in Poland. Source: Polish National Bank 2009, 49. Note: Data after excluding the impact of exchange rate movements.

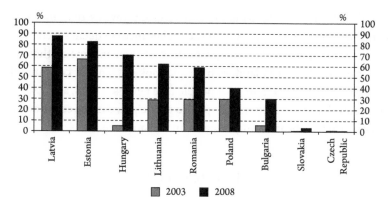

Figure 7.6 Share of Foreign Exchange Loans within the Banks' Household Loan Portfolio in International Comparison Source: Hungarian National Bank 2009.

While foreign-denominated loans were cheaper, they posed a risk few borrowers understood at the time: Domestic currency can lose its value relative to the currency in which the loan is denominated. This weakness became apparent in late 2008 when both Poland and Hungary experienced steep devaluations of their currencies. The Hungarian forint dropped 20 percent in a few days in October 2008 as the international financial crisis reached the region. That year, the Polish zloty also saw a decline in its value. Housing prices began a long-term slide in the entire region at the same time, and while loan delinquencies rose, an American-style collapse seemed unlikely as of 2011 because mortgage lenders had required high down payments and generally shunned home equity loans.

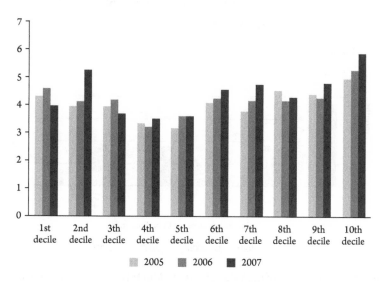

Figure 7.7 The Distribution of Consumer Debt by Income Deciles in the Czech Republic. Source: Czech National Bank 2009, 30.

The distribution of the loans by income group reveals that, in the Czech Republic and in Hungary, people in the higher income deciles were carrying about the same debt burden as a proportion of their income as those in the poorer groups, while in Poland, rich people took out smaller consumer loans relative to their incomes than poor people (see figures 7.7, 7.8, and 7.9).[4] These figures show that lower income groups also participated in the consumer credit expansion, thereby broadening demand on consumer markets.

Tiers of Credit

For lenders to redistribute money, they have to solve the information asymmetry problem. Even when they have collateral, as in mortgage lending, lenders

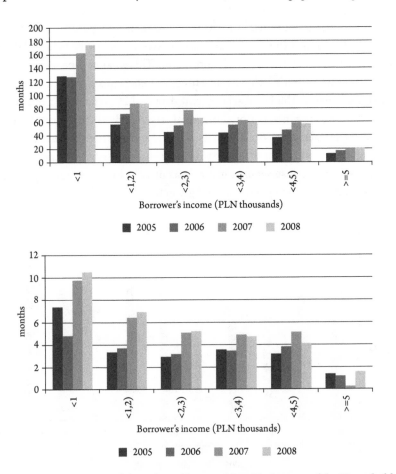

Figure 7.8 Average Ratio of the Value of Loan to Monthly Income of the Household Taking out the Loan in Poland: Housing Loan (top) and Consumer Loan (bottom).
Source: Polish National Bank 2009, 46.

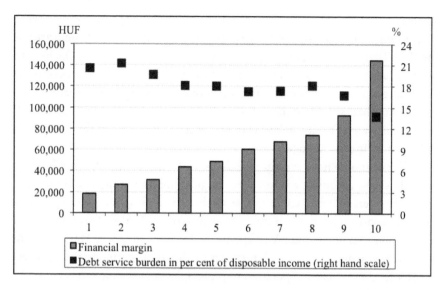

Figure 7.9 Debt Service Burden of Indebted Households in Income Deciles and Their Average Financial Margin in Hungary, 2007. Note: Financial margin means the income that remains after the basic costs of living (housing, public utilities, and food) and the installment payments are deducted from the disposable income and that is available to cover the potential increase of the installment payment. Source: Hungarian National Bank 2007.

face high costs when they have to repossess and liquidate property. With other types of credit, such as personal and revolving loans, ensuring proper repayment is even more important. The tools at the banks' disposal are much less powerful than the ones the state can deploy, even though, to a limited extent, banks can rely on the power of the state. Going to court, however, is slow and cumbersome and rarely cost-effective, given the small amounts involved.

The consumer credit market has four segments. The first two segments are operated by retail banks, and the second of these is by far the largest and the most dominant.[5] Credit in these tiers is dispensed to upper-, middle-, and working-class customers. Below this, one finds the "fringe," comprised of two layers: in the third tier, legally operating banks specialized in payday loans and the underworld of loan sharks lending to the poor on the margins of society, in the fourth tier. Each tier has developed its own method of dealing with information asymmetry.

Retail Banks

VIP customers

While retail banks operate a highly formalized and impersonal system of credit, each bank has a narrow circle of elite customers who are served through "private banking." These so-called very important people (VIPs)[6] do their banking with the help of special personnel assigned to their cases. These important clients usually hold large accounts with the bank, but some are put on the VIP list because of their political power or celebrity status. The list can also include top managers of important corporate clients. For members of the VIP list, terms are always negotiable, exceptions are possible, and decisions are tailored to their specific circumstances. They do not have to stand in line, fill out forms, or argue with tellers as the bank sends its clerks to their homes or offices at their convenience.

VIP customers have multiple dealings with the bank that often handles their business accounts, advises them on portfolio investment, and provides a range of personal financial services to them, including maintaining checking and saving accounts and issuing various loans. Banks, therefore, have a fairly good idea about their VIP clients' economic situations. Many of them are also in the public eye, which provides further information to the bank. As most VIP clients have a reputation to protect, banks have more leverage over them than they do over other customers. Their large accounts can also act as quasicollateral.

Mass Consumer Credit

The vast majority of the banks' clientele participates in a different world of bank credit. People in this category are processed through a highly impersonal, bureaucratic, and rationalized system that developed only in the first decade of the century. This is the tier that is by far the largest, and it is the one that is responsible for the expansion of consumer credit and that has the largest redistributive impact.

The regular bank client applies by completing various forms. In some banks, the lending officer fills out the form after interviewing the applicant. The information is standardized, and it is partially verified using direct checks (e.g., calling the person's work place to find out if she really works there), by means of cross-checks (e.g., looking for inconsistencies in the information supplied by the applicant), by obtaining authorized documents (e.g., paystubs) and by consulting external databases. The monitoring and control of these accounts are also highly automated, and clerks follow hard-and-fast rules whenever they interact with their clients. They rarely see the client face to face except on the other side of the teller window. Most communication with regular clients is by mail or by phone.

Identifying

When applying for a loan, each applicant must fill out a form that has two parts: identification and sorting. Identification, the first part, distinguishes the applicant as a unique individual who can be found and held accountable for the loan, while making the individual available for surveillance and sanctioning. All modern states have some form of identification for their subjects from passports and driver's licenses to social security cards and birth certificates (Rule et al. 1983; Torpey 1998). Before the rise of the modern state, people were identified by various measures of belonging, including lineage and residence. Modern state identification (IDs), on the other hand, makes an attempt to tie identity to biological characteristics of the person's body. The picture ID produces a likeness of facial features and records height, weight, and eye and hair color along with age (date of birth). None of these features is unique individually, but in combination, these pieces of information are likely to fit only one or a very few individuals. Fingerprints have also been added to the arsenal. Physical identification is useful only if the person is present but unidentified. Modern states have a large network of contact points, from airports and traffic checks to the department of motor vehicles and the welfare office, through which people are constantly passing. Those who show up can then be identified with the help of physical markers.

Credit files rarely contain pictures of borrowers, and application forms never ask for eye color or height. Physical markers are unimportant, because the lender has a different kind of identification problem. When there is trouble, the borrower is unlikely to show up at the bank and the lender must find the delinquent customer. Under these circumstances, belonging is a better form of identification because it allows the bank to track down the missing borrower through her connections. This is why one's address is so important and it is also why lenders prefer owners to renters, as owners have more durable ties to their place of residence. For the same reason, phone numbers are collected, and landlines are preferred over cell phones. This is the reason that lenders demand to know the exact location of a borrower's workplace and why large and more permanent work organizations are favored. This form of identification prizes the stability of the identifying relationships. To gain control, lenders use stable ties to people and places to prevent borrowers from disappearing.

Sorting

The second part of the form is necessary to sort the client, to place her with similar others by looking for commonalities. This is crucial to establish the credit-worthiness of the applicant. The purpose of sorting is to put the applicant in a group of similar people with existing payment records by using a system of classification. Unlike the classification systems used by the welfare state that operate with legal categories, banks use statistical ones. While the difference between legal and statistical categories can be blurry, statistical categories do not require causal justification, nor do they necessarily by themselves lend to well-defined and explicit consequences. Belonging to an occupation, industry, or education level does not explain—or result in—entitlement to or exclusion from credit. Rather, it is the statistical combination and the predictive power of the various factors that matter.[7] This is because creditors sort by forward-looking criteria, solely on the basis of the expected future consequences of their redistributive action, while the welfare state decides by looking backward at eligibility that individuals have already earned.

The better the sorting the better the lender can estimate the applicant's future behavior. In principle, the lenders could devise their own, optimal categories, but that would require precise instructions and definitions that the applicant would have to follow, making the application process unwieldy, long, and error prone. Moreover, the lender would lose the ability to use data from other sources that mostly deploy conventional classification systems. For instance, to find the unemployment rates of specific occupational categories in order to make an educated guess at people's likelihood of losing their job, the lenders must be able to match their occupational groupings with the ones used in official statistics. Sorting is an attempt to overcome information asymmetry by using information from other, comparable cases in a methodical fashion.

Once the applicant is properly sorted in the first instance, a second sorting takes place. With statistical tools, the bank establishes if the person is creditworthy or not, sorting her into the "deserving" or the "undeserving" category. This is done by applying weights to each piece of information gathered about the applicant, calculating a weighted sum expressing the likelihood that the applicant is deserving, and using a certain threshold above which the decision to lend will be positive.

Creating Reputation

Dealing with people with whom one has not had personal experience requires a system of reputation. Reputation systems serve two purposes. They punish or reward bad or good behavior committed in the past and they help others avoid or seek out bad or good characters in future dealings. They thus both control and inform. Historically, the information that built one's reputation was circulated through social networks in the form of gossip and rumors (Landa 1995; Olegario 1999). Reputation systems depend on information sharing and collective memory. The reputation system in contemporary lending is embodied in the credit registries (also known as credit bureaus). These registries work much like the ones states use to conduct their own business. There are two kinds of consumer credit registries in central Europe: those that collect and share solely negative information and those that include the full performance record of borrowers.[8] Because banks are competitors, information sharing about customers is not a simple matter. Information about clients is a valuable commodity that banks often acquire at a cost. Knowing who is a good and who is a bad risk is crucial for the bank's success; therefore, handing this information to other lenders cuts the bank's competitive edge.

Blacklists and full records create different incentives for clients. The blacklist is an invitation for malefactors to switch identities in order to erase their record once they are found out. The list contains only negative information, thus getting off the list or not being recognized as being on it carries only benefits. Individuals can forge their documents or find proxy applicants for loans to free themselves from the burden of their history of bad conduct. Blacklists make no distinction between applicants with perfect records and those with no previous experience.

Full records, on the other hand, provide a complete picture of past behavior, allowing banks to evaluate the total debt exposure of their clients. While for blacklists no information is good information, for full lists no record is not much better than a negative one, and, therefore, their usage encourages people to build their reputation. This means that people must invest in presenting their credit histories. They must take on and repay loans not just to be able to afford purchases but also so that they can borrow in the future.

Full-information credit bureaus for consumers require much cooperation among lenders and are hard to develop in transition countries because of the high concentration of retail banking. Big banks such as OTP, CS, or PKO have a lot to lose by sharing their vast amount of information with new, smaller banks that have little to contribute to the credit bureau. Big banks would rather keep the information they have about clients and use it to their own advantage, as releasing information on good clients would be an invitation for the other banks to poach clients. Information sharing about bad clients has a slightly different calculus. While there is some advantage for the big bank to withhold information about its former bad customers and see its competitors lose money lending to them,[9] alerting other lenders permits the unpaid lender to punish nonpayers by shutting them out of the entire market. As a result, most transition countries have blacklists. By the early 2000s, Poland and the Czech Republic had managed to build a working full-reporting system; Hungary embarked on this project only in late 2011.

One law originally designed to address different concerns but that nevertheless has a strong effect on credit is the law on shielding personal data. All three countries have strong laws to protect the privacy of personal information. Such laws were created in the aftermath of the collapse of Big Brother state socialism, when people were eager to shelter themselves from an all-knowing state. Blanket data protection laws thwart the creation of credit bureaus because they prohibit the release of personal credit information to any registry without the explicit permission of the client. In all these countries, banks argued successfully that nonpayment is such a gross violation that it forfeits the borrower's right to data privacy.

In Poland and the Czech Republic, where full-record credit bureaus have existed for almost a decade, banks were able to circumvent privacy regulations, and the Polish credit bureau collects not just information on payment behavior but also sociodemographic data that include income, occupation, and family information. These credit bureaus, just as banks' US counterparts, also register the history of inquiries into each account. The history of inquiries, which is available to other lenders, can influence their decisions in making their own loans. Inquiries that are not followed by loans serve as warning signs that, even if the record looks clean, previous lenders must know something unfavorable about the person that is not apparent in the record.

Quantification

Reputations are conveyed not just through standardized narratives as presented by the credit record in the registry. Polish and Czech credit bureaus also offer a single number or credit score that summarizes a person's creditworthiness. Numbers are powerful not just because of their air of scientific objectivity but also because of their ultimate simplicity, easy communicability, and instant comparability (Porter 1995).[10] The vast power of quantifying a person's reputation can cut both ways. While banks can legitimize their selection process by pointing to its scientific nature, which makes challenges to their decisions difficult, the same numbers can empower customers with high scores to demand better terms from banks in a competitive market place.

Quantification, like sorting, creates comparability, and, as such, it provides new information from similar cases. But it also ensures that the reputation sticks. With its simplicity and seeming objectivity, judgments expressed as a single number are more difficult to avoid or contest.

"Fringe" Banking

Payday Lenders

Not everyone is served by the retail banks. There are also "fringe" credit institutions that offer consumer credit for the poor who usually have no bank accounts and would not qualify for a loan from a bank. Payday lenders constitute the third tier. One such company is the British Provident Financial.[11] Provident is active in Hungary, Poland, the Czech Republic, Slovakia, Romania, and Mexico. It offers short-term, unsecured personal loans with an annual percentage rate (APR) between 200 and 500. The loans are administered by officers who visit the applicants in their homes and build a personal relationship with them. After their first visit, they make an assessment, and if the decision is positive, the money is handed to the applicant physically on a second house visit. Collection is also done in person at the home of the client at mutually agreed-on times.

The loan officer usually lives in the vicinity of the applicant and has local knowledge of the applicant's circumstances. Provident claims to employ more than 4,000 officers in Hungary, 13,500 in Poland and 5,000 in the Czech Republic and Slovakia.[12] Ironically, Provident's services in many ways are similar to the treatment regular banks offer to their elite customers, except here, at the bottom of the economic hierarchy, personal attention acts as a strong form of control. Provident's method of overcoming the problem of information asymmetry is much more expensive than the formalized and highly mechanized processing of regular bank customers and all the costs of this labor-intensive lending are pushed onto the destitute client. Interest rates are high not just because those who borrow from payday lenders are riskier but also because operating costs are massive relative to the loaned amount.

Usury

Provident is a fully legitimate operation, which is preferable to loan sharks who are numerous and especially active in economically depressed regions. There is no systematic study of loan sharking and usury in postcommunist Central Europe, but there is plenty of anecdotal evidence that in poor areas such as Roma communities, loan sharks are often the only source of credit poor locals can turn to (Ferge 2010, 2000; Bjerkan and Huitfeldt 2004; Gelei and L. Murányi 2009).

In a small village in northern Hungary, for instance, where registered unemployment stands around 20 percent, the majority of the residents subsist on welfare. Loan sharks, who live in the community and therefore know their clients well, work with their own family members. The male and female members of the loan shark family often have a division of labor. Women often set up the transaction, while men enforce payment. They lend small amounts of money at a very high interest rate to people in need, who are often elderly, sick, or suffering from alcoholism. Because written records are rare, disputes are frequent about the terms of the loan and whether the borrower paid and how much. It is common that, each time a debtor goes to receive his welfare payment, the loan shark or one of his relatives escorts him to the welfare office and collects a cut on the spot. In some cases, the lender himself can collect his victim's welfare or pension with the intimidated victim's written permission. Physical violence and psychological pressure are important tools in loan sharking. There have been instances in which the debtors were kidnapped and kept in de facto debt slavery. They were forced to work and, in some cases, driven into prostitution or other criminal activity. Loan sharks overcome information asymmetry by exercising coercion, an extreme level of control.

While retail banks pick up the slack left behind the welfare state, fringe banking thrives on whatever is left of welfare services. Payday lenders and loan sharks exist largely because the poor receive stable, if meager, support from the welfare state in the form of family allowances, old age and disability pensions, unemployment compensation, or other forms of cash assistance.

Conclusion

With the retrenchment of the welfare state, consumer credit emerged as an alternative way to redistribute incomes to the middle class in order to provide effective demand for domestic consumer markets. This process arrived in Central and Eastern Europe only recently. The expansion of this credit was due to the enormous growth of formalized lending by retail banks. To supplement the state's role, lenders had to solve the problem of information asymmetry, which required cooperation in a competitive market; they also needed to cut the cost of lending. This was hard because initially the market of retail banking was highly concentrated, and the dominant bank in each country was reluctant to share information and join a common credit registry that would supply the two main solutions to the information asymmetry problem: more information and inexpensive control. The concentrated market also gave little incentive to the giants to expand consumer credit. Newcomers, on the other hand, initially did not have the volume to make the formalized lending viable and profitable.

Like the welfare state, banks redistribute income from those who have it to those who need it, but they follow different principles. Welfare state provisions are based on the ideas of social insurance and solidarity, whereby the ones most in need, as defined by some societal criteria, will receive resources. Consumer credit, on the other hand, operates on the basis of subjective needs, and banks, being competitive businesses that pursue profit and not bureaucratic monopolies, will lend to those who seem to be in a position to repay the loan.

The emerging dominant system of mass consumer credit in Central Europe prizes stability. People who are employed by large companies for a long period will be preferred. The system discriminates against the self-employed who may be rejected even if they earn more, simply because their income flow is less predictable. The availability of the applicant is rewarded, therefore people in the countryside who live in areas where telephone landlines are hard to come by are at a disadvantage. The value put on stability and availability is the reason that people on welfare or who receive a pension—stability created by welfare transfers—can also go into debt, albeit only on the fringe. The steadiness of their income flow and their lack of resources to relocate makes them good clients, but lending to them is profitable only at very high interest rates because they borrow small amounts and their risk of missing payments—as opposed to defaulting—is high.

In contrast to the welfare state that protects old people, mass consumer credit in Central Europe strongly discriminates against the aged. Most banks have an upper age limit—usually between 60 and 65—on eligibility to apply. Credit benefits most the younger age groups. Early in their life cycle, young people must invest in their households: Buy a home, furnish it, and purchase appliances, yet they have little savings. Not surprisingly, they are among those most interested in borrowing (Tóth and Árvai 2001).

Credit comes with strings attached. The installments must be paid regularly. If one becomes unemployed even temporarily, debt makes job loss even more painful. Anyone who carries a mortgage or a car payment and is fired, leaves a job voluntarily, or gets sick will find it difficult not just to hang onto her house or car but to avoid getting on the list of bad debtors.[13] This increases the employers' power over their indebted employees. By verifying employment and income, employers play a role in helping their employees to get the loan, but once the loan is secured the debt acts as a disciplinary force. The obligation to the bank increases the worker's commitment to her job, enhancing the employer's powers. Welfare works in the opposite direction. The safety net it provides eases anxieties about job loss.

With the ability to take bank loans, people depend less and less on financial support from their family and friends. With a vigorous mortgage market, young people can move out of their parental home sooner and more easily. Bank credit, therefore, weakens already fraying family ties (see chapter 9). In this respect, credit and welfare have similar effects. Credit also forces people to be more rational and calculative. They must draw up a budget and plan ahead. They must wrestle with time as money in the form of interest and depreciation (or appreciation) and meet payment schedules punctually.

Despite its success, consumer credit cannot solve the problem of suboptimal income distribution. While borrowers enjoy a temporary increase in consumption, the long-term effect of consumer credit is a reduction in the borrower's capacity to purchase unless the loan is used either to earn income (e.g., by buying a car that is also used to provide taxi services) or as a way to reduce expenses (e.g., when residential renting is so expensive that buying a home saves money even with mortgage interest and the other costs of ownership factored in). Credit redistributes income primarily not from rich to poor but from future to present. Thus consumer credit will expand and contract in cycles. What remains permanently in place is a new system of social control.

Notes

1. There is some debate about how the accounting system used under socialism can be made comparable with the calculations based on market prices that are used now; the exact numbers are therefore in dispute. What is not in dispute, however, is that there was a large drop in GDP.
2. Hungary and Poland also had a sprawling network of rural credit cooperatives that survived during communist rule. Their typical customers were rural workers whose financial service needs centered on agricultural production and small-scale construction.
3. One early entrant to this market in all three countries was the postal service that created a post bank. In none of these countries was this attempt successful.
4. Loans to households also include credit to the self-employed. This might partially explain why Poland is different. It still has an agricultural sector that, although it has shrunk since the end of communism, still is one of the largest in the EU and that is dominated by small private farmers who are poor but need loans for running their farms.
5. We also include here leasing companies.
6. The English acronym for very important person is the actual banking term used in Polish, Czech, and Hungarian.
7. In some cases, lenders use clear rules (e.g., no one under 18 years of age can receive credit) that are similar to legal categories. Unless those simple rules are legally mandated, the bank, unlike the state, is not obliged to disclose them to its clients. Moreover, these are always exclusionary criteria.
8. There are also commercial registries where nonlending institutions (e.g., phone and utility companies) share negative information.
9. Big banks will know about more bad customers than any smaller bank.
10. This quantification of credit-worthiness has had enormous consequences in the United States, where credit scores are now used not just in gauging credit-worthiness but as a general measure of character and reliability.
11. Another one is Beneficial Kredyt, a subsidiary of Household International owned by HBSC. Beneficial Kredyt operates in Poland.
12. See http://www.providentfinancial.hu/pages/szervezetunk.
13. Some banks offer insurance against sickness and unemployment, but it is usually expensive and debtors rarely buy it.

References

Babeau, André and Teresa Sbano. 2003. "Household Wealth in the National Accounts of Europe, the United States and Japan." *OECD Working Paper Series*. Available: http://www.oecd.org/officialdocuments/publicdisplaydocumentpdf/?cote=STD/DOC%282003%292&docLanguage=En
Bjerkan, Lise and Anniken Huitfeldt. 2004. "Roma Minorities in the Czech and Slovak Republics: Development of a Survey Methodology." *FAFO Paper* 2004: 18.
Boorstin, Daniel. 1973. *The Americans: The Democratic Experience*. New York: Random House.
Borocz, Jozsef and Akos Rona-Tas. 1995. "Formation of New Economic Elites: Hungary, Poland and Russia." *Theory and Society* 24(5): 751–781.
Brenton, Paul and Daniel Gros. 1997. "Trade Reorientation and Recovery in Transition Economies." *Oxford Review of Economic Policy* 13(2): 65–76.
Cao, Yang and Victor Nee. 2000. "Comment: Controversies and Evidence in the Market Transition Debate." *American Journal of Sociology* 105: 1175–1189.

Christensen, Betina Sand and Tue Mollerup Mathiasen. 2002. "Household Financial Wealth: Trends, Structures and Valuation Methods." Paper presented at the 27th General Conference of The International Association for Research in Income and Wealth, Stockholm, Sweden, August, 2002.

Clayton, Richard and Jonas Pontusson. 1998. "Welfare-State Retrenchment: Entitlement Cuts, Public Sector Restructuring, and Inegalitarian Trends in Advanced Capitalist Societies." *World Politics* 51(1): 67–98.

Coricelli Fabrizio, Fabio Mucci and Debora Revoltella. 2006. "The 'New Europe' Household Lending Market." In *Financial Development, Integration and Stability: Evidence from Central, Eastern, and South-Eastern Europe,* edited by Klaus Liebscher, Josef Christl, Peter Mooslechner, and Doris Ritzberger-Grünwald, 277–302. Northampton, MA: Edward Elgar.

Czech National Bank. 2009. *Financial Stability Report.* Available: http://www.cnb.cz/ miranda2/export/sites/www.cnb.cz/en/financial_stability/fs_reports/fsr_2008- 2009/FSR_2008-2009.pdf

Diamond, Douglas. 2006. "Thinking about Subsidies to Housing Finance." In *Housing Finance: New and Old Models in Central Europe, Russia, and Kazakhstan,* edited by József Hegedüs and Raymond J. Struyk, 79–98. Budapest: Open Society Institute.

Djankovic, Simeon and Peter Murrell. 2002. "Enterprise Restructuring in Transition: A Quantitative Survey." *Journal of Economic Literature* 40(3): 739–792

Duenwald, Christoph, Nikolay Gueorguiev, and Andrea Schaechter. 2005. "Too Much of a Good Thing? Credit Booms in Transition Economies: The Cases of Bulgaria, Romania, and Ukraine." *IMF Working Paper* No. 05/128. Available: http://ssrn.com/abstract=887997.

Égert, Balázs, Peter Backe, and Tina Zumer. 2006. "Credit Growth in Central and Eastern Europe: New (Over)Shooting Stars?" *ECB Working Paper* No. 687. Available: http://ssrn. com/abstract=936896

Erturk, Ismail, Julie Froud, Sukhdev Johal, Adam Leaver, and Karel Williams. 2007. "The Democratization of Finance? Promises, Outcomes and Conditions." *Review of International Political Economy* 14(4): 553–575.

Eyal, Gil, Ivan Szelenyi, and Eleonor Townsley. 1998. *Making Capitalism without Capitalists.* New York: Verso.

Ferge, Zsuzsa. 1997. "The Changed Welfare Paradigm: The Individualization of the Social." *Social Policy and Administration* 31(1): 20–44.

―――. 2010. "Key Specificities of Social Fabric under New-Capitalism." *Corvinus Journal of Sociology and Social Policy,* 1/2: 3–28.

Gelei, József and László L. Murányi. 2009. "Egy Település Szolgálja az Uzsorás Család Gazdagodását." (A Village Serves the Enrichment of the Loan Shark Family.) *Új Néplap* September 3, 2009. Available: http://www.szoljon.hu/jasz-nagykun-szolnok/bulvar/ egy-telepules-szolgalja-az-uzsoras-csalad-gazdagodasat-273548.

Gerber, Theodore P. 2000. "Membership Benefits or Selection Effects? Why Former Communist Party Members Do Better in Post-Soviet Russia." *Social Science Research* 29: 25–50.

Gracés, Jorge, Francisco Ródenas, and Stephanie Carretero. 2003. "Observations on the Progress of Welfare-State Construction in Hungary, Poland, and the Czech Republic." *Post-Soviet Affairs* 4: 337–371.

Greenspan, Alan. 2005. "Innovation and Structural Change Boost Access to Consumer Credit." Address to Federal Reserve System's Fourth Annual Community Affairs Research Conference, April 8, 2005, Washington, DC.

Greskovits, Bela. 1998. *The Political Economy of Protest and Patience. East European and Latin American Transformations Compared.* Budapest: Central European University Press.

Heidenreich, Martin. 2003. "Regional Inequalities in the Enlarged Europe." *Journal of European Social Policy* 13(4): 313–333.

Heyns, Barbara. 2005. "Emerging Inequalities in Central and Eastern Europe." *Annual Review of Sociology* 31: 163–197.

Hungarian National Bank. 2007. *Jelentés a pénzügyi stabilitásról (2007. április)*. Available: http://www.mnb.hu/Kiadvanyok/mnbhu_stabil/mnbhu_stab_jel_20070410
——. 2009. *Jelentés a pénzügyi stabilitásról*. Available: http://www.mnb.hu/Kiadvanyok/mnbhu_stabil/mnbhu_stab_jel_20091104

Jaffe, Dwight M. and Thomas Russell. 1976. "Imperfect Information, Uncertainty, and Credit Rationing." *The Quarterly Journal of Economics* 90(4): 651–666.

King, Lawrence P. and Ivan Szelenyi. 2005. "Post-Communist Economic Systems." In *The Handbook of Economic Sociology*, edited by Neil J. Smelser and Richard Swedberg, 205–229. Princeton, NJ: Princeton University Press.

Kolodko, Gregorz W. 2000. "Transition to a Market and Entrepreneurship: The Systemic Factors and Policy Options." *Communist and Post-Communist Studies* 33: 271–293.

Kornai, Janos. 1980. *Economics of Shortage*. Amsterdam: North Holland.

——. 1992. *The Socialist System. The Political Economy of Communism*. Oxford, UK: Oxford University Press.

Krugman, Paul. 2009. *The Conscience of a Liberal*. New York: W.W. Norton.

Landa, Janet Tai. 1995. *Trust, Ethnicity, and Identity. Beyond the New Institutional Economics of Ethnic Trading Networks, Contract Law, and Gift-Exchange*. Ann Arbor: University of Michigan Press.

Langley, Paul. 2007. "The Uncertain Subjects of Anglo-American Financialization." *Cultural Critique* 65: 66–91.

——. 2008. "Financialization and the Consumer Credit Boom." *Competition & Change* 12(2): 133–147.

Leyshon, Andrew and Nigel Thrift. 1999. "Lists Come Alive: Electronic Systems of Knowledge and the Rise of Credit-Scoring in Retail Banking." *Economy and Society* 28(3): 434–466.

Lux, Martin. 2009. "The Czech Republic." In *Management of Privatised Housing. International Policies and Practice*, edited by Vincent Gruis, Sasha Tsenkova and Nico Nieboer, 149–172. Chichester, UK: Wiley-Blackwell.

Marron, Donncha. 2007. " 'Lending by Numbers': Credit Scoring and the Constitution of Risk within American Consumer Credit." *Economy and Society* 36(1): 103–133.

Mitra, Pradeep, Marcelo Selowsky and Juan Zalduendo. 2010. *Turmoil at Twenty. Recession, Recovery, and Reform in Central and Eastern Europe and the Former Soviet Union*. Washington, DC: World Bank.

Murrell, Peter. 1995. "The Transition According to Cambridge, Mass." *Journal of Economic Literature* 33(1): 164–178.

Nee, Victor. 1989. "A Theory of Market Transition: From Redistribution to Markets in State Socialism." *American Sociological Review* 54: 663–681.

——. 1991. "Social Inequalities in Reforming State Socialism: Between Redistribution and Markets in China." *American Sociological Review* 56: 267–282.

Nesporova, Alena. 2002. "Why Unemployment Remains So High in Central and Eastern Europe?" Geneva: ILO 2002/43.

Nocera, Joseph. 1994. *A Piece of the Action: How the Middle Class Joined the Money Class*. New York: Simon and Schuster.

Olegario, Rowena. 1999. " 'That Mysterious People': Jewish Merchants, Transparency, and Community in mid-Nineteenth Century America." *Business History Review* 73(2): 161–189.

Piven, Frances Fox and Richard A Cloward. 1993. *Regulating the Poor: The Functions of Public Welfare*. New York: Vintage.

Polish National Bank. 2009. *Financial Stability Report*. June. Available: http://www.nbp.pl/en/systemfinansowy/financial_stability_2009.pdf

Porter, Theodore M. 1995. *Trust in Numbers: The Pursuit of Objectivity in Science and Public Life*. Princeton, NJ: Princeton University Press.

Poznanski, Kazimierz Z. (ed.) 1995. *The Evolutionary Transition to Capitalism*. Boulder, CO: Westview.

Przeworski, Adam. 1991. *Democracy and the Market: Political and Economic Reforms in Eastern Europe and Latin America*. Cambridge, UK: Cambridge University Press.

Rodrik, Dani. 1992. "Foreign Trade in Eastern Europe's Transition: Early Results." NBER Working Paper No. W4064. Available: http://ssrn.com/abstract=226883.

Rona-Tas, Akos. 1994. "The First Shall Be Last? Entrepreneurship and Communist Cadres in the Transition from Socialism." *American Journal of Sociology* 100: 40–69.

Rule, James B., Douglas McAdam, Linda Stearns, and David Uglow. 1983. "Documentary Identification and Mass Surveillance in the United States." *Social Problems* 31(2): 222–234.

Sachs, Jeffrey and David Lipton. 1990. "Poland's Economic Reform." *Foreign Affairs* 69(3):4 7–66.

Shiller, Robert. 2003. *The New Financial Order: Risk in the Twenty-First Century*. Princeton, NJ: Princeton University Press.

Stark, David. 1996. "Recombinant Property in East European Capitalism." *American Journal of Sociology* 106: 1129–1137.

Starke, Peter. 2006. "The Politics of Welfare State Retrenchment: A Literature Review." *Social Policy and Administration* 40(1): 104–120.

Stiglitz, Joseph E. and Andrew Weiss. 1981. "Credit Rationing in Markets with Imperfect Information." *The American Economic Review* 71(3): 393–410.

Szelenyi, Ivan and Eric Kostello. 1996. "The Market Transition: Toward a Synthesis?" *American Journal of Sociology* 101(4): 1082–1096.

Torpey, John. 1998. "Coming and Going. On the State Monopolization of the Legitimate 'Means of Movement.'" *Sociological Theory* 16(3): 239–259.

Tóth, István János and Zsófia Árvai. 2001. "Liquidity Constraints and Consumer Impatience." *National Bank of Hungary* Working Paper Series.

Vanhuysse, Pieter. 2006. *Divide and Pacify: Strategic Social Policies and Political Protests in Post-Communist Democracies*. Budapest: Central European University Press.

8

Financing Constraints on the Private Sector in Postsocialist China

YASHENG HUANG

In chapter 7 of this volume, Akos Rona-Tas describes one particular institutional change in the financial sector in postcommunist Eastern European countries, the rise of a consumer credit market. Complementing the conventional market transition theory (Nee and Matthews 1996) that focuses on the supply side of market, such as entrepreneurial firms, Rona-Tas highlights the demand side. His study analyzes how cultural values and financial institutions were transformed as customers were provided incentives to borrow money for consumption. This chapter has a similar focus as it considers the financing constraints that have faced the growth of the Chinese private sector.

There has been a substantial reversal—as well as some progress—in the financial treatment the government has accorded to the Chinese private sector in the last three decades. The reversal of the financial policies governing the private sector has been especially apparent in the years since 1989, when, as Barry Naughton points out in chapter 6 of this volume, the state became more activist. The views and data reported and summarized here are based on past and ongoing research projects that have examined detailed data on private firms, rural households, and qualitative data, such as documents from the banking sector and related policy measures.

A number of definitional and measurement issues concern the size of China's private sector, and these need to be explained at the outset. Since 1978 and even since 1989, the Chinese government has fostered growth in the private sector and facilitated privatization. A detailed perusal of microdata, however, shows that, by the end of the 1990s, the size of the indigenous private sector—firms owned by Chinese entrepreneurs—was miniscule among industrial firms conventionally classified as large and medium firms.

This portrayal contrasts with a common view among China economists that China made substantial strides in private sector development into the 1990s.

The next section of this chapter proposes a hypothesis explaining why China's indigenous private sector is undersized. The argument and empirics concentrate on the rural sector, because the countryside was the origin of Chinese private entrepreneurship in the 1980s. The size of the rural economy meant that the state's rural policies affected not just rural China but the overall pace and trajectory of China's entire economic transition. Research reveals a substantial reversal of financial policy in the 1990s, from a stance of pro-rural entrepreneurship in the 1980s to one that was detrimental to rural entrepreneurship. There is a link between this policy reversal and the slow growth of the indigenous private sector in the 1990s. (An explicit and direct demonstration of these two developments requires far more space than this chapter affords.) The last section of the chapter points to some broad implications of the findings.

Private Sector Growth in Postsocialist China

Similar to the previous Soviet bloc countries, China's communist period (1949–1978) was dominated by the planned economy, which was primarily composed of state- and collectively-controlled firms. Since China opened its door to the world economy in 1979, the economic and social landscape of production, service provision, and distribution has been fundamentally transformed. Among various changes was the rise and dramatic growth of indigenous private firms originating in the rural areas. Moreover, China's entry into the world economy coincided with an ever-deepening globalization that resulted in a huge influx of foreign direct investment (FDI) into the country and enabled China to become a global manufacturing power. Together, indigenous private firms and foreign-invested enterprises (FIEs) have contributed a large proportion of industrial output value, which had been dominated by state or collectively owned firms before the economic reforms began in 1978.

Before describing private sector growth, I must clarify what I mean by "private firms." The ownership of firms in a transitional economy is so complicated and fluid that just defining China's private sector is itself a worthy and difficult research question. Some scholars have used state and nonstate categories of firms as a way to assess private sector development in China (Bai, Li, and Wang 2003). The term *state-sector firms* refers to traditional state-owned enterprises (SOEs), whereas *nonstate sector firms* encompasses a wide variety of firms, including so-called collective enterprises, private firms, shareholding enterprises, domestic joint-ownership firms, and FIEs. In some cases, the boundary between the state and the nonstate sectors is not clear and requires having some textual knowledge of the Chinese economy and making a number of assumptions about how that economy operates. For example, some scholars also treat SOEs that have issued shares on the stock exchanges as part of the nonstate sector, while others do not.

The complexity of the concept of nonstate firms by and large accounts for the vastly different estimates that have been offered for the size of the private sector. For example, some scholars show that the share of the nonstate sector in industrial output value was 68.4 percent in 1997 (Wang 2002). But, variously, the Chinese National Bureau of Statistics (NBS) calculates that the nonstate sector accounted for only 21.2 percent of industrial value-added output in the same year (NBS 1999a).

To reconcile the discrepancies resulting from the various definitions of private firms, I present estimates based on firms' control rights, including their rights to appoint management, to dispose of assets, and to set their own strategic direction. Control rights are a more meaningful measure of firm ownership than revenue rights are. An operational difficulty in applying this definition, however, is that it is not easy to know whether a firm in China has private or governmental control rights.

To solve this problem, I will follow the approach used by Sean Dougherty and Richard Herd (2005), who define firm ownership in terms of the structure of their shareholding. Their research is based on a unique dataset compiled by the NBS that covers more than 160,000 industrial firms between the years 1998 and 2003. In this dataset, one critical piece of information regarding the shareholding structure of firms is that it provides a solution to the uncertainty over the exact ownership—control rights—of Chinese firms. One caveat, however, is that the NBS dataset is biased toward large firms—defined as those with at least 5 million yuan in sales. The estimates based on this dataset reflect the private share of the industrial value-added output produced by the largest firms in China, not the private share of the entire industry.

In line with Sean Dougherty and Richard Herd's (2005) definition of private firms,[1] I reexamine the same dataset that they used but extend their methodology to the NBS data for 2005. My estimates, which reveal a far smaller indigenous private sector as compared with theirs, are based on different assumptions about what types of firms have private control rights. Unlike their presumption that legal person shareholding firms are privately owned, I treat firms of this kind as SOEs. Stripped of confusing linguistic connotations, these firms are in most cases—especially in the 1990s—in essence SOEs establishing or holding significant equity stakes in other firms; the affiliates or subsidiaries of SOEs are, by definition, SOEs themselves. In terms of control rights, these firms should be more properly classified as SOEs.

Another departure from the work of Dougherty and Herd's (2005) is that I report separately the data series on indigenous and foreign private sector firms, respectively. There is a substantive reason for doing this. It is well documented by now that in the 1990s the Chinese state systematically favored foreign firms at the expense of indigenous private sector firms (Huang 2003), although the situation has arguably been reversed since 2007, when the Chinese government unified the corporate income tax rates of foreign and domestic firms. Because foreign and domestic private firms received very different policy treatments, it is important to distinguish between them in any discussion of the private sector in China.

Table 8.1 presents my estimates of private sector growth in China based on the NBS data. The contribution of the private sector to Chinese economic growth was on an increasing trend after the turn of the century. For example, indigenous private sector firms produced 5.9 percent of all profits in 1998, 10.6 percent in 2001, and 19.1 percent in 2005. Despite their growing importance, however, it is striking how small (vis-à-vis the state sector firms) the indigenous private sector firms were as recently as 2001. The estimates reflect the position of those firms among China's indigenous private sector that stand at the top of the corporate chain, rather than an average of all private firms' contribution, for the NBS dataset covers only the largest industrial firms. A

Table 8.1 **Estimates of Private-Sector Shares in Chinese Industrial Value-Added Profits and Long-Term Debt**

Private Firms	Year		
	1998	2001	2005
Indigenous	17.2	27.8	50.5
(1) Individual share capital >0.5	5.9	10.6	19.1
(2) Legal person share capital >0.5	11.3	17.2	31.4
Foreign: (capital >0.5)	11.7	16.9	20.7
Sum of indigenous and foreign (not including legal person share)	28.9	44.7	71.2

Note: We follow the classification and methodology used by Dougherty and Herd (2005). We classify firms in the nonstate category as those with more than 50 percent of share capital held by individual investors and foreign firms. We also present the firms with more than 50 percent of shares controlled by legal persons. We understand these sorts of firms as state-owned enterprises and do not include firms falling in this category when we describe the private sector growth.

Source: National Bureau of Statistics database of industrial firms with more than 5 million yuan in sales. For details of sources, see Huang (2008).

mitigating factor that may also be apparent in the data is the mid-1990s policy of "grasping the big, letting go of the small," mentioned in Naughton's chapter in this volume, which created many large monopoly SOEs but also contributed to the downsizing and privatization of hundreds of thousands of smaller SOEs. These two factors partially explain why my estimates of private sector firms are relatively small.

Although the data is limited to the larger industrial firms, the conclusion is straightforward: Contrary to the widely held perception that the private sector grew quickly and steadily after the start of economic reforms in 1978, I found that the flourishing of the indigenous private sector firms has been a recent development. At the end of the twentieth century, the size of the indigenous private sector among large industrial firms was miniscule (5.9 percent in 1998). It was only in and after 2005 that the indigenous private sector became relatively sizable (at 22 percent of the total industrial value-added output).

In comparison with the small size and slow growth rate of indigenous private firms in the 1990s, FIEs'[2] contributions represented a larger share. As table 8.1 shows, the percentage share of FIEs was about twice that of indigenous private firms (excluding the legal person shareholding firms) in 1998 (11.7 percent vis-à-vis 5.9 percent). This ratio declined to 16.9 in 2001 and reached a near parity in 2005. So the indigenous private sector began to grow much faster than foreign firms after 1998.

Yet the data on aggregate size obscure the extent to which indigenous private firms are undersized because there are far more indigenous private sector firms than there are FIEs in the NBS data. For example, the 5.9 percentage share of indigenous private firms in 1998 was spread among 19,322 firms, whereas the 11.7 percentage share represented by FIEs was produced by 15,934 FIEs; these figures reveal that the percentage share of an average indigenous private firm was much smaller than that of an average FIE.

China has made progress in its economic transition as the steadily increasing share of the private sector demonstrates. Between 1978 and 2001, the proportion that indigenous and foreign private firms collectively represented among all large firms rose from 0 percent to 38.8 percent. This implies an annual growth rate in the size of the private sector by about 1.7 percent a year. One can argue this is consistent with the gradualist perspective of Chinese reforms, according to which the size of the private sector grew steadily over time.

Even if the gradualist perspective is accurate, it still begs the question of why, during a period when GDP growth was exceedingly fast, the indigenous private sector seemed to grow relatively slowly. I propose that financing constraints were an important factor.

Financing Constraints and Policy Reversals

The business environment, broadly defined, includes both informal and formal institutional arrangements that protect property rights, encourage human capital mobility, provide access to finance, and offer third-party arbitration when a dispute arises. Media reporting has revealed that rent seeking, corruption, and a lack of property rights protection are rampant in reform-era China. I focus here on the workings of China's financial institutions and its banks specifically, in terms of their ability to channel resources to firms. In the late 1990s, the Chinese banking sector reported high nonperforming loan ratios, and there have been several rounds of recapitalization for Chinese banks since then. There is now a lot of knowledge about such "balance sheet" issues, but the operating issues of Chinese banks—in particular, how banks choose to lend or not to lend to firms—is an important factor to scrutinize.

The general picture is well known—Chinese banks favor state sector firms at the expense of the private sector. Beyond this point, however, it is important to highlight just how severe these credit biases are. To this end, I put China's financing constraints into comparative perspective by employing the unique cross-country data collected by the World Bank Environment Survey (WBES). To be consistent with this volume's theme of the process of transition under way in China and Eastern Europe since 1989, I focus on countries in these two parts of the world. Data from other countries are also used to provide a benchmark.

The World Bank designed and implemented the WBES from 1999 to 2000. The survey was carried out in 81 countries and involved more than 10,000 firms operating in these countries. It was designed to capture firm managers' views on many aspects of the business environment pertaining to their operations. An important feature of the WBES was its emphasis on entrepreneurial firms, and the vast majority of the firms it covered were owned privately. Of the entire WBES sample, only 12 percent of the firms reported some government ownership, and these firms were not controlled by the government. The WBES sampling framework is highly representative, and the firms' industry composition is roughly designated in accordance with their contributions to the GDP of the sampled countries. Firm size is considered too, with at least 15 percent of the sample having been set aside for small firms (those with fewer than 50 employees) and at least another 15 percent for large firms having more than 500 employees. In addition, at least 15 percent of the sample comprises firms with foreign ownership, while at least 15 percent of the firms export 20 percent of their output.

The WBES asks many detailed questions in regard to the entrepreneurial firms' business environment, including inquiries about financing constraints. For instance, question 38 asks, "Please judge on a four-point scale how problematic the following factors are for the operation and growth of your business." The response choices are: 1 (no obstacle), 2 (minor obstacle), 3 (moderate obstacle), or 4 (major obstacle). The WBES provides a choice of 11 factors for the respondent firms to rate, one of which is what the WBES terms the general financing constraint (GFC). I use firms' perceived GFC as a primary indicator of the financing constraints they encountered in their operations and management.

Table 8.2a presents the percentage shares of firms in a number of countries that ranked the GFC as a major hindrance to their business (i.e., a score of 4 in response to Question 38) or as a moderate/major obstacle (a score of either 3 or 4). Higher numbers indicate greater financing constraints perceived by the firms. For China, 66.3 percent of the firms sampled gave the GFC in China a rank of 4 (i.e., they gave the financial system a rank of 4 on this measure or constraint), the second highest proportion among all the countries in the WBES. (The country that received the highest financing constraint score was Moldova at 69.1 percent.) A higher percentage of Chinese firms ranked the GFC as a major issue than did their counterparts in the transition economies in Eastern Europe. For example, except for Kyrgyzstan, whose proportion, at 64 percent, was roughly the same as China's, the figures for European transition economies were all less than 60 percent. As many as 80.2 percent of Chinese firms agreed that the GFC was a moderate/major obstacle to business, a level similar to their counterparts in Romania, Belarus, Croatia, and Kazakhstan (in all of which the figure was around 80 percent).

To better understand the business environment in transition economies, I also included data showing the WBES averages for the GFC scores. These data indicate that the percentages of firms in transition economies as a whole—including China—ranking the GFC as major or as moderate/major are substantially higher than the WBES averages. The figures for these two measures of the GFC are 36.3 percent and 63.5 percent, respectively, while the averages for the selected transition economies are 55.5 percent and 79.2 percent, respectively. China has the highest GFC scores of all transition economies.

Secondly, I further contrast China with a number of Asian countries. Such factors as culture or geography make this a suitable comparison. I ask whether the severe financing constraints in China are idiosyncratic of transition economies or a common problem encountered in Asian countries. On average, private firms in other Asian countries did not face the same level of financing constraints as their Chinese counterparts experienced. For example, in India, a country that policy makers and scholars often compare with China, only 25.5 percent of private firms judged the GFC to be a major problem and 52.1 percent regarded GFC as a major/moderate concern (as against 80.2 percent in China). Singapore is another example, where there is a similar Confucian

Table 8.2a **Perception of General Financing Constraints in China, Selected Transition Economies, and Other Countries**

| | Perceived Financing Constraints | | |
| | (1–4, from least severe to most severe) | | |
Countries	Percentage of firms giving a score of 4	Percentage of firms giving a score of 3 or 4	Per capita dollar (PPP), 2001
China	66.3	80.2	4,260
Other Transitional Economies			
Russia	51.8	79.5	8,660
Romania	59.4	80.5	5,980
Belarus	54.9	82.3	8,083
Croatia	56.7	73.3	5,950
Georgia	58.1	78.3	2,860
Kazakhstan	48.8	79.5	6,370
Kyrgyzstan	64.0	87.2	2,710
Lithuania	35.9	69.8	7,610
World Business Environment Survey Average	36.3	63.5	n/a
Other Asian Counties			
India	25.5	52.1	2,450
Indonesia	41.0	50.0	2,940
Malaysia	22.1	41.0	8,340
Philippines	35.0	57.0	4,390
Singapore	9.1	30.3	24,910

Note: General financing constrains based on Question 38a in the World Business Environment Survey: "Please judge on a four-point scale how problematic are the following factors for the operation and growth of your business." 1=No obstacle; 2=Minor obstacle; 3=Moderate obstacle; 4=Major obstacle.

Source: General financing constrains data are from World Business Environment Survey. Per capita income data are from World Bank (2003).

culture but where the percentage of firms that ranked GFC as a major or major/ moderate concern was much smaller, at 9.1 and 30.3, respectively.

Another issue is the variance of constraints experienced by different types of private firms in China. Using the same WBES data, I break down the private firms into FIEs and indigenous private firms. Table 8.2b reports the questions in regard to business environment as perceived by these two categories of private firms. For all the four selected factors relating to the business environment, indigenous private firms perceived more constraints than the FIEs did. Firms were asked to rank from 1 to 4 the extent of the financing constraints they experienced, with 4 referring to a much greater extent of financing constraints and 1 representing minor constraints. The result of this survey was that the average score assigned to financing constraints by indigenous private firms was 3.48, while it was much lower for FIEs, at 2.93.

The next question to consider is whether these financing constraints were a constant feature of the Chinese transitional economy since the country started its market reforms or if, instead, they constituted a phenomenon limited to the time of the WBES in 1999 and 2000. Financing constraints for private firms in urban areas were most likely a constant feature of the Chinese economy during the period of interest to this volume. However, for rural private entrepreneurship, financing constraints increased over time after the beginning of the 1990s.

The evidence for the latter proposition comes in two forms. One is qualitative. Huang (2008) conducted a detailed examination of thousands of bank documents, which documents show a clear pattern. In the 1980s—even as early as 1979—such Chinese rural financial institutions as rural credit cooperatives were encouraged to lend to private household businesses, while bank loans were used as a tool to promote nonfarm businesses and to promote a transition from farming to service and industrial ventures.

Across a broad range of dimensions, including credit rationing, interest rate regulation, collateral guarantees, loan decisions, government intervention, and entry barriers, the 1980s witnessed substantial liberalization in rural China. All or nearly all of these rural financial liberalization policies, however, were reversed after 1989. Informal finance was also encouraged in the 1980s, with some of its activities even achieving a quasilegal status. All of this was reversed in the 1990s. A number of bank documents went so far as to criminalize informal finance, while a number of entrepreneurs engaged in this activity

Table 8.2b **Firms' Perception of Business Environment in China**

From 1 to 4 From no obstacle to a major obstacle	Foreign-Invested Enterprises	Indigenous Private Firms
General constraint—financing	2.93	3.48
General constraint—corruption	1.93	2.13
Business regulations	1.79	1.90
Labor regulations	1.62	1.70
General constraint—taxes and regulations	1.86	2.17

Source: World Bank Business Environment Survey (2000).

were arrested and jailed; one was even executed in 1991. Although informal finance persisted well into the 1990s and continues to operate up to the time of this writing, its activities became much more clandestine after 1989 and were substantially curtailed. This finding complements the argument in the Naughton chapter in this volume.

One more telling characteristic is that informal finance in the 1990s was limited to a small number of regions (such as Wenzhou and parts of Fujian provinces, as documented by Tsai 2002). By way of contrast, according to a number of bank reports, informal finance was widespread geographically in the 1980s, existing in such locations as Hebei, Guizhou, and Guangxi provinces.

Qian and Huang (2011) have gone beyond simply relying on qualitative evidence and have examined statistical analysis of a large-scale rural household survey data series that was undertaken over the years 1986 to 2002. The surveys in this series, conducted by the Ministry of Agriculture in multiple waves (in 1986–1991, in 1993, and in 1995–2002), followed a consistent sampling strategy and were of the type known as fixed-site rural household surveys (FSRHS).[3] For each survey, an average of 300 to 400 villages nationwide were sampled according to their levels of socioeconomic development and by their geographical locations. Within each village, 20 to 120 households were randomly selected. FSRHS provides household-level information for many variables, including income, expenditures, household assets, and the numbers of household members, along with their employment, ages, and gender. The most important information provided is the household's access to bank loans and to informal finance.

There are two important features about the findings reported in Qian and Huang (2011). First, the data are contemporaneous, that is, the data collection has the same timing as the research questions. This is more reliable than research findings that are based on retrospective questions that may be subject to selection biases or to respondents' memory lapses. (Only for an issue such as a rural financial reversal would there be no difference between findings based on contemporaneous data and findings based on retrospective data.)

The second feature is that the statistical technique used in the paper allows the researchers to control for the economic and demographic characteristics of rural borrowers, i.e., for changes in income levels and other variables reflecting financing constraints. The result is that one can discern the net effect that can be attributed to policy reversals.

After controlling for a variety of factors, Qian and Huang (2011) show that rural households received far more loans, both from formal and informal financial institutions, in the second half of the 1980s (over the years 1986–1991) than in the second part of the 1990s and in the early 2000s (during the period 1994–2002). The paper also demonstrates that, in the 1980s, variables

Table 8.3 **Retrospective Analysis of Financing Options for Chinese Private Firms**

	(1) Percentrage of firms reporting receiving bank loans in the founding year		(2) Percentage of firms reporting receiving informal loans in the founding year	
	(1a) Privately founded firms	(1b) Privately founded firms in rural areas	(2a) Privately founded firms	(2b) Privately founded firms in rural areas
1984	25.0	36.4	29.2	18.2
1985	26.5	50.0	20.6	33.3
1986	23.3	15.8	27.9	15.8
1987	29.0	38.5	34.2	46.2
1988	27.0	27.8	23.8	16.7
1989	16.2	27.3	23.5	27.3
1984–1989 average	24.5	32.6	26.5	26.3
1990	21.3	25.0	27.7	28.1
1991	16.2	16.7	27.0	30.0
1992	23.8	25.0	27.8	22.5
1993	18.8	26.4	34.2	18.9
1994	18.2	27.6	33.2	36.2
1995	19.6	25.7	32.9	29.7
1996	19.1	25.6	31.3	30.8
1997	20.9	29.2	35.6	29.2
1998	22.3	34.3	30.9	31.4
1999	21.8	34.6	34.6	34.6
2000	18.4	28.0	28.6	24.0
2001	15.0	13.8	27.0	41.4
1990–2001 average	19.6	26.0	30.9	29.7

Source: Question 8 in Renmin University (2002).

such as the political status of the rural households—whether a household had a party member or a village cadre—did not matter when it came to loan access, whereas in the 1990s it mattered substantially (i.e., households with a higher political status systematically got more loans). Also in the 1980s, those rural households that engaged in nonfarm businesses got more loans than other households did, but in the 1990s these same households got fewer loans as compared with other households. This is evidence that, in the 1980s, rural financial institutions promoted rural nonfarm entrepreneurship, which is consistent with the bank documents. In the 1990s, on the other hand, rural financial institutions hampered rural nonfarm entrepreneurship.

Financial Policy Reversal and Private Sector Development

Is there any connection between the financial reversal documented in the previous section and the modest development of China's indigenous private sector discussed at the beginning of the chapter? To answer this question directly is difficult, as it would require a counterfactual analysis. One direct piece of evidence is what occurred in the region of Wenzhou in Zhejiang province. Wenzhou did not reverse its financial policies in the 1990s, and, not coincidentally, experienced the most robust development of the entire indigenous private sector. This experience suggests that it is likely that financial policy reversals hampered the development of China's private sector as a whole. In this connection, it is only logical to argue that the statist orientation of policy developments in China after 1989, despite the accelerated pace of urbanization and globalization since then, had a detrimental effect on the pace and trajectory of China's development of its private sector, arguably the most important aspect of the country's economic reforms.

The financial policy reversal should not have mattered for private sector development. Private firms are based in urban areas, whereas the policy reversal occurred in the rural areas. But to conclude this would amount to a static and incorrect interpretation of Chinese reforms. First of all, in China, the indigenous private sector has been overwhelmingly rural, and private sector surveys conducted in urban areas even show that a large number of the founders and entrepreneurs originally came from the rural areas. Even in the most urbanized area of the country, Shanghai, rural residents were running approximately 40 percent of the indigenous private sector firms in the early 1990s, according to some surveys (see Huang 2008 for more details).

Secondly, there is both contemporaneous and retrospective evidence that financial policy reversal occurred in urban China as well in this period. The contemporaneous evidence comes from fixed-asset investment data. Since fixed-asset investments are heavily debt financed, they can be used as a proxy for the financial treatment of private sector firms. Huang (2008) has undertaken a detailed analysis of this topic. Using a variety of definitions of private firms, his work (2008) shows that fixed asset investments that were accounted for by indigenous private sector firms contracted substantially after 1989 relative to the fixed-asset investments accounted for by state and collective firms. In the 1980s the private sector averaged around 20 percent of total fixed-asset investments, while after 1993 this proportion declined to around 14 percent. There are some uncertainties about the exact classifications of firm ownership, however. Using the broadest definition of *private firms*, this study by Huang (2008) demonstrates that the share of total private sector fixed-asset investments did not manage to surpass the level prevailing in the 1980s until the period from 2002 to 2005. Thus, during the entire decade of the 1990s, the relative share of the private sector in fixed-asset investments was smaller than it was in the 1990s, again resonating with the Naughton argument in chapter 6 of this volume.

The other piece of evidence comes from surveys of private sector firms located in urban areas. These survey series (conducted in 1993, 1995, 1997, 2000, 2002, and 2004) were organized by the All-China Federation of Industry and Commerce.[4] The main drawback of this body's survey method is that it relied on retrospective questions since none of the surveys was actually conducted in the 1980s. Still, the study provides helpful data, for two reasons: First, the 1993 survey is sufficiently close chronologically to the decade of the 1980s that the retrospective bias is present but probably within a tolerable limit. That survey is thus quasicontemporaneous and can be compared with those conducted in later years. Second, the findings based on retrospective questions should be considered as a part of a package of evidence that includes both contemporaneous surveys and real data (i.e., fixed-asset investments). It is the congruity between these different types of evidence that provides confidence in the findings.

The 2002 survey can be used as a representative example, since the other surveys show similar results. What this particular survey reveals is that over time private firms relied less and less on formal finance and increasingly on informal finance. This finding should be interpreted with a few caveats. It is possible that the best among the private firms that were founded in the 1980s survived into the time of the 2002 survey, in part simply because they had more support all along from formal financial institutions. This supposition would imply that firms without support failed to survive and so no longer existed at the time of the 2002 survey. So it is theoretically possible that survivor bias is at play here. Adopting a survivor bias perspective requires making an implausible assumption that Chinese banks had the foresight to support the firms with the potential to perform best. Such an assumption would be inconsistent with the track record of Chinese banks, which instead have a history of supporting failing SOEs.

Another type of survival bias is more credible. Those private firms that were supported by banks in the 1980s had greater odds of surviving until the 2002 survey because they had greater access to capital. If this is the case, then the fact that only a small share of private firms with credit access—around 13 to

15 percent as late as 2001—survived would be a sign of serious constraints on China's private sector.

The 2002 survey was nationwide and included 3,258 firms drawn from all the provinces of China. Almost all the firms in that survey appear to be privately operated (*siying qiye*) rather than individual (*geti*) businesses. Privately operated firms are usually larger than individual businesses, which employ only up to eight employees. This survey provides information on the firm's size, status of development, organization, and operation; its management system and decision-making style; the socioeconomic background of enterprise owners and their social mobility and social networks; the source and composition of employees; employee-employer relations; and the income, expenditures, and assets of the entrepreneurs.

Of most interest here is the information on entrepreneurs' views on a range of issues related to government-business relations, the overall business environment, and the availability of financing. Question 8 in the survey asks the respondents to check off their sources of startup capital from the following choices: savings from running small businesses, savings from running small-scale production operations, donations from friends and relatives, wages, informal loans, bank loans, and inheritance. Given that all Chinese banks are state owned, I adopt a conservative classification scheme and classify bank loans as formal finance and the remaining choices as informal finance.

For all private firms, the percentage that reported a reliance on formal finance at the startup stage declined over time. During the period from 1984 to 1989, an average of 24.5 percent of private firms reported receiving formal finance; this ratio declined to 19.6 percent during the 1990 to 2001 period, a decline of 4.9 percentage points. The outcomes of policy reversals in the 1990s are more salient for private firms founded in the rural areas. During the 1984 to 1989 period, an average of 32.6 percent of rural private firms reported having received formal finance. This figure, however, dropped to 26 percent in the 1990 to 2001 period, a decrease of 6.6 percentage points.

This development contrasts with a growing reliance on informal finance. For all private firms founded during the 1984 to 1989 period, on average, 26.5 percent reported receiving informal finance; for those founded in the 1990 to 2001 period, 30.9 percent did so. For those private firms founded in the rural areas, a similar pattern emerged, as 26.3 percent of the firms founded in the 1984 to 1989 period reported receiving informal finance while 29.7 percent did so in the 1990 to 2001 period. The 1990s, therefore, witnessed a decline in the share of private firms able to tap into resources through the formal financial sector and a corresponding growth in firms' reliance on the informal sector. The evidence from the 2002 survey is entirely consistent with other types of evidence presented in this chapter.

Conclusions

The finding that a smaller percentage of private firms had access to formal finance, while a larger percentage of them turned to informal finance in the 1990s as compared with the 1980s, is striking. Some analysts have argued that the emergence of informal finance indicates the government's tolerance of greater play for market forces and private decision making outside the state's direct control (Tsai 2002). The evidence offered here, however, demonstrates that this viewpoint is not quite accurate. A better indicator of the government's altered views would be the greater legal tolerance for informal finance rather than a rising share of informal finance in a firm's total capital. Documentary evidence, in fact, suggests that the opposite was in fact the case—in the 1980s there was a greater policy tolerance of informal finance than in the 1990s. Thus, the prominence of informal finance in the 1990s was not due to reforms but instead to a contraction of formal finance. All else being equal, firms would naturally prefer formal to informal finance.

Xinghai Fang's (2005) research reveals that informal finance is extremely expensive, as it demonstrates that the curb market rate in Beijing for small private firms in the late 1990s was as high as 18 percent, compared with a rate of just 6 percent on formal loans. Similarly, Shleifer and others have shown that informal contracts are not enforceable, so that informal finance carries a greater default risk.

This financial reversal has significant economic implications. One hypothesized effect is the relatively small size of the Chinese indigenous private sector during a time when the GDP averaged double-digit growth every year. The other possibility is the decline of rural household income growth rates (but not of levels) in the 1990s. During the decade when rural financing constraints were most severe, the rural household income indeed grew at its slowest rate (see Huang 2008 for more details). More research needs to be done to demonstrate this connection, but it is plausible to argue that there is one.

Why did China reverse its rural financial policies in the 1990s? The answer is that we do not know. Still, it could credibly be argued that the leadership change in 1989 was the catalyst for these policy changes. In the 1980s, the forging of Chinese economic policy was led by those who first rose to national prominence as capable managers of rural affairs and as pioneers of rural reforms. Zhao Ziyang and Wan Li are the best representatives of that cohort of leaders. In the 1990s, to the contrary, China was led by technocrats, namely Jiang Zemin and Zhu Rongji, who had made their name in the most urban and most state-controlled city of the country, Shanghai. In a top-down system such as China's, it would be surprising if the credentials, ideas, and perspectives of top leaders did not affect economic policy making. These suggestions imply, as the Fewsmith chapter in this volume argues, that the 1989 events cast a long political as well as an economic shadow.

Acknowledgment

The writing of this chapter benefited substantially from the excellent research by and discussions with Enying Zheng. All errors are mine.

Notes

1. Their methodology involves two steps. First, they divide the firms into state and nonstate. State firms, in turn, comprise two types of subfirms: SOEs and collective firms in which collective share capital exceeds 50 percent. The second step is to classify all those firms in the nonstate category as being those having more than 50 percent of their share capital held by legal persons, individual investors, and foreign firms.
2. The study by Sean Dougherty and Richard Herd (2005) adopts a conservative definition, covering only those firms with foreign share capital exceeding 50 percent.
3. The dataset is available from the University Services Center of the Chinese University of Hong Kong. Only information from six provinces, Liaoning, Shandong, Hubei, Guangdong, Yunnan, and Gansu, has been released.
4. There was another private sector survey conducted in 1991, but it was limited to what is termed "individual businesses," that is, small single proprietorships having only a few employees. The 1993 and the private sector surveys thereafter began to focus on larger private firms that have multiple shareholders and a large number of employees. The data from the 2004 survey have not been released, although the Chinese press has made references to its summary findings.

References

Bai, Chong-En, David D. Li, and Yijiang Wang. 2003. "Thriving on a Tilted Playing Field." In *How Far across the River? Chinese Policy Reform at the Millennium*, Nicholas C. Hope, Dennis Tao Yang, and Mu Yang Li, eds., 97–121. Palo Alto, Calif.: Stanford University Press.

Dougherty, Sean and Richard Herd. 2005. "Fast-Falling Barriers and Growing Concentration: The Emergence of a Private Economy in China." Paris: Organization for Economic Cooperation and Development.

Fang, Xinghai. 2005. "Reconstructing the Micro-Foundation of China's Financial Sector." In *Financial Sector Reforms in China*, Yasheng Huang, Tony Saich, and Edward S. Steinfeld, eds., 19–28. Cambridge, Mass.: Harvard University Asia Center.

Huang, Yasheng. 2003. *Selling China: Foreign Direct Investment during the Reform Era*. New York: Cambridge University Press.

———. 2008. *Capitalism with Chinese Characteristics: Entrepreneurship and the State*. New York: Cambridge University Press.

Lee, Ching Kwan. 2007. *Against the Law: Labor Protests in China's Rustbelt and Sunbelt*. Berkeley: The University of California Press.

National Bureau of Statistics. 1999a. *Guanyu tongjishang ruhe fanying suoyuzhi. Jiegou wenti de yanjiu [Research on Statistical Reporting on Ownership Structures]*. Beijing: Zhongguo tongji chubanshe.

Naughton, Barry. 2007. *The Chinese Economy: Transitions and Growth*. Cambridge, Mass.: MIT Press.

Nee, Victor and Rebecca Matthews. 1996. "Market Transition and Societal Transformation in Reforming State Socialism." *Annual Review of Sociology* 22: 401–436.

Qian, Meijun and Yasheng Huang. 2011 "Financial Reversal in Rural China," Working paper.

Renmin University. 2002. Private Sector Survey. Done in collaboration with the Chinese Academy of Social Sciences and the Beijing Academy of Social Sciences. Beijing.

Tsai, Kellee S. 2002. *Back Alley Banking: Private Entrepreneurs in China*. Ithaca, N.Y.: Cornell University Press.

Wang, Yuanjiang. 2002. *Zhongguo minyin jingji touzi tizhi yu zhengce huanjin [The Investment System and the Policy Enviroment for China's People-Run Economy]*. Beijing: Zhongguo jihua chubanshe.

World Bank. 1999. *World Business Environment Survey: Measuring Conditions for Business Operation and Growth*. Washington, D. C.: The World Bank.

World Bank. 2003. *World Development Indicators*. Washington, D. C.: The World Bank.

PART V

RESHAPING SOCIAL INSTITUTIONS

9

Changing Family Formation Behavior in Postsocialist Countries

Similarities, Divergences, and Explanations

THEODORE P. GERBER

When state socialist regimes collapsed throughout Eastern Europe and the Soviet Union from 1989 to 1992, few observers saw the family as a central changing social institution. Nor did they envision the significant impact of the system's demise on family formation behavior. Instead, most scholarly and policy analyses focused on the profound changes the postsocialist transition ordained in terms of economic life, politics, and culture. The ongoing nature, continuing relevance, and complex inter-relationships of the changes in these realms have been explored in depth in other chapters this volume. For example, in chapter 10, Wang Feng and Yang Su show that, even as market institutions have supplanted direct state control over economic activity in China, the Chinese political regime has actually enhanced its capacity to intervene economically and socially, demonstrating flexibility, innovation, and resilience in the process. In China, moreover, market reforms spurred an extended period of dramatic economic growth, whereas in Eastern Europe and the former Soviet Union they precipitated sharp economic crises, as József Böröcz demonstrates in chapter 5 using a novel approach to measure economic performance. Against the backdrop of such variable and counterintuitive developments in the political economy of postsocialist countries, it is small wonder that changing family formation patterns have received less attention.

However, in recent years researchers and policy makers have come to recognize what the Russian demographer Sergei Zakharov (2008) has aptly called the "quiet revolution": virtually all the Eastern European and post-Soviet countries experienced a common set of dramatic, rapid, and unprecedented changes in marriage and fertility patterns, and these changes may prove to have equally

or even more significant long-term consequences for their societies as the economic, political, and cultural transformations. A growing literature, much of
it developed by demographers from the region, has documented the emergent
family formation patterns and sought to understand why they have taken place
so swiftly, whether they are temporary or permanent in nature, and what their
likely consequences will be in the future. Twenty years after the collapse of
state socialism, no consensus has been reached on these issues. This chapter
describes the main patterns in question, notes some of the important variations among countries, discusses the principal explanations that have been
proposed, and considers the potential consequences. It concludes with ideas
for testing the competing explanations.

Changing Patterns: A Tale of Two Decades?

Each of the former state socialist societies has its own distinctive history, culture, and contemporary economic, political, and social circumstances. These
factors combine to produce variations in marriage and fertility levels, as well as
in their prevailing trends. At the same time, several broad tendencies characterize the postsocialist experience. Economic reforms shifted economies from
state-administered to market-based systems, albeit unevenly and at different
speeds. The countries experienced economic crises in the immediate aftermath of reforms, though the duration and severity of these crises varied, as
József Böröcz shows in chapter 5 of this volume. Political reforms eliminated
Communist Party rule and strict constraints on civil liberties, implementing
in their place some form of democracy and protections of individual freedoms,
though elements of authoritarian control remain present, even resurgent,
especially in some of the former Soviet countries. With the end of extensive
restrictions on the capacity to organize groups outside the party-state, voluntary organizations, independent media outlets, and other components of civil
society emerged, though the countries varied considerably in the number,
strength, and independence of these institutions. These societies all opened
up culturally, in the sense that socialist-era censorship and limits on the free
exchange of cultural artifacts, ideas, and images with Western societies were
effectively removed. Finally, barriers to the free movement of people within
and across national borders fell, which led to increases in both international
and domestic migration.

As this brief summary suggests, there are enough common elements in
the processes of postsocialist transformations experienced by the Eastern
European and former Soviet countries to expect that a similar set of parallel
changes in the area of family formation may also have taken place. Moreover,

to the extent that economic circumstances, cultural norms, and political institutions and policies affect family formation, common developments in these areas could have some degree of uniform impact on marriage and fertility patterns.

The countries of Eastern Europe and the former Soviet Union also share a distinctive historical legacy in terms of family formation that predated the state socialist period. At least as early as the nineteenth century, Russia and other European countries east of a line running from Trieste to Saint Petersburg exhibited a distinctive "Eastern European" family formation pattern: Marriage was more universal and took place at younger ages than in Western Europe (Hajnal 1965; Coale, Anderson, and Haerm 1979; Coale 1992). This pattern persisted in Russia and other Eastern European countries during the first half of the twentieth century, a period when many Western European countries began to reflect and replicate Eastern European patterns of younger and more universal marriage. In Russia, the massive societal disruptions associated with world wars, revolutions, and famines predictably led to short-term declines in marriage rates and increasing average ages at first marriage, but the impact of these historical episodes was only fleeting (Scherbov and Van Vianen 1990).

In light of the long-term stability of the Eastern European family formation pattern in this region of the world, the rapid shifts in marriage and fertility behavior following the collapse of state socialism are especially striking. Several distinct patterns and tendencies have emerged. Marriage rates have declined. Those who do marry typically do so at older ages than people generally did in the state socialist era. In addition, nonmarital cohabitation and nonmarital childbearing have become more common, while fertility rates have fallen precipitously, and in many cases women now wait until they are older before bearing children than they did under the previous regime. The institution of marriage thus appears to have been significantly weakened, and low fertility rates have become the norm. These trends have been described and discussed by other researchers (e.g. Caldwell and Schindlmayr 2003; Kalmijn 2007; Frejka 2008; Zakharov 2008), but these scholars generally deal only with the 1990s. One purpose of the present study is to extend these analyses into the 2000s and consider the implications of more recent developments in the trends that prevailed in the first postsocialist decade.

In order to provide some empirical illustrations of changing family formation behaviors, I depict the trends that unfolded from 1989 to 2007 using statistical measures that describe these phenomena for eight countries: Russia, Armenia, Kyrgyzstan, the Czech Republic, Hungary, Poland, and Bulgaria. All data come from the TransMONEE database, a compilation based on national sources produced by the United Nations Children's Fund's (UNICEF's) Regional Office for Central and Eastern Europe and the Commonwealth of

Independent States, which is available online (http://www.unicef-irc.org/databases/transmonee/). The TransMONEE data provide information on all 28 countries of Eastern Central Europe (ECE) and the former Soviet Union (FSU). I limit my presentation to eight countries because it is difficult to plot clearly the trends in all the region's countries due to the variety in initial levels and in the timing of changes in the rates analyzed. In choosing which countries to include in the charts, I sought to cover the geographic range of the region (from ECE and Southern Central Europe to the Balkans, Eurasia, the Caucasus, and Central Asia). I excluded countries that have experienced sustained military conflicts during the last 20 years, such as the former Yugoslav republics (because military conflict is likely to have a pronounced and possibly idiosyncratic impact on family formation, which would further complicate an already complex picture). I also prioritized countries where the data are more complete, consistent, and reliable.

Declining Marriage

The best available macrolevel measure of marriage behavior is the age-specific marriage rate, which is the number of marriages in a given year divided by the number of people (at midyear) in the age range of 15 to 44 years old, the span of ages during which the vast majority of marriages take place. This measure is somewhat better than the "crude" marriage rate (the number of marriages divided by the total population), because it at least restricts the denominator to those who are old enough to marry and young enough that they still have fairly high probabilities of marrying if they have not done so already. Yet the age-specific marriage rate is far from perfect. Ideally, to capture annual fluctuations in marriage entry behavior, the denominator would include only that part of the population that is actually at risk of getting married during a particular year. This would exclude not only those too young to marry but also those who are already married. By failing to remove already married individuals from the denominator, the age-specific marriage rate tends to produce offsetting trends over time, because as rates of marriage increase in a particular year, the effect (other things being equal) is to reduce the size of the marriage-eligible population in subsequent years; thus, even if the rate of marriage entry among those at risk is stable, the age-specific rate may well decline, depending on the stability of rates among those entering the risk set because they turn 15. Moreover, other factors shaping the number of those eligible to marry are seldom equal; for example, relative cohort size can also play a major role, given that there is considerable variation in marriage rates by age within the broad 15 to 44 range. Unfortunately, governmental statistical bodies seldom collect data on the size of their marriage-eligible populations, so actual measures of the annual rates of marriage entry among those at risk can only be estimated from survey data from individual countries. Nonetheless, the age-specific marriage rate is suitable for identifying general tendencies. For the purposes of broad comparisons, it is the best available measure. In this context, marriage refers exclusively to legal marriages, not to cohabiting unions.

As figure 9.1 depicts, former state socialist countries all experienced declines in the age-specific marriage rates for most of the 1990s. In the countries under consideration here, the decline was steepest in Kyrgyzstan, which began the period with the highest rate of marriage entry. It was most moderate in Poland, perhaps reflecting the influence of Catholicism. Figure 9.1 also shows that marriage rates were declining in three of the four Soviet republics examined prior to the collapse of the Soviet Union at the end of 1991. The exception is Kyrgyzstan, which (along with Uzbekistan and Kazakhstan) experienced a curious and short-lived rise in marriage rates during the perestroika era, perhaps reflecting a response to expectations of increasing dowries due to inflation or to renascent traditional values (Dommaraju and Agadjanian 2008).

The trends in marriage rates began to diverge in the 2000s. In Bulgaria, the Czech Republic, and Hungary, they remained essentially stable throughout the decade. Elsewhere they rebounded, in some cases in the early 2000s and steeply (Russia, Armenia, Kyrgyzstan), while in other places, later and more modestly (Estonia and Poland). It is difficult to say whether the increases in

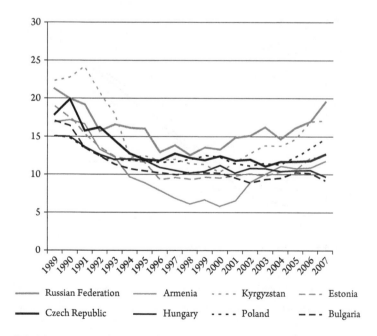

Figure 9.1 Marriages per 1,000, Ages 15 to 44. Source: TransMONEE database, http://www.unicef-irc.org/databases/transmonee/

marriage rates observed reflect actual increases in the rate at which eligible people entered into marriages as opposed to changes in the denominator (an increase in the proportion of unmarried people within the age range and/or changes in relative cohort size due to aging). Available country-level studies using survey data tend to confirm that true marriage rates (among those at risk for marriage) fell during the 1990s. But, largely for the lack of more recent data, these studies do not address the 2000s (Hoem et al. 2009; Philipov and Jasilonienne 2008; Gerber and Berman 2010). Thus, while declining marriage rates for most of the first decade of postsocialism were a common pattern, developments during the 2000s are less certain and appear to be more heterogeneous. In all likelihood, the declines in marriage ceased in about 2000, and in some but not all countries, countertrends emerged at that point or later in the 2000s. Declining marriage rates can reflect an overall decline in marriage propensities that affects all age groups more or less equally, or they can reflect an emergent tendency to delay marriage rather than forgo it altogether (see Goldstein and Kenney 2001). One way to analyze the delay process is to consider the average age at first marriage, as shown for women in figure 9.2. This measure exhibits fairly monotonic increases in all the countries considered: Throughout ECE and the FSU, both sexes are tending to wait longer before entering a first marriage. The rate of increase was slow or negligible at first but took off during the late

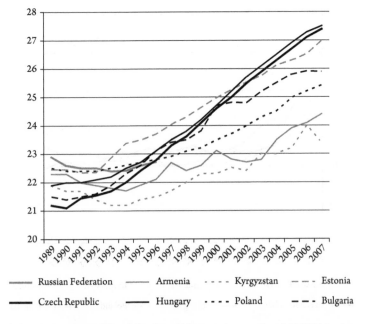

Figure 9.2 Average Age at First Marriage, Women. Source: TransMONEE database, http://www.unicef-irc.org/databases/transmonee/

1990s, especially in ECE. Russia is a possible exception: The official data suggest virtually no increase in the average ages at first marriage during the early 1990s, and no official data are available after 1998 (due to changes in government data-collection protocols.) But according to survey-based estimates (Zakharov 2008), the mean age at marriage began increasing in Russia in the late 1990s.

The evident trend of increasing age at first marriage implies that the declining marriage rates of the 1990s could have been delaying effects rather than being a sign that more people are forgoing marriage altogether. Although some studies (Hoem et al. 2008; Gerber and Berman 2010) suggest that at least part of the decline reflected across-the-board drops in marriage rates (as opposed to pure delay), it is not possible to tell definitively whether total cohort marriage rates (the percentage of a cohort that ever marries) fell during this period until the cohorts in question reach their fifties. In any case, an increasing tendency to delay marriage will generally result in a decline in cohort marriage rates because some individuals who delay miss the opportunity to marry when they are young and never get another chance.

Fertility

The total fertility rate (TFR) is the expected number of children a woman will have in the course of her lifetime assuming that the age-specific fertility rates that obtain in the country during that year obtain in the future. The TFR is, therefore, an ideal age-adjusted measure of period fertility. As portrayed in figure 9.3, the ECE and FSU countries each experienced substantial declines in their total fertility rates during the 1990s. The declines were steepest in those countries with initially higher fertility rates (Kazakhstan and Armenia). The TFRs stabilized during the early 2000s and, in some cases, began to inch upward again at some point in that decade. However, for the most part, the improvements in TFRs during the 2000s were modest, especially when viewed against the backdrop of the steep declines of the 1990s. By 2007 all the countries except Kyrgyzstan and Estonia had TFRs well below 1.5, qualifying them as very low fertility countries. In most developed countries, a TFR of 2.1 is required to "replace" the current population in the long run.

As in the case of marriage, short-term declines in TFRs can reflect delays in childbearing rather than long-term declines. This may be the case in some of the former socialist countries: Starting in the early to mid-1990s, the average age at first birth increased monotonically, though at different rates, in all the sample countries except Armenia (see figure 9.4). Russia, again, is another possible exception: The average age at first birth fell during the initial transition

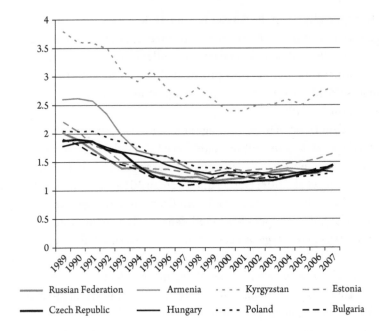

Figure 9.3 Total Fertility Rate. Source: TransMONEE database, http://www.unicef-irc.org/databases/transmonee/

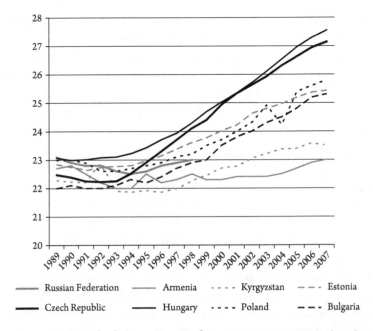

Figure 9.4 Average Mother's Age at First Birth. Source: TransMONEE database, http://www.unicef-irc.org/databases/transmonee/

period, until regaining its 1989 level in 1998 (the last year when Russian data were available). Given the timing of the declines in TFRs, it is noteworthy that the increases in average age at first birth date to the mid-1990s rather than to the outset of the transition period. Delayed childbearing has been especially pronounced in Hungary and the Czech Republic, where the average ages shot upward dramatically from less than 23 to more than 27. Overall, the patterns suggest that some of the moderate increases in fertility observed in the latter half of the 2000s resulted from "catch-up" childbearing by women having their first births in their late twenties and early thirties. If these women have additional children, then TFRs will continue to grow modestly, though overall cohort fertility rates are unlikely ever to approach those of the socialist era (Frejka 2008). When women delay childbearing, they often end up with fewer children than they may have wanted due to difficulties having children at older ages (Kohler et al. 2002).

In Russia and Ukraine women tend to have one child but stop there (Perelli-Harris 2005). Survey-based research suggests this pattern intensified in Russia during the 1990s and early 2000s: Women continued to have their first child at relatively young ages, but they had second children at rapidly declining rates, while in Bulgaria a growing number of women postponed or avoided first births. Among those who did have children in Bulgaria, however, the rate of transition to a second birth remained stable (Philipov and Jasiloniene 2008). This helps explain the unusual combination of trends in Russia, where declining fertility accompanied decreasing ages at marriage and first birth (Hollander 1997). Altogether, these patterns indicate that the fertility declines in these countries reflect a combination of both delayed fertility and across-the-board declines in fertility—in technical terms, both tempo and quantum effects—and also that the specific patterns of fertility decline vary from one country to the next.

Nonmarital Fertility

Another striking development in the former state socialist countries, as depicted in figure 9.5, is the sharp rise of nonmarital births as a percentage of total births in all countries. These rates rose dramatically even in the more religiously conservative countries such as Armenia, Kyrgyzstan, and Poland. Estonia and Bulgaria experienced the sharpest increases: By 2007 more than half of all births were to unwed mothers. In the space of two decades, nonmarital childbearing went from being a relatively minor, if not entirely insignificant issue, to an area of major social concern. Apart from Estonia, no country's

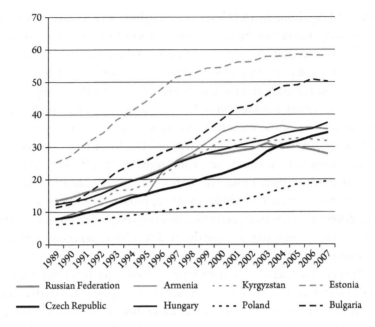

Figure 9.5 Percentage of Nonmarital Births. Source: TransMONEE database, http://www.unicef-irc.org/databases/transmonee/

rate of nonmarital births exceeded 15 percent in 1989, but by 2007 all except Poland had rates of 28 percent or higher.

Cohabitation

In many Eastern European and post-Soviet countries nonmarital cohabitation has increased dramatically. There is no macrolevel data demonstrating this, but it is evident from survey-based estimates in a number of studies of individual countries or subsets of countries (Kalmijn 2007; Philipov and Jasilioniene 2008; Hoem et al. 2009; Gerber and Berman 2010). The increase in nonmarital unions casts the decline in marriage and the growth in nonmarital childbearing throughout the region in a different light. To some extent, nonmarital unions have emerged as a substitute for the institution of legal marriage. Moreover, many mothers who are unmarried at the time of their first birth are in cohabiting unions: In Russia, at least, much of the growth in nonmarital childbearing results from the increase in cohabitation rather than an increase in births to single mothers (Perelli-Harris and Gerber 2011). This does not mean that nonmarital childbearing is a "benign" phenomenon: If cohabiting unions are less stable than marriages in Russia, then the increase in the proportion of births to cohabiting mothers will lead to an increase in single mother-headed households.

Explanations

Three broad classes of explanation for these trends can readily be identified, which focus respectively on the economic crisis, on long-term normative shifts, and on political and institutional factors. Each explanation applies to the shifts in both marriage and fertility behavior, which is not surprising given how closely the two are linked.

Economic Crisis and Uncertainty

An obvious candidate to explain the declining rates of marriage and fertility in the former socialist countries is the economic crises that befell them following the collapse of the state. Economic explanations for both marriage and fertility abound. Many researchers have found, for example, that in the United States men require a minimal level of economic resources before they can take on the responsibilities of marriage and parenthood, and they do not make attractive marriage partners unless they have good economic prospects (Easterlin 1976; Goldscheider and Waite 1986; Lichter et al. 1991; Lloyd and South 1996; Oppenheimer, Kalmijn, and Lim 1997). Recent studies indicate that, with the rise in female labor force participation, better economic prospects also make women more attractive marriage partners (Qian and Preston 1993; Sweeney 2002). Applying this logic, the rising unemployment and declining wages of men and women during the postsocialist crisis period would make fewer of them suitable marriage partner candidates and thus would reduce marriage rates as long as these phenomena persisted. Consistent with the economic explanation for marriage decline in post-Soviet Russia, economic crises in Latin American countries since the 1920s have typically produced nearly immediate declines in marriage, even as other demographic consequences occur only after lags of one or more years (Palloni, Hill, and Aguirre 1996).

The same logic applies to fertility: Limiting the number of children per family is a rational response to economic hardship: Children cost money, and so in times of economic duress or slowdown, fewer individuals think they can afford them. Historical studies from a variety of contexts have documented the responsiveness of fertility to economic change (e.g., Lee 1990; Palloni et al. 1996). A related argument emphasizes not individual-level economic hardship as such but the uncertainty or social anomie produced by macrolevel dislocations, rising unemployment, and inflation. Even individuals not directly affected by downsizing and wage cuts may fear such problems in the future and thus refrain from such long-term commitments as marriage or childbearing (Kohler et al. 2002; Perelli-Harris 2006; Kalmijn 2007).

Scholars commenting on marriage and fertility decline in ECE and the FSU often assert that deteriorating wages and growing unemployment are the primary causes (Heleniak 1995; Vannoy et al., 1999; Cartwright 2000; Kohler et al. 2002; Kohler and Kohler 2002; Sobotka et al. 2003; Buhler 2004; Perelli-Harris 2005; see also Kantorova 2004). Several analyses of the sharp decline in marriage rates in the former East Germany following German unification in 1989 cite economic crisis and uncertainty due to the loss of state welfare benefits and insecure employment as the causes (Eberstadt 1994; Adler 1997; Rudd 2000). Economic explanations for declining marriage and fertility also abound in political and media circles, at least in Russia (Zakharov 1999; Anderson 2002). Their appeal is so intuitive that Caldwell and Schindlmayr (2003) suggest many scholars downplayed family formation trends in former socialist countries during the 1990s on the assumption that any changes were just ephemeral responses to economic crises and would quickly reverse with the restoration of growth. Historical evidence suggests that, once conditions improve, fertility typically regains its precrisis level (see Ashton et al. 1984; Lee 1990; Anderson 2002). So, one way to assess the power of the economic explanation is to ask whether the demographic trends reversed once the economies of the former state socialist countries stabilized and resumed growth.

The economic crisis explanation is clearly wanting. Although the countries in the sample experienced a short-term decline in per capita GDP, all except Kyrgyzstan rebounded quite strongly, as is seen in figure 9.6. The turnaround came quickly in the three Central European countries, as well in Estonia: Growth resumed in the early 1990s and continued throughout the 2000s. Russia's economy stabilized in the mid-1990s, but growth did not really resume until after the August 1998 financial crisis. There is no evidence of a reversal in the signature family formation tendencies in these countries following the resumption of growth, and, if anything, the Czech Republic, Estonia, Hungary, and Poland, which experienced the earliest and most impressive economic growth, show the fewest signs of reversing demographic patterns. The delaying of marriage and childbearing took hold only after the recoveries had begun in most countries. The countries such as Armenia, Kyrgyzstan, and Russia that experienced the steepest declines in the initial phases of market transition also appear to have experienced the sharpest changes in family formation behavior. However, whether this is the case or not depends on whether absolute or relative decline in GDP is the measure of its extent. Moreover, the pattern holds mainly for marriage and fertility decline, not for delayed marriage and fertility or nonmarital childbearing.

If, as the economic crisis explanation implies, transition-related economic shocks were the driving force behind shifting family formation behaviors, then it follows that the demographic shifts should not have started before the

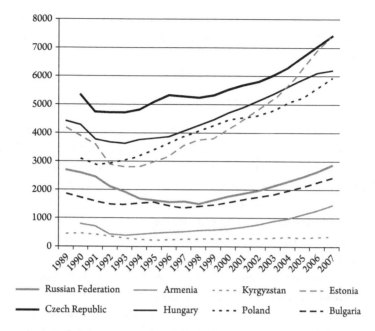

Figure 9.6 Per Capita Gross Domestic Product, $1,000s of constant 2000 Dollars.
Source: TransMONEE database, http://www.unicef-irc.org/databases/transmonee/

collapse of state socialism. The TransMONEE data do not afford much opportunity to address this question, but recent studies of individual countries have concluded that at least the decline in marriage and increase in cohabitation began earlier in the 1980s (Hoem et al. 2009; Gerber and Berman 2010).

Microlevel empirical studies of Russia cast further doubt on the economic explanation. Kohler and Kohler (2002) found no negative association between labor market uncertainty and fertility at the individual level; women or couples who were directly affected by the labor market crisis actually had a higher probability of having a child in the period from 1994 to 1996 than those who were affected to a lesser extent. In an analysis of 1994 microcensus data, Kharkova and Andreev (2000) conclude that economic crisis is not the primary cause of fertility decline in Russia. Consistent with this view, Gerber and Berman (2010) find that variables associated with economic well-being exhibit few associations with individual-level marriage and cohabitation entry rates in Russia from 1985 to 2000.

The former socialist countries are not unique in the persistence of demographic patterns that originated at the same time as extensive economic difficulties. In the United States, the recessionary "retreat from marriage" continued, albeit at a slower tempo, during the economic boom of the 1990s (Lichter, McLaughlin, and Ribar 2002). The persistence of shifts in family formation behavior, despite the economic recoveries in most former state socialist countries, suggests that something other than economic crisis must be the main driving factors.

Changing Norms/Culture: "Second Demographic Transition"

The main alternative explanation interprets the emergent demographic behaviors as the result of broad and long-term changes in norms and values that many other countries experienced in the mid-1960s through the end of the 1980s. In this period, first Northern and Western Europe, the United States, Australia, and New Zealand and eventually Southern Europe and Japan as well exhibited declining marriage rates, increasing age at first marriage, and more widespread nonmarital cohabitation (van de Kaa 1987; Qian and Preston 1993; Lesthaeghe 1995; Goldstein and Kenney 2001; Raymo 2003; Surkyn and Lesthaeghe 2004). Some link these trends to a broader "second demographic transition" (SDT) that also includes delayed childbearing, declining cohort fertility, increasing divorce and out-of-wedlock births, smaller household size, and growing proportions of single-parent families (van de Kaa 1987; Lesthaeghe 1995; Raymo 2003; Sobotka et al. 2003; Surkyn and Lesthaeghe 2004).

Most scholars who embrace the notion of a SDT see ideational changes (shifts in norms and value orientations) as the main factor behind these trends in demographic behavior. Beginning in the 1960s or 1970s, societies undergoing the transition began to turn away from traditional values and altruistic orientations in regard to children. They embraced alternative lifestyles, emphasizing individual fulfillment and self-expression rather than sacrifices to the family and the collective good, even encouraging what some have labeled "hedonistic individualism" (Mayer 2004). Young adults no longer felt bound by tradition to marry and have children; instead, they saw their lives as opportunities to realize their personal goals for self-expression and enjoyment (Preston 1986). These shifts may have been rooted in post-World War II economic prosperity, longer-term secularization, rising education levels, and the feminist movement (van de Kaa 1987; Inglehart 1990; Lesthaeghe 1995; Inglehart and Baker 2000; Lesthaeghe and Neels 2002). Whatever their origin, ideational shifts in the direction of this rather diverse set of norms make marriage and childbearing, associated with responsibility to others and sacrifices of individual freedom, less attractive.

The SDT perspective has become popular as an alternative to the economic crisis explanation of family formation patterns in postsocialist ECE and the FSU (Zakharov 1999, 2008; Lesthaeghe and Surkyn 2002; Sobotka et al. 2003; Frejka 2008; Philipov and Jasilioniene 2008; Sobotka 2008; Hoem et al. 2009; Gerber and Berman 2010). Its proponents observe that the cultural opening of state socialist societies began before the full-fledged collapse of their regimes, exposing their citizens to Western norms of individualism, sexual expression, feminism, and consumerism, as well as Western family formation models (Sobotka et al. 2003; Thornton and Philipov 2009; Gerber and Berman 2010). Perhaps state socialist institutions delayed the rise of the norms associated with the SDT, but socialist regimes could not forestall their diffusion for long.

The SDT perspective has its appeal, but it, too, has some potential problems. First, its proponents infer normative change from the behaviors it is meant to explain rather than demonstrate empirically that normative change occurred. Without long-term panel studies or repeated public opinion surveys using the same questions over a long period of time, it is impossible to directly measure shifts in attitudes. Some have tried doing so using comparative surveys (Lesthaeghe and Surkyn 2002), but the correspondence between the measures of these surveys and the underlying SDT concepts is inexact, and the surveys do not go back far enough to test for long-term aggregate shifts. Moreover, survey data on attitudes toward family formation in individual countries often suggest that early childbearing and multiple children remain the normative ideal (see, e.g., Kostowska et al. 2008 on Poland; Koytcheva and Philipov 2008 on Bulgaria; Stropnik and Sircelj 2008 on Slovenia).

Second, the structural, social, and economic conditions usually linked to the SDT in other parts of the world, such as increasing education levels, high female labor force participation, secularization, and economic prosperity, either obtained in most state socialist countries well before the late 1980s or did not apply at all at the time of the purported shift in values. For example, female labor force participation in Soviet-era Russia was among the highest in the world, and women maintained their presence in the workforce during the transition era, despite fears they would disproportionately suffer from job losses (Gerber and Mayorova 2006). Moreover, patterns of individual-level variation implied by the SDT approach do not always hold up well empirically in studies of the region: Among Russian women, higher education is associated with higher rates of marriage (Gerber and Berman 2010) and lower rates of nonmarital births (Perelli-Harris and Gerber 2011), whereas the SDT logic would predict that the most educated women are the most likely to reject traditional views of marriage and childbearing. Therefore, scholars who apply the SDT concept to ECE and the FSU usually claim it has taken on a particular, distinctive character there (Sobotka 2008). Yet the specific nature of that distinctive character is hard to pinpoint and could well vary from one country to the next, so the notion of normative change loses theoretical coherence and becomes more of a descriptive characterization.

Third, critics of the SDT theory often note that the discrete components of the syndrome of family behaviors linked to it rarely appear together in the same context. So it is with the former state socialist countries: Russia, for example, has declining fertility and marriage rates and rising divorce but also stable or declining average ages at first marriage and first births. Across countries, different measures of the social strength of marriage as an institution, such as the average age at first marriage, the total marriage rate (the percentage that ever marries), and divorce rate, are weakly correlated (Kalmijn 2007), which implies societies may not adhere to consistent norms about marriage as an institution. For these reasons, the SDT perspective, while promising, requires additional elaboration and empirical testing in the context of ECE and the FSU.

Politics: Changing Institutions and Policies

A third perspective on changes in family formation behavior in former socialist countries, developed most extensively by Tomas Frejka (2008; see also Kalmijn 2007; Sobotka 2008), emphasizes the changes in institutions and policies associated with the demise of state socialism. In terms of institutions, proponents of this view note that many aspects of state socialism promoted early marriage and childbearing. These include: guaranteed employment security throughout one's career, free health care and education (which reduce the costs of raising children), preferential treatment of families with children in housing allocation, state supported child care, generous maternity leave, and child benefits. For their part, state socialist authorities worried about low fertility rates in their countries during the 1960s and sought to bolster childbearing using a diverse array of changing policies, including discouraging the use of modern contraception in the 1970s and 1980s (Frejka 2008). The lack of access to contraception at a time when Western European countries were embracing the birth control pill is evident in high rates of both abortions and marriages entered due to pregnancy (Cartwright 2000). Also, the broader context of authoritarian control and mutual suspicion that pervaded these respective societies may have enhanced the importance of the nuclear family as an arena of solidarity and agency (Gerber and Berman 2010). In these concrete ways, state socialist institutions and policies thwarted any incipient tendency for postmaterialist values in regard to family formation by making the practices of early marriage and childbearing perfectly rational responses to the institutional and policy context.

The collapse of state socialism did not just initiate economic crisis and cultural change. More importantly, it destroyed key institutional and policy supports for early marriage and childbearing. The shift to a market-based economy entails the loss of a sense of economic security, as one can no longer count on lifelong employment at a relatively low but sufficient and stable wage. Just as young people embrace the consumerist values associated with the SDT, they also come face to face with the reality that they have no guarantees of being able to realize their material goals: Hard work, luck, and perhaps two-career partnership arrangements are necessary to sustain a desirable standard of living. Uncertainty is not so much the hallmark of economic crisis per se as it is endemic to market-based economic institutions in which governments withdraw from regulating the economy and the myriad forms of state support for childbearing and the nuclear family recede. Consumerism and individualism made little sense in the low-risk but also low-reward environment of the state socialist economy, but under market conditions not only do individuals have to rely on themselves and their networks to obtain goods and services previously provided by the state, they also have new freedoms and opportunities to realize their individualistic material and expressive goals. A rational person facing these incipient uncertainties will hesitate before entering into the type of long-term commitments that marriage and childbearing entail: In these concrete circumstances of spiraling inequality in life chances, it becomes more sensible to cohabit before legally marrying and to wait to have children until one can assess a partner's career trajectory.

The political-institutional perspective does not so much reject the economic crisis and normative change arguments as contextualize them and provide a deeper explanation of how specific aspects of the postsocialist experience interacted with economic crisis and helped produce the normative changes associated with declining marriage, increasing nonmarital cohabitation, and lower fertility. As Wang and Su remind us in chapter 10 by demonstrating the persistence of active economic interventions and aggressive social policies in the contemporary Chinese state, it is an oversimplification to describe the postsocialist condition as inevitably involving the demolition of socialist-era institutions and policies. Nonetheless, the Eastern European and most former Soviet countries all have undertaken, albeit to varying degrees, precisely such a process of curtailing state involvement in the economy and society. Therefore, the political-institutional perspective offers an attractive integrating theoretical framework for understanding changing family formation patterns in these countries, one that helps account for some of the anomalies that arise in relation to the economic crisis and SDT perspectives.

The political/institutional perspective also effectively links developments in the realm of family formation behaviors to two of the larger themes running throughout the other contributions to this volume: the retreat of the state from the management of economic and social life and the attendant growth of socioeconomic inequalities. In the introductory chapter to this volume, Nina

Bandelj and Dorothy J. Solinger describe how the withdrawal of state regulation of the economy yielded increased inequality throughout the formerly socialist world. In chapter 7, Akos Rona-Tas illustrates how the shift from state-based to private regulation of credit produces an alternative form of social control. The political-institutional explanation for changing family formation patterns draws attention to the possible repercussions of declining state intervention and growing inequality in other, noneconomic realms of social life.

Despite its promise, the political-institutional theory has not been systematically tested using empirical data. Developing and applying suitable empirical assessments is an important item on the agenda for understanding changes in family formation in contemporary ECE and the FSU. I propose some ideas for such assessments in the conclusion of this chapter.

Consequences

Although no decisive conclusions have yet been reached, most researchers examining family formation processes in the former state socialist world now believe that the revolutionary shifts in marriage and childbearing brought on by regime changes are likely to remain in place for the foreseeable future rather than reverse in response to improvements in the economy. Governments in the region have recently introduced policies to enhance fertility, such as Russia's maternity capital benefits, but experience shows that these policies have limited long-term effects. If so, what are the likely economic, political, and social consequences? Although few researchers have studied this topic extensively, some fairly intuitive repercussions can readily be proposed.

Most obviously, continuing low fertility rates—which are closely related to low rates of marriage—will likely cause the populations of these countries to shrink. Although rising mortality rates in such countries as Russia have received more media attention, declining fertility affects population size more than increasing mortality does (Anderson 2002). Is shrinking population size necessarily a negative development? After all, European countries such as Italy, Spain, and Germany have experienced very low fertility (TFRs below 1.5) for many years running. Certainly, many governments think that shrinking populations are a cause for concern. In his 2006 presidential address, Vladimir Putin declared the demographic crisis the country's "most acute" problem. Russian officials are, of course, particularly worried about staffing the country's large military and populating its extensive territory, especially in the face of rapid population growth in China and instability in Central Asia. Countries without these concerns may have less to fear, but shrinking populations are generally thought to be a source of economic problems. A trend toward smaller cohorts of young workers would exert downward pressure on economic growth simply because there would be fewer people producing output. In the postindustrial age, that relationship may not be as strong as it was in prior eras, but it nevertheless is a legitimate source of concern. Another potentially serious complication is that the rapid shrinking of younger cohorts implies a distorted age structure as those born in the 1990s and after enter their working years: At that point, the ratio of dependents (retirees and children) to working adults will be quite high, which is likely to produce obvious economic and political challenges. Shrinking populations and growing dependency ratios will stimulate political debates over topics as diverse as mandatory military service, immigration and naturalization policies, retirement ages and benefits, and the priorities of the welfare state.

Nonmarital childbearing is generally associated with economic deprivation in the United States, and some early studies of countries such as Russia identify single-mother households as a key factor associated with poverty (see Perelli-Harris and Gerber 2011). If this trend continues, it is possible that family structure will come to play an ever-greater role in the socioeconomic stratification of individuals and households in former socialist countries.

Finally, the rise of smaller families, often based on cohabiting relationships rather than marriage, may gradually erode the social fabric of these societies. State socialism, with its low levels of generalized trust and endemic shortages, reinforced a historically rooted social structure based on tightly defined social networks (see, e.g., Ledeneva 1998). Family relationships served as the single most important basis for network ties. As families shrink in size and become less stable, they may not perform this function as well. Fewer marriages and children mean fewer in-laws, siblings, cousins, and uncles. Over time, the changes in family formation behavior may exert subtle but growing pressure on society to forge new bases for solidaristic attachments, perhaps even encouraging citizens to participate more in voluntary associations. Alternatively, a weakening of social networks could produce a protracted and ugly deterioration of social structure. Assuming that networks are undermined, whether and how they will be replaced will probably vary from country to country depending on economic, cultural, and political factors.

Conclusion

Throughout the former socialist world rates of marriage entry and childbearing have declined, and these events tend to take place at later ages than they did under socialism. Nonmarital cohabitation and childbearing have also become more widespread. Although the pace and timing of these changes vary across

ECE and the FSU, their basic direction is similar enough to conclude that some common force is at work. Economic crisis and normative change have been proposed as playing just such a role. However, the end of severe economic problems associated with the market transition—recession, unemployment, inflation—has not led to a restoration of socialist-era family formation behaviors, and it is hard to account for the precise timing of the putative normative shifts based on the structural factors usually associated with them.

The political-institutional explanation for the changes in family formation behavior offers an attractive alternative: It accounts for the precise timing of the changes in family formation behavior, foregrounds the distinctive institutional context of postsocialism, and incorporates both economic and cultural reasoning. This explanation emphasizes the myriad ways that state socialist institutions and policies created material and normative incentives for nearly universal marriage and childbearing. However, the political-institutional explanation has only recently been proposed, which perhaps reflects the lack of communication between demographers and researchers who study the political and economic dimensions of postsocialism, and it has not been subject to a rigorous empirical test. What might such a test entail?

Institutional and policy changes vary at the macro level. While different groups of residents in a country (or a region, to the extent that regional or local governments make relevant policies) may respond differently to the introduction of new institutions and policies, they all experience essentially the same policy context. Thus, the logical analytical strategy for testing whether changes in institutions and policies affect family formation behaviors in the proposed manner is to conduct macrolevel pooled time-series analyses that examine how national-level variables are related over time in the broad ECE and FSU regions.

Case studies of single countries using individual-level data are not well suited to testing the political-institutional perspective on changing family formation behaviors, precisely because the institutional and policy changes affect all the residents within the country and vary across a single dimension, time. Yet, case studies have been the mainstay of demographic analyses of former socialist countries. A pooled time-series analysis of multiple ECE and FSU countries can capitalize on cross-country variations in the timing and extent of reforms and policy changes.

A recent paper takes a promising first step in the direction of such an analysis (Billingsley 2010). Seeking to adjudicate between the economic crisis and SDT explanations by associating fertility decline (stopping births altogether) with the former and postponement with the latter, the author identifies three sets of ECE and FSU countries experiencing early postponement of births, early stopping of births followed by postponement, and decline with little or no postponement, respectively. Billingsley estimates pooled time-series regressions analyzing the associations among four economic measures and age-specific birthrates within each group of countries, finding a complex and somewhat contradictory pattern of economic effects. She does not include measures of changes in norms, institutions, or policies in the analysis.

A thorough and convincing test of the political-institutional perspective and its alternatives would include precisely such measures, along with the economic variables. Moreover, a range of dependent variables should be analyzed: marriage and cohabitation entry, age at first marriage, nonmarital childbearing rates, birth rates by parity, and divorce. The most immediate challenge to conducting these types of analyses is that there are few of the necessary measures beyond standard indices of macroeconomic performance and more controversial measures of economic and political liberalization. Data sets with time-varying measures of the extent of market reforms, democratization, social conflict, uncertainty, inequality, family-related norms, policies supporting childbearing and marriage (such as maternity leaves, childbearing and marriage subsidies, and divorce regulations), the availability of contraception, the role of family versus voluntary associations in social capital formation, and other related variables must be painstakingly constructed by researchers with detailed knowledge of the countries in question. In this capacity, individual-level survey data can also play a role: Previous cross-sectional attitude surveys and both recent and future retrospective studies of family formation can be used to derive time-varying measures of attitude changes and of appropriate dependent variables. Once reasonable measures have been obtained, the analysis will also have to confront the methodological challenges posed by endogeneity, unobserved heterogeneity, multicollinearity, nonstationarity, and serial autocorrelation that typically plague pooled time-series analyses. However, a range of econometric techniques is available for this purpose.

A tremendous amount of data collection and statistical analysis work is required for observers to be in a position to systematically test the validity of the political-institutional perspective on the sweeping changes in family formation behavior that the former socialist countries of ECE and the FSU have experienced in the last 20 years. Most likely, this enterprise will require the collaboration of a team of experts on the respective countries.

Acknowledgments

The author thanks Barbara Heyns and the editors for helpful suggestions. Address correspondence to: tgerber@ssc.wisc.edu.

References

Adler, Marina A. 1997. "Social Change and Declines in Marriage and Fertility in Eastern Germany." *Journal of Marriage and the Family* 59:37–49.

Anderson, Barbara A. 2002. "Russia Faces Depopulation? Dynamics of Population Decline." *Population and Environment* 23.

Ashton, Basil, Kenneth Hill, Alan Piazza, and Robin Zeitz. 1984. "Famine in China in 1958–61." *Population and Development Review* 10:613–645.

Billingsley, Sunnee. 2010. "The Post-Communist Fertility Puzzle." *Population Research and Policy Review* 29:193–231.

Buhler, Christoph. 2004. "Additional Work, Family Agriculture, and the Birth of a First or a Second Child in Russia at the Beginning of the 1990s." *Population Research and Policy Review* 23:259–89.

Caldwell, John C. and Thomas Schindlmayr. 2003. "Explanations of the Fertility Crisis in Modern Societies: A Search for Commonalities." *Population Studies* 57:241–263.

Cartwright, Kimberly. 2000. "Shotgun Weddings and the Meaning of Marriage in Russia: An Event History Analysis." *History of the Family* 5:1–23.

Coale, Ansley J. 1992. "Age of Entry into Marriage and the Date of the Initiation of Voluntary Birth Control." *Demography* 29:333–341.

Coale, Ansley J., Barbara Anderson, and Erna Haerm. 1979. *Human Fertility in Russia since the Nineteenth Century.* Princeton, N.J.: Princeton University Press.

Dommaraju, Premchand and Victor Agadjanian. 2008. "Nuptiality in Soviet and Post-Soviet Central Asia." *Asian Population Studies* 4:195–213.

Easterlin, Richard A. 1976. "The Conflict between Aspirations and Resources." *Population and Development Review* 2:417–425.

Eberstadt, Nicholas. 1994. "Demographic Shocks after Communism: Eastern Germany, 1989–93." *Population and Development Review* 20:137–152.

Frejka, Tomas. 2008. "Determinants of Family Formation and Childbearing during the Societal Transition in Central and Eastern Europe." *Demographic Research* 19:139–170.

Gerber, Theodore P. and Danielle Berman. 2010. "Entry to Marriage and Cohabitation in Russia, 1985–2000: Trends, Correlates, and Implications for the Second Demographic Transition." *European Journal of Population* 26:3–31.

Gerber, Theodore P. and Olga Mayorova. 2006. "Dynamic Gender Differences in a Post-Socialist Labor Market: Russia, 1991–1997." *Social Forces* 84:2047–2075.

Goldscheider, Francis K. and Linda J. Waite. 1986. "Sex Differences in the Entry into Marriage." *American Journal of Sociology* 92:91–109.

Goldstein, Joshua R. and Catherine T. Kenney. 2001. "Marriage Delayed or Marriage Forgone? New Cohort Forecasts of First Marriage for US Women." *American Sociological Review* 66:506–519.

Hajnal, John. 1965. "European Marriage Patterns in Perspective." In *Population in History: Essays in Historical Demography,* D. V. Glass and D.E.C. Eversley, eds., 101–143. Chicago: Aldine.

Heleniak, Timothy. 1995. "Economic Transition and Demographic Change in Russia, 1989–1995." *Post-Soviet Geography* 36:446–458.

Hoem, Jan M., Dora Kostova, Aiva Jasilioniene, and Cornelia Muresan. 2009. "Traces of the Second Demographic Transition in Central and Eastern Europe: Union Formation as a Demographic Manifestation." *European Journal of Population* 25:239–255.

Hollander, D. 1997. " In Post-Soviet Russia, Fertility Is on the Decline; Marriage and Childbearing Occurring Earlier." *Family Planning Perspectives* 29:92–94.

Inglehart, Ronald. 1990. *Culture Shift in Advanced Industrial Society.* Princeton, N.J.: Princeton University Press.

Inglehart, Ronald and Wayne E. Baker. 2000. "Modernization, Cultural Change, and the Persistence of Traditional Values." *American Sociological Review* 65:19–51.

Kalmijn, Matthijs. 2007. "Explaining Cross-National Differences in Marriage, Cohabitation, and Divorce in Europe, 1990–2000." *Population Studies* 61:243–263.

Kantorova, Vladimira. 2004. "Education and Entry into Motherhood: The Czech Republic during State Socialism and the Transition Period (1970–1997)." *Demographic Research* special collection 3, article 10.

Kharkova, Tatiana L. and Evgueny M. Avdeev. 2000. "Did the Economic Crisis Cause the Fertility Decline in Russia? Evidence from the 1994 Microcensus." *European Journal of Population* 16:211–233.

Kohler, Hans-Peter, Francesco C. Billari, and Jose Antonio Ortega. 2002. "The Emergence of Lowest-Low Fertility in Europe during the 1990s." *Population and Development Review* 28:641–680.

Kohler, Hans-Peter and Iliana Kohler. 2002. "Fertility Decline in Russia in the Early and Mid 1990s: The Role of Uncertainty and Labor Market Crises." *European Journal of Population* 18:233–262.

Kostowska, Irena, Janina Jozwiak, Anna Matysiak, and Anna Baranowska. 2008. "Poland: Fertility Decline as a Response to Profound Societal and Labour Market Changes?" *Demographic Research* 19:795–854.

Koytcheva, Elena and Dimiter Philipov. 2008. "Bulgaria: Ethnic Differentials in Rapidly Declining Fertility." *Demographic Research.* 19:361–402.

Ledeneva, Alena. 1998. *Russia's Economy of Favours: Blat, Networking, and Informal Exchange.* Cambridge, U.K.: Cambridge University Press.

Lee, Ronald. 1990. "The Demographic Response to Economic Crisis in Historical and Contemporary Populations." *Population Bulletin of the United Nations* 20:1–15.

Lesthaeghe, Ron. 1995. "The Second Demographic Transition in Western Countries: An Interpretation." In *Gender and Family Change in Industrialized Countries*, Karen Oppenheim Mason and An-Magritt Jensen, eds., 17–62. Oxford, U.K.: Clarendon.

Lesthaeghe, Ron and K. Neels. 2002. "From the First to the Second Demographic Transition: An Interpretation of the Spatial Continuity of Demographic Innovation in France, Belgium and Switzerland." *European Journal of Population* 18:325–360.

Lesthaeghe, Ron and Johan Surkyn. 2002. "New Forms of Household Formation in Central and Eastern Europe: Are They Related to Newly Emerging Value Orientations?" *UNECE, Economic Survey of Europe* 1:197–216.

Lichter, Daniel T., Diane K. McLaughlin, and David C. Ribar. 2002. "Economic Restructuring and the Retreat from Marriage." *Social Science Research* 31:230–256.

Lichter, Daniel T., Felicia B. LeClere, and Diane K. McLaughlin. 1991. "Local Marriage Markets and the Marital Behavior of Black and White Women." *American Journal of Sociology* 96:843–867.

Lloyd, Kim M. and Scott J. South. 1996. "Contextual Influences on Young Men's Transition to First Marriage." *Social Forces* 4:1097–1119.

Mayer, Karl Ulrich. 2004. "Whose Lives? How History, Societies, and Institutions Define and Shape Life Courses." *Research in Human Development* 1:167–187.

Oppenheimer, Valerie Kincade, Matthijs Kalmijn, and Nelson Lim. 1997. "Men's Career Development and Marriage Timing during a Period of Rising Inequality." *Demography* 34:311–330.

Palloni, Alberto, Kenneth Hill, and Guido Pinto Aguirre. 1996. "Economic Swings and Demographic Change in the History of Latin America." *Population Studies* 50:105–132.

Perelli-Harris, Brienna. 2005. "The Path to Lowest-Low Fertility in Ukraine," *Population Studies* 59:55–70.

———. 2006. "The Influence of Informal Work and Subjective Well-Being on Childbearing in Post-Soviet Russia." *Population and Development Review.* 32:729–753.

Perelli-Harris, Brienna and Theodore P. Gerber. 2011. "Nonmarital Childbearing in Russia: Second Demographic Transition or Pattern of Disadvantage?" *Demography* 48:371–342.

Philipov, Dimiter and Aiva Jasilioniene. 2008. "Union Formation and Fertility in Bulgaria and Russia: A Life Table Description of Recent Trends." *Demographic Research* 19:2057–2114.

Preston, Samuel H. 1986. "Changing Values and Falling Birth Rates." *Population and Development Review* 12, Supplement: Below-Replacement Fertility in Industrial Societies: Causes, Consequences, Policies, 176–195.

Qian, Zhenchao and Samuel H. Preston. 1993. "Changes in American Marriage, 1972 to 1987: Availability and Forces of Attraction by Age and Education." *American Sociological Review* 58:482–495.

Raymo, James M. 2003. "Educational Attainment and the Transition to First Marriage among Japanese Women." *Demography* 48:83–103.

Rudd, Elizabeth C. 2000. "Reconceptualizing Gender in Postsocialist Transformation." *Gender & Society* 14:517–539.

Scherbov, Sergei and Harriet Van Vianen. 2001. "Marriage and Fertility in Russia of Women Born between 1900 and 1960: A Cohort Analysis." *European Journal of Population* 17:281–294.

Sobotka, Tomas. 2008. "The Diverse Faces of the Second Demographic Transition in Europe." *Demographic Research* 19:171–224.

Sobotka, Tomas, Krystof Zeman, and Vladimira Kantorova. 2003. "Demographic Shifts in the Czech Republic after 1989: A Second Demographic Transition View." *European Journal of Population* 19:249–277.

Stropnik, Nada and Milivoja Sircelj. 2008. "Slovenia: Generous Family Policy without Evidence of Any Fertility Impact." *Demographic Research* 19:1019–1058.

Surkyn, Johan and Ron Lesthaeghe. 2004. "Value Orientations and the Second Demographic Transition (SDT) in Northern, Western, and Southern Europe: An Update." *Demographic Research*, special collection 3, article 3.

Sweeney, Megan M. 2002. "Two Decades of Family Change: The Shifting Economic Foundations of Marriage." *American Sociological Review* 67:132–147.

Thornton, Arland and Dimiter Philipov. 2009. "Sweeping Changes in Marriage, Cohabitation and Childbearing in Central and Eastern Europe: New Insights from the Developmental Idealism Framework." *European Journal of Population* 25:123–156.

Van de Kaa, D. J. 1987. "Europe's Second Demographic Transition." *Population Bulletin* 42:1–57.

Vannoy, Dana, Natalia Rimashevskaya, Lisa Cubbins, Marina Malysheva, Elena Meshterkina, and Marina Pisklakova. 1999. *Marriages in Russia: Couples during the Economic Transition.* Westport, Conn.: Praeger Publishers.

Zakharov, Sergei. 1999. "Fertility, Nuptiality, and Family Planning in Russia: Problems and Prospects." In *Population under Duress: The Geodemography of Post-Soviet Russia,* George J. Demko, Grigory Ioffe, and Zhanna Zayonchkovskaya, eds. 41–57. Boulder, Colo.: Westview Press.

———. 2008. "Russian Federation from the First to the Second Demographic Transition." *Demographic Research* 19: 907–972.

10

Communist Resilience

Institutional Adaptations in Post-Tiananmen China

WANG FENG AND YANG SU

On June 4, 2009, an emblematic scene from Tiananmen Square was broadcast to a world audience. On the twentieth anniversary of the 1989 bloody crackdown against student protests, the journalists and visitors who were at the square encountered neither protests nor signs of commemoration; instead they saw only desperate-looking groups of well-dressed men, each holding an umbrella. One could quickly discern that these middle-aged men were undercover government security agents as they interceded to determine who could enter the square and what was allowed to occur there. These umbrellas, supposedly meant to shield the bright summer sunshine, were actually shields that could be used to block any attempt to photograph the agents. These interactions between journalists and the plain-clothed security men were almost humorous, a far cry from the images of tanks, blood, and death that marked the night 20 years ago.[1]

A similar sense of quiet and wariness prevailed at this spot on past anniversaries. Political dissidents who had demonstrated 20 years earlier were, as of 2009, mostly in jail or in exile. College students, the main force of those demonstrations, generally shifted their attention to careers in business and, ironically, became among the most ardent of the regime's supporters. The 20 years following the protests would never again see young Chinese wage open protest against the regime, save their occasional outbursts of nationalistic zeal. The most visible public defiance of those two decades came from the Falungong religious cult, whose groups of practitioners within China were severely diminished by harsh waves of suppression. On sensitive occasions such as the anniversaries of June 4, initial deployments of large numbers of uniformed soldiers gave way over time to more subtle forms of protest management.

The scene of the umbrella-holding men signaled an increasing professional-ism within the corps and growing confidence in the country's mandate as the regime persisted in the wake of the collapse of socialist states elsewhere. The posting of barely disguised security personnel was also a testimonial to insti-tutional changes in state-society relations. Many factors have contributed to the resilience of the Chinese communist state, which, as of 2009, had clearly eluded what seemed a looming political crisis brought on by the events in 1989 (Goldstone 1995). These changes include the Communist Party's co-opting of private business people into the party (Tsai 2007), improved governance and administrative reforms (Yang 2004), and, most notably, a booming economy that has continued to raise the living standards of the population despite the lack of democratic reforms (Pei 2006) and irrespective of mounting inequality (Riskin et al. 2001).

In this chapter, we explore three types of institutional change introduced since 1989 and review specific state adaptations that have strengthened the resilience of Chinese communist rule. First, echoing the analyses made by Barry Naughton and Yasheng Huang in chapters 6 and 8 of this volume, respectively, we document a renewed state dominance in the economy that, we argue, has served as the foundation for continued state control not only over the economy but also over society. Second, we discuss how this political-economic arrangement has contributed to one of the most important social changes in China, namely, rising inequality. This new, post-1989 political-eco-nomic order has served as a structural basis for that inequality. At the same time, that arrangement has also allowed the Chinese state to reclaim the role of redistributor, a role it had begun to relinquish as the state plan initially faded, thereby lending enhanced legitimacy to the regime. Third, we examine changes in the state's methods for managing public protests that break out in response to inequality and related injustices. These changes have contributed to the stability of communist rule in the 20 years since tanks left Tiananmen Square in the early summer of 1989.

The Economy: Growing Out of the Plan, But Not Away From the State

A critical development that lies at the heart of the ongoing resilience of Chinese communist rule has been the spectacular economic growth of the years fol-lowing 1989, especially in the first decade of the twenty-first century, growth that came about as a result of the underappreciated role of the state.

On September 5, 2009, the main story covered by every major Chinese news outlet was that, in 2008, for the first time in history, the combined profit of China's largest 500 companies exceeded that of the 500 largest firms in the United States; moreover, it even surpassed that of the 500 largest companies in the world.[2] Chinese corporations' superior performance came in part on the heels of the drastic downturn in profits experienced by American businesses, which suffered severely from the US-led global economic crisis of those years. This much-reported news item certainly amounts to a stunning demonstration of the rising might of the Chinese economy; at the same time, it also speaks volumes about the prominent role of state ownership in an economy that is often mischaracterized as being in a transition toward extensive privatization.

This news of the re-emergence of the state's role in the economy appeared after three decades of economic reform beginning in the late 1970s. The reforms led China away from the planned economy model and have significantly increased the share of the non state-owned sectors. The Chinese economy, in Barry Naughton's words, had "grown out" of the socialist plan by the early 1990s (Naughton 1996). Yet, in the decade following, a different trend emerged that has seen the economy moving away from market reforms based on private property rights (see Huang 2008 and in chapter 8 of this volume). There has been a trend of expanded influence of the Chinese state over the economy, not only in terms of policies and regulations but also in its actual control over firms' ownership.

Changing urban employment patterns illustrate how the state has, if anything, expanded its dominance over the economy. As first glance, figure 10.1 appears to portray precipitous declines in employment in both the state- and collectively owned sectors since the early 1990s, especially starting in the mid-1990s. Between 1995 and 2004, in just one decade, the share of urban employees in the state sector was reduced by more than half, from constituting about 60 percent to 25 percent, an astonishing accomplishment if the goal was to achieve the withering of the hand of the state. In terms of absolute numbers, public employment plummeted from 126 million in 1995 down to 67.1 million in 2004, a whopping reduction of more than 45 million in less than a decade.

The change was especially drastic in the late 1990s, when in just the three years from 1997 to 2000, 20 million employees disappeared from the payrolls of the so-called public sector. Where did they go? Some were laid off, and some were forced to retire early, but that is only part of the overall story. Many former state employees ended up in one of three other categories: in the cooperative economy, in a limited liability company, or in shareholding corporations. The first two categories emerged in the official statistical yearbooks only after 1997, and by 1998, the three groupings together comprised 6.2 million workers; by 2004, they accounted for 16.28 million people; and by 2008, they amounted to a total of 23.58 million employees. The numbers in the third category, the shareholding corporations, doubled within one decade, from 4.1 million in

Figure 10.1 Divergent Paths in Urban Employment, 1978 to 2008. Source: China
Statistical Yearbook 2005/2008, table 5.4.

1998 to 8.4 million in 2008. In total, as figure 10.1 demonstrates, these three
categories were employing more than 30 million people by 2008. A significant
share of those 45 million workers who disappeared from the state-owned sector after the mid-1990s, therefore, may well have ended up being absorbed into
these three newly created categories. Moreover, it was these categories, along
with the private sector, that absorbed a large share of the new entrants to the
labor market.

The big question, then, becomes, are the firms in these newly created categories private, or are they state-owned? The three categories, especially the
two that were newly created in the wake of the enterprise reforms of the late
1990s, are by no means outside the state's aegis. To the contrary, many of them
are previously state-owned companies now operating under a new form of
governance but remaining under the state's control, while others are jointly
owned by the state and private capital. An analysis of ownership restructuring among China's state-owned industrial enterprises in 1998 shows that only
about one-quarter of the more than 4,000 enterprises that were restructured
became privately or foreign-owned, with the rest remaining in the hands of the
state. In more than 80 percent of the restructured enterprises, the government
was involved in selecting the chief executive officer (Lin and Zhu 2001). One
study conducted in 2001 found that 70 percent of 6,275 large- and medium-
sized restructured state-owned enterprises had officials who were previously
members of their firms' Communist Party committee serving as the directors
of the board (Pei 2006:31).

Many of the restructured economic organizations, in other words, were reorganized in line with what David Stark (1996) labeled recombinant property rights arrangements, based on his studies of the Hungarian transitional economy. If we add up the number of Chinese employees working in what is called the public economy as of 2008, that is, in state-owned and -controlled or -participating organizations (including employees in state, collective, cooperative, joint ownership, limited liability, and shareholding companies), we find that they total 103.5 million. The number of employees in private, foreign-owned, and Hong Kong and Macao-invested firms, as well as self-employed urban laborers came to almost the same total, or 103.6 million in that same year. So in urban China, a full one-half of the labor force in 2008 was still under the direct or indirect control of the state.[3] As Huang explains in chapter 8 of this volume, the conclusion is similar if one uses a different measure, industrial output. These newly emerged sectors that are under the control of the state, along with the traditional state-owned sector, occupy the most advantageous position in the postreform Chinese economy, both in terms of capital endowment and in revenue. Leading the list of the 500 largest Chinese companies in 2008 are firms that are either entirely owned or controlled by the Chinese state. State-owned and -controlled companies represented more than 60 percent of these top 500 corporations. The largest 20 on the list are all state-owned companies with monopoly status.

Moreover, in the last two decades and especially in the 2000s, the economic power of the Chinese state has risen at a speed that has far outpaced its impressive economic growth. As figure 10.2 (using numbers from China's National Bureau of Statistics) shows, over the last decade the year-to-year growth rate of government revenue constantly exceeded the rate of growth of GDP per capita. The pattern remains the same if we compare the growth rate of taxes to that of GDP, with the former constantly exceeding the latter. In the same figure, we use the lowest two lines to represent the household income for the urban and rural areas respectively, and we can see that, between 1998 and 2008, unadjusted for inflation, China's GDP per capita grew 3.34 times, a rate greater than per capita household income either in urban (2.91 times) or in rural areas (2.20 times). Yet government revenue increased in the same period at a rate of 6.21 and taxes at a rate of 5.85, far outpacing the growth of the economy. The relative shift between state and individual economic power is even more dramatic when the comparison is with the rise in personal incomes. In a decade's time, the share of government revenue as a proportion of the total GDP almost doubled, from 11.7 percent in 1998 to 20.4 percent in 2008. These numbers depict a clear shift of economic resources toward the hands of the government during China's recent economic boom.[4]

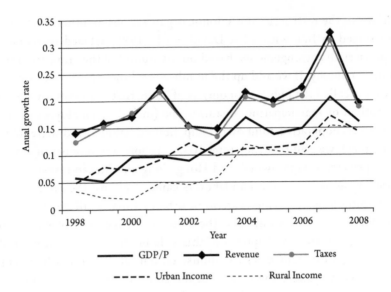

Figure 10.2 Changes in Gross Domestic Product per Capita, Government Revenue, Taxes, and Household Income, China, 1998 to 2008. Source: China Statistical Yearbook 2009, various tables.

Growth with Inequality

What have been the social consequences of such rapid growth in this state-dominated economy? Rising economic inequality has been one of the most prominent among them. Over a relatively short period, even as economic growth was lifting perhaps as many as 200 million Chinese people out of poverty, the state reversed itself from being one of the most egalitarian to one of the most unequal societies in the world, experiencing a rate of increase in inequality unsurpassed in recent world history (Riskin, Zhao and Li 2001; Wang 2008; Davis and Wang 2009).

The state has been directly responsible for what has amounted to an ever-enlarging gap between the haves and the have-nots. For the state continues to monopolize key economic sectors, and a substantial increase in the rate of state revenue extraction has left a steadily smaller share of the expanding economy for individual households, especially those located away from the bureaucratic power center. As a result, employees in the large state sector are increasingly doing better than those in most of the private sector.

Furthermore, the state's prominent role also helps shape the way people perceive the inequality, to the effect of damping social discontent. First, employees in the state sector, who are most closely related to state power and who are on the winner's side of the equation, tend to consider their advantage to be deserving and justified, and their numbers have increased along with the expansion of the state. Second, decades ago the state created and perpetuated economic and social categories, thereby serving to distinguish urban, rural, and migrant populations from one another and to differentiate employees along the lines of industrial sectors and work units. These state-devised "boundaries and categories" have made it more likely that individuals will engage in comparisons of their economic status within their own boundaries and categories and avoid a much more acute sense of relative deprivation had cross-boundary comparisons been pervasive (Wang 2008). Since the 1950s, there has always been much less inequality within such groupings than within the population at large. A third measure with the same result is that welfare spending by the government has not only helped to reduce regional and individual inequalities but also to portray an image of a government that cares.

Employees working in organizations belonging to the state-monopolized sectors receive a large share of the rent that the state extracts and therefore enjoy an income level much higher than others. In 2008, urban employees in state-owned work organizations received the highest average earnings of any occupational group, at 30,287 yuan per annum, versus 18,103 yuan for those in collectively owned enterprises, and 28,552 yuan for those in other ownership forms. Moreover, between 1996, the year when massive layoffs in state-owned enterprises spread, and 2008, the latest year for which official statistics are available, employees in state-owned work organizations in urban China received a 4.9-fold increase in earnings, versus the 4.2 and 3.4 increase, respectively, in the other two categories.[5]

Employees in particular jobs in the state-monopolized sectors were especially privileged. In 2005, at the Bank of China, for instance, the average annual income for the more than 200,000 employees was 88,548 yuan, an amount more than five times the average for all state employees in that year. In two state-controlled companies that generate electricity, Datang and Huanneng, the average annual income was as high as 103,500 and 105,828 yuan, respectively, and in the state-controlled telecommunications firm China Mobile, average annual income amounted to as much as 143,292 yuan that year (Wang 2008:151). At the same time, the state also makes arrangements to avoid large income disparities within sectors, organizations, or work units. Intraorganization income distribution is relatively egalitarian (Wang 2008).

As a result of this combination of between-category inequality and within-category equality, China's rapidly rising overall level of inequality has not had the psychological effect on Chinese citizens that it might have in places where an increase in inequality has not followed such a pattern, such as the countries of postsocialist Europe (Bandelj and Mahutga 2010). In a 2004 national survey, for instance, respondents were asked to assess the degree of inequality they perceived in the country, as well as in their own work organizations, neighborhoods, and local areas generally. The share of urban respondents who perceived their workplaces' inequality as especially high was only one-third of the percentage of those who believed that inequality was too great across the country as a whole, 14.7 versus 44.5 percent; the percentage of those who rated the degree of inequality in their workplaces as moderate was more than twice as high as the percentage of those who judged this to be the case for the whole country, 37.3 versus 15.9 percent, respectively (Wang 2008:167).

A major reason for the relatively equal income distribution within work organizations is the hybrid nature of the property rights arrangement in many firms, such that the state still controls these organizations and has a say in their salary distributions. While the overall level of inequality nationwide has risen sharply, many urban residents do not experience that level in their own immediate vicinity. A perception of vast inequality at the national level, therefore, has not translated into localized resentment, which explains, in part, why rising inequality has not, as widely expected, served as the basis for social unrest.

The increasing concentration of economic resources in the hands of the government has also enabled the state to play an active role as a benevolent redistributor and so to mitigate the public's perception of inequality. The growth of resources in the hands of the state has allowed it to expand its investment in previously neglected areas, such as social welfare spending. Over the two decades after 1989 and especially in the first decade of the new century, the government also devoted new investment to infrastructure, by launching a number of high-profile projects. These programs include the year 2000's "Develop the West" program, which allocated a large portion of state investment funds to the poverty-stricken Northwest. Other examples include the establishment of a minimum livelihood guarantee program (*zuidi shenghuo baozhang* or *dibao*) first for impoverished urban and then for extremely poor rural households; the elimination of the agricultural tax; the initiation of subsidies for compulsory schooling in rural areas; and, eventually, the creation of a national basic health insurance and an old-age social security scheme.

These expenditures and programs have helped craft an image of the central government as a benevolent redistributor, thereby garnering broad support both for the reform program as a whole and for the Chinese government itself (Han and Whyte 2009; Whyte 2010). Simultaneously, these efforts fuel a continuing public expectation that the state should play a major role in the economy and in the provision of social welfare. As shown in table 10.1, a 2004 national survey of the perceptions of distributive justice in China[6] indicated that, while the sentiment favoring state intervention was strong, with 58 and 35 percent, respectively, of the survey respondents agreeing with the statements that the state has a responsibility for reducing income inequality and for capping the highest income levels, the public expectation that the state ought to guarantee basic livelihood is even higher. Seventy-seven percent of the respondents agreed that the government should provide jobs for those who want to work; 79 percent believed that it is the state's duty to provide a minimum livelihood guarantee. Thus, two and half decades after the start of China's economic reforms, more than a decade after the end of the "iron rice bowl" employment system, and more than five years after the massive layoff of employees in state-owned enterprises, an overwhelming majority of Chinese citizens still had hopes that the state would be responsible for employment.

Moreover, only a small proportion of Chinese citizens believed that such areas of basic social and economic guarantees as health care, support for the elderly, and elementary education are wholly or even mostly their own responsibilities. As shown in the lower panel of table 10.1, in the same 2004 national survey, only 19 percent of respondents believed that health care was mostly or wholly an individual responsibility, while 25 percent took this stand with

Table 10.1 **Public Expectation of State's Role and Responsibilities, China, 2004**

	State Role			
	Reducing Income Inequality	Regulating Top Income	Providing Work for All	Ensuring Minimum Livelihood for All
Strongly Disagree	1.9	6.74	0.49	0.34
Somewhat Disagree	10.49	26.03	3.83	2.54
Neutral	30.03	31.82	19.75	15.94
Somewhat Agree	35.83	25.41	46.24	42.08
Strongly Agree	21.75	9.99	29.68	39.11
	State versus Individual Responsibility			
	Health Care	Caring for Elderly	Primary and Secondary Education	Employment
State Fully	10.54	13.91	17.22	8.61
State Mainly	21.81	21.51	26.66	21.9
Equally	48.76	39.32	34.11	43.43
Individual Mainly	12.8	14.86	14.13	19.42
Individual Fully	6.09	10.39	7.88	6.65

Note: The results are the authors' calculations.

Source: China National Survey of Perceptions of Distributive Injustice, N = 3,263.

respect to support of the elderly. Just 22 percent thought that primary and secondary education should be personally financed, while only 26 percent judged that it was their own responsibility to secure employment. In comparison, larger percentages of respondents thought that all these services were mainly or wholly the responsibility of the state: The percentages were 32, 35, 44, and 30, respectively. The Chinese public, as late as 2004, continued to hold the state responsible for the allocation of social welfare; at the same time, that the state has risen to the task in many ways is a hopeful development.

Changing Modes of Protest Management

Up to the present, the regime has been able to prevent significant challenges of revolutionary proportions. This success has been achieved despite an upsurge of social protest in China beginning around the mid-1990s. The number of *mass incidents,* a government term for acts of resistance, increased almost tenfold in only a little more than a decade, from 8,709 in 1993 to 87,000 in 2005 (Yu 2007), among which an escalating number were labor disputes (Gallagher 2005). Even official statistics report a sevenfold increase in the number of disputes during these years, from less than 50,000 cases in 1996 to more than 350,000 in 2007. *Collective labor disputes,* the term used to indicate the involvement of groups of participants, also rose rapidly, as evidenced in figure 10.3, from only around 3,000 cases per year in 1996 to close to 13,000 in 2007, with as many as 270,000 individuals taking part in them in 2007. That the regime

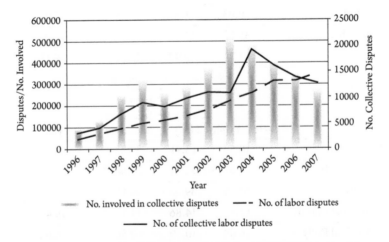

Figure 10.3 Labor Disputes and Participants, China, 1996 to 2007. Source: China Labor Statistical Yearbook (中国劳动统计年鉴, 国家统计局人口和就业统计司; 人力资源和社会保障部规划财务司编, 中国统计出版社) 2008.

did not experience a revolutionary crisis was not because of a lack of discontent but because of the state's success in managing grievances.

Theorists often attribute the occurrence of a revolution to the inflexibility of the old regime in coping with a looming crisis (e.g., Skocpol 1979; Goldstone 1991; Tocqueville 1955). Observers have expressed a similar pessimism over the likely outcome of reforms in communist systems (Kornai 1959, 1989). Pessimism has been borne out elsewhere in the once socialist world, but China's leaders over the decades following 1979, when the reforms began, have proved to be extraordinarily adaptive not only in regard to economic matters but also with respect to the management of dissent.[7]

Having been involved for several decades before its 1949 victory with revolutionary, anti-Japanese and civil wars, the Communist Party was engaged for a long time in a rhetorical exercise using the language of war in its dealings with social problems, whether crime, deviation from the party line, or outright defiance. The extreme version was practiced during the political campaigns under Mao Zedong, such as the Cultural Revolution. In that era, no act of indiscretion was treated as small, and all offenses were taken to be against the revolution (and, accordingly, against "the people" and state as a whole).

This tendency of politicizing behavior of every sort survived into the first years of the reform era. Any organized expression of grievance or dissent was seen as a threat to the core of the system, and the response was to extensively root out any perceived conspiracies. The analysis of and the response to the 1989 Beijing popular movement were typical in linking domestic dissent to "enemy forces from abroad." Protesters' acts were, correspondingly, politicized as issues of national security. Attempts at public venting on less weighty occasions were dealt with in a similar fashion. Calls for more open dialogue and efforts at producing liberal publications and cultural products during the pre-Tiananmen years were deemed to be "bourgeois liberalization."

The state's war-framing mode of addressing social control has gradually been altered over the recent two decades, representing an important institutional adaptation. This adaptation evolved over time and is evident in speeches by the party's general secretary in twenty-first-century congresses of the CCP. In September 1997, for instance, General Secretary Jiang Zemin called for "strengthening national security [and] watching out for activities of infiltration, subversion or separation by *enemy forces from abroad and inside the country*" (emphasis ours), a perspective used in referring to activities the regime viewed as undesirable. The same speech contained a continued use of such terms as the *people's democratic dictatorship* along with accusations of *bourgeois liberalization*.[8] Jiang also repeated the same linguistic framework of "enemy forces" in his address at the following party congress held in 2002, although that time he did not employ such words and terms as *dictatorship* and *bourgeois liberalization.*[9] It was not until the 17th Party Congress, held in 2007, which was Hu Jintao's second congress as general secretary, that the phrase *enemy forces* was not enunciated; at this time the concept of the harmonious society became a new catchphrase.[10]

Consequently, the Chinese government in recent years has begun drawing a key distinction between political and nonpolitical dissent, thereby shifting to a two-track approach toward social control. Political dissent—as in the speeches and activities of democracy movement dissidents, religious leaders, union activists, and ethnic division agitators—was now taken to be targeting the legitimacy of the system itself, and the state's response, one of harsh repression, became invariably swift. Though the state's behavior has involved many violations of human rights, it has been effective in preventing local dissent from gaining a national audience, in keeping economic grievances from becoming political expression, and in preventing disparate groups of petitioners from forming alliances. Through these tactics, the Chinese government succeeded in deflecting revolutionary crisis in the 20 years subsequent to 1989.

At the same time, the regime seems to have become increasingly tolerant of, and at times even accommodating to, protests targeting local government officials or business owners. One telling indicator of this change is that the official term to describe such actions has gone from *mobbing crowds* (暴徒) or *illegal associations* (非法集会) to the more neutral *mass incidents* (群体性事件). The new terminology signals the depoliticization of the majority of citizen protests and an acceptance of them as an inevitable fact of life. Thus, the prior taboo banning any public discussion of the subject of social protest was terminated (Yu 2007; Su and He 2010).

As recently as December 2008, Zhou Yongkang, the Chinese official in charge of law and order, emphasized two principles in regard to "mass incidents." The first of these concerned pre-emption and held that local governments "should nip the bud of problems at the grassroots level and reduce the contradictions that could give rise to mass incidents."[11] This principle laid down an interpretative framework that attributed protest to local officials' negligence, and many local leaders were dismissed on this ground.[12] The second principle demanded that local government agencies appear, in Zhou's words, at the "first site" at the "first moment" whenever a protest breaks out.[13] This served as another attribution framework, entailing blaming local leaders under whose watch a protest escalates into a high-profile event. Failing to appear at the site of protest became an unforgivable oversight should the event escalate into a mass incident.[14]

If Zhou outlined the general principles, other pronouncements tempered his words by warning against using violence to crack down on mass incidents. In another high-profile national policy clarification, Meng Jianzhu, the minister of public security, admonished the police to refrain from or to limit using weapons or policing devices in dealing with protests (Zhong 2008). A document issued by the CCP Disciplinary Investigation Committee stipulated that the "indiscriminate use of police force" can be subject to "double dismissals" from both one's official post and one's party membership for those local leaders found responsible (Li and Yu 2008). An op-ed piece published on December 1, 2008 by the *Beijing Daily*, a newspaper known for its close heeding of the central party line, called for "a new way of thinking in handling mass incidents."

Such shifts in framing and tactics at the end of the first decade of the twentieth century created a new political culture among local leaders, who dreaded any form of escalation of protest. To the extent that a demonstration gained publicity beyond the jurisdiction in question, particularly when it drew the attention of higher-level authorities, local leaders often were blamed and disciplined. This fear was encapsulated in a widely circulated picture of a kneeling Jiang Guohua, party secretary of Mianzhu City in 2008. The photo, taken after the Sichuan earthquake in which thousands of children died due to substandard school buildings, shows a group of grieving parents who had staged protests and vowed to appeal to the authorities in Beijing. Secretary Jiang and members of his staff not only showed up at the protest site but also knelt down to plead to the parents to end the public spectacle (Zhang and Chen 2008).

Another high-profile protest, one that escalated into riots, took place in Weng'an, Guizhou province, in 2008. This one attracted the attention of then party general secretary Hu Jintao, who reportedly gave personal instructions to investigate the situation and to discipline local leaders. Following the protest, the county secretary and the chief of the county's public security bureau were both dismissed. The province's party secretary came to the county to announce the dismissal and gave a postmortem analysis blaming the inattention and lapses of the local government and charging that authority with being the source of the discontent.[15] In cases such as these, though the protesters did not obtain tangible benefits, they nevertheless were vindicated when the leaders against whom they had complained were disciplined for their bureaucratic failings.

Beyond these individual cases, a more systematic analysis of protest events and their management confirms that there was a fundamental shift in protest management by the state at that point.[16] The findings offer evidence of what has been a new form of dispute resolution appearing in a number of locales that Su and He dub "street as courtroom" (Su and He 2010). In this format, local officials bring court hearings and decisions to the street and, in many cases, rule in favor of those who are able to combine their petitions with street protest.

The authors find that the degree of accommodation involved in this approach appears to have differed depending on whether the target of a demonstration was the government itself or the government's interests or whether, instead, the government was largely a third party to the dispute. When meeting a protester's demand could endanger the economic interests of the government, a favorable resolution has been unlikely. In January 2006, for example, a group of fishermen in Dalian City, Liaoning, blocked the construction of a state project, protesting against the pollution and noise generated by the project. Authorities from the city government, the urban police bureau, and the construction company arrived at the protest site immediately. The prompt hearing of the grievances on site and the restraint that was shown resembled the street as courtroom approach, but instead of accommodating the protesters' requests, the local officials and police officers "educated and persuaded" the 40 protesters to leave.

The style of state response displayed in the street as courtroom system has been particularly salient in labor disputes, although its elements have also been common in other protests. An analysis of 500 newspaper reports shows that this new approach of accommodating protest has not been confined to the research site of Su and He (2010), which was located in the economically advanced province of Guangdong; in fact, examples were discovered in Sichuan, Anhui, and Guizhou provinces. This should not be surprising in light of the national policies stipulated and the admonishment against violence by the country's public security chief. Similar dispute-resolution mechanisms seem to be common in Shanghai, a region that has attracted much foreign investment.

According to a Shanghai newspaper, in January 2008, the Civil Cases Department of the city's Xuhui District Court opened a "Green Channel" to resolve wage dispute cases that were staged in the street. In the first such case, "the judge approached the 18 migrant workers protesting on the street and awarded them back pay amounting to 10,000 RMB." According to the reporter, "The entire resolution process lasted for only nine days" (Li 2008). There are reasons to believe that, in the economically more developed regions such as Guangdong and Shanghai, the governments engage in the street as courtroom approach in a more complete fashion, probably at least in part because of the availability of funds that can be used in the adjudication. The local governments in these areas also appear to be more willing to go after the international companies who evade their responsibilities than to blame the domestic parties involved in the dispute.

That there are new modes of handling conflict, however, should not be taken to imply that contemporary Chinese protest incidents are never repressed. There are also newspaper reports of cases in which protesters were detained, imprisoned, and even assaulted with gunfire. For instance, in one dramatic case in Longnan, Gansu province, in November 2008, 30 rioters were arrested after a crowd burned 20 vehicles and set fire to 110 rooms.[17] In the previously cited case in Weng'an, Guizhou, while the authorities dismissed two key county officials, they also blamed "black hands" behind the riot and arrested more than fifty individuals.[18]

In the bloodiest crackdown of protests since the 1989 Tiananmen Square movement, police opened fire on protesters in Shanwei City, Guangdong, reportedly killing at least three persons and wounding eight.[19] These cases indicate that police violence remains an alternative to the newer accommodating mode of government reaction. Accommodation, however, had become relatively common and increasingly the norm rather than the exception as of 2009. In all these cases entailing repression, local leaders were judged by higher authorities to be excessive and negligent, rulings that lend support to our argument.

Conclusion

In this chapter we examine institutional changes and state adaptations that are at the core of understanding the social order and state resilience in the two decades that followed the 1989 Tiananmen Square demonstrations in China. The Chinese state, rather than retreating, has increased its control over the key sectors of the economy and has accelerated its own resource extraction. That new political economy has both laid the foundation for rising inequality while at the same time paving the way for state redistribution aimed at reducing inequality. This development, at least as of that point, refigured state-societal relations and, as a critical byproduct, headed off the revolutionary crisis that seemed to be looming in the late 1980s. Myriad social problems notwithstanding, the government, as of the twentieth anniversary of the 1989 protests, seemed to be enjoying an extended period of stable rule, marked by the euphoria and hype displayed at the Beijing Olympic Games in 2008 and the sixtieth anniversary of Communist Party rule in 2009.

In the two decades after 1989, China saw tremendous growth in the private economic sector and a corresponding decline in state-owned enterprises, yet the state remained the most important player in the economy. By the year 2009, in addition, the state had emerged not only with strong and increasing control over the key sectors of the economy but also had accelerated its resource extraction. The economy had grown out of the plan (Naughton 1996) but not away from the state. Government-guaranteed jobs and welfare were long gone by that time, but the state was still seen as a major provider. Economic inequality had skyrocketed, yet to the extent that social protests increased, they were not organized to display social discontent over rising inequality but to protect people's personal livelihood and property. Dissent erupted when people were laid off from their jobs, not paid their wages, or had their houses torn down or their land taken away (O'Brien and Li 2006; O'Brien 2008; Yu 2007).

Besides, in dealing with social conflict, the local state had begun to cultivate an image of a third-party judge in a range of geographical areas. That new approach meant no longer treating all defiance as a crime against the state and thus avoiding precipitously stepping into the role and position of target. Corruption, one of the main sources of grievance and protest, was thus seen by the public as more the sin of "corrupt officials" (贪官) than as a lack of benevolence on the part of the "emperor" (皇帝). This state-society relationship, new in contemporary China, echoed a style of statecraft promoted by many rulers in Chinese history.[20]

With neither meaningful elections nor a free media, the political system was nonetheless able to extend more freedom to its citizenry than ever before. It had started to manage, rather then repress, most incidents of social unrest, if only to prevent them from taking on a larger political meaning. One scholar has called this process "liberalization and pluralization" without elections (Mertha 2008).

It is unclear, however, how long that situation could last. The resilience of the economy itself could one day be called into question, given the volatility of the global environment and the challenges of domestic factors, including rising resource costs, a rapidly aging population, and rampant corruption. Moreover, state-sponsored economic monopolies, while allowing the state to continue and even to enhance its control over the economy, and also supplying the state with easy revenue, in the long run can suffocate innovation and competition and thereby reduce economic responsiveness and efficiency.

Perception management notwithstanding, the buildup of inequality between haves and have-nots is showing no sign of slowing down.[21] Above all, it is too early to judge whether the Chinese experiment of liberalization without democratic elections will ultimately succeed in transforming an authoritarian state into a free society (Mertha 2008; Su and He 2010).[22] The tight control over the media and cultural discourse, while effective thus far in the sense of manipulating public perceptions and heading off political turmoil, could, eventually, have the effect of converting social discontent into a "social volcano," not to mention that these practices encounter international disapprobation and, at times, inflict egregious human rights violations. The measures of protest management are experimental and ad hoc, subject to the whims of the current leader, devoid of a constitutional foundation or institutional guarantees (Su and He 2010). In an era that witnessed the collapse and rebuilding of other communist regimes, China is celebrating its fortune in avoiding the woes and pains that have accompanied democratization elsewhere. Yet it is unknown whether the Chinese way, maintaining authoritarian rule while in some ways permitting the evolution of a more open society, is just deferring political turmoil to a future time.

Notes

1. http://www.cnn.com/video/#/video/bestoftv/2009/06/03/ac.shot.wednesday.cnn?iref=videosearch.
2. See, for example, http://www.chinadaily.com.cn/bizchina/2009-09/07/content_8660864.htm, or http://news.xinhuanet.com/fortune/2009-09/05/content_12002226.htm (accessed October 5, 2009).
3. Counting employees in the newly emerged categories as private leads to a very different assessment, as in Naughton: "By the end of 2004 the urban private sector, without counting foreign-invested firms, employed about twice as many workers as the traditional state sector: 55 million, compared with less than 30 million in SOEs" (2007:106). Naughton's comparison of employment by sector also shows that, in 1978, 14 percent of the total labor force was employed by state-owned enterprises, plus 4 percent in government and public service units. In 2004, the shares changed to 4 and 5 percent. Adding the contribution of the "new corporate" category, 3 percent, to state-owned enterprises and government and public service units would add up to only 12 percent in 2004, compared with 18 percent of total labor force in the state sectors in 1978 (Naughton 2007:182). In 2004, however, there is a new category, the urban informal sector, that captured 13 percent of the total labor force and whose nature of employment is not totally clear.
4. These numbers are calculated from the China Statistical Yearbook 2009.
5. Calculated from China Statistical Yearbook 2009, table 4.16.
6. A detailed introduction to the survey can be found in Whyte 2010.
7. Here we do not attempt to explain why the Chinese state is able to undergo such a shift but simply document some aspects of change that may help account for the puzzle of regime resilience (and regime vulnerabilities; see discussion).
8. Jiang Zemin, Report to the 15th CCP Congress, September 12, 1997.
9. Jiang Zemin, Report to the 16th CCP Congress, November 17, 2002.
10. Hu Jintao, Report to the 17th CCP Congress, October 24, 2007.
11. Reported by *Chongqing Evening News,* December 18, 2008.
12. One such report is in the *Guizhou Daily,* July 1, 2008.
13. *Chongqing Evening News,* December 18, 2008.
14. In this same interpretative framework, a newspaper reported that a vice governor of Anhui province was in the company of mistresses in the days when a large-scale protest was going on. *Information Daily,* November 2, 2006.
15. *Guizhou Daily,* July 1, 2008.
16. The authors searched a database that includes newspapers in Chinese published in mainland China and other Chinese-speaking regions, such as Hong Kong, Taiwan, and Singapore. The research generated more than 600 relevant articles, from which we selected some 50 protest events taking place between 2006 and 2008. Most of the information gleaned centered on government intervention and the outcome of the case. We then differentiated and compared state reactions to labor disputes and to other types of protests. The term *mass incident* and the policy implications that relate to the concept apply to collective action incidents of all types. The authors excluded only protest attempts deemed by the government to challenge the system as a whole.
17. *Chongqing Morning News,* November 21, 2008.
18. *Guizhou Daily,* July 1, 2008.
19. BBC News, 2005. http://news.bbc.co.uk/2/hi/asia-pacific/4517706.stm
20. One relatively recent example was the case of Chen Tonghai, who was given a death sentence for taking bribes amounting to nearly $30 million. He was the head of Sinopec,

China's largest state-controlled company and the highest-ranked Chinese company listed on the Fortune Global 500.

21. In 2005, consumption by urban Chinese households in the top one-fifth income bracket was equivalent to about 95 percent of combined consumption of the lowest 60 percent, approaching that of the United States in 2008. Moreover, the richest one-fifth of urban Chinese households not only consumed more than the rest but also saved more: Their savings comprised more than half of all urban household savings (as calculated from the difference between income and expenditure). Urban households in the lowest one-fifth income level had only 1.8 percent of their income saved, and the next highest one fifth, only 7.7 percent. Spending disadvantages among the lower social strata in education and medical care also position these groups to form a permanent underclass in the society (Wang and Wang 2009).

22. The increasing concentration of resources in the hands of the central and local governments, through the means of rent extraction and in the absence of external political checks, nurtures a tendency for predatory behavior on the part of the state (Pei 2006.

References

Bandelj, Nina and Matthew C. Mahutga. 2010. "How Socio-Economic Changes Shape Income Inequality in Central and Eastern Europe." *Social Forces* 88(5):2133–2161.

Cai, Yongshun. 2006. *State and Laid-Off Workers in Reform China: The Silence and Collective Action of the Retrenched.* London: Routledge.

Davis, Deborah and Wang Feng, eds. 2009. *Creating Wealth and Poverty in Post-Socialist China.* Palo Alto, Calif.: Stanford University Press.

Gallagher, Mary. 2005. "'Use the Law as Your Weapon!' Institutional Change and Legal Mobilization in China." In *Engaging the Law in China: State, Society, and Possibilities for Justice*, N. J. Diamant, S. B. Lubman, & K. J. O'Brien, eds. Palo Alto, Calif.: Stanford University Press.

Goldstone, Jack. 1991. *Revolution and Rebellion in the Early Modern World.* Berkeley: University of California Press.

———. 1995. "The Coming Chinese Collapse." *Foreign Policy* 99:35–52.

Han, Chunping and Martin King Whyte. 2009. "The Social Contours of Distributive Injustice Feelings in Contemporary China." In *Creating Wealth and Poverty in Post-Socialist China*, Deborah Davis and Wang Feng, eds., 193–212. Palo Alto, Calif.: Stanford University Press.

Huang, Yasheng. 2008. *Capitalism with Chinese Characteristics: Entrepreneurship and the State.* Cambridge, U.K.: Cambridge University Press.

Kornai, Janos. 1959. *Overcentralization in Economic Administration: A Critical Analysis Based on Experience in Hungarian Light Industry.* Oxford, U.K.: Oxford University Press.

———. 1989. *The Socialist System: The Political Economy of Communism.* Princeton, N.J.: Princeton University Press.

Li, Shengnan. 2008. "法院帮农民工讨薪 (Court Helps Farmers Claim Back Pay)," *Information Evening News* January 28, A12.

Li, Yajie and Yu Qinghong. 2008. "《关于违反信访工作纪律处分暂行规定》 颁布实施违规用警力处置群体事件将追责 ('Preliminary Regulations on Disciplinary Actions on Violations of Xingfang Work' Issued; Undisciplined Use of Police Forces to Be Curbed)." *Haikou Evening News* July 23, A05.

Lin, Yimin and Tian Zhu. 2001. "Ownership Restructuring in Chinese State Industry: An Analysis of Evidence of Initial Organizational Change." *The China Quarterly* 168:305–341.

Mertha, Andrew C. 2008. *China's Water Warriors: Citizen Action and Policy Change.* Ithaca, N.Y.: Cornell University Press.

Naughton, Barry. 1996. *Growing out of the Plan: Chinese Economic Reform 1978–1993.* Cambridge, U.K.: Cambridge University Press.

———. 2007. *The Chinese Economy: Transition and Growth.* Cambridge, Mass.: MIT Press.

O'Brien, Kevin, ed. 2008. *Popular Protest in China.* Cambridge, Mass.: Harvard University Press.

O'Brien, Kevin J. and Lianjiang Li. 2006. *Rightful Resistance in Rural China.* Cambridge, U.K.: Cambridge University Press.

Pei, Minxin. 2006. *China's Trapped Transition: The Limits of Developmental Autocracy.* Cambridge, Mass.: Harvard University Press.

Riskin, Carl, Zhao Renwei, and Li Shi, eds. 2001. *China's Retreat from Equality.* Armonk, N.Y.: M. E. Sharpe.

Skocpol, Theda. 1979. *States and Social Revolution.* New York: Cambridge University Press.

Stark, David. 1996. "Recombinant Property in East European Capitalism." *American Journal of Sociology* 101(4):993–1027.

Su, Yang and Xin He. 2010. "Street as Courtroom: State Accommodation of Labor Protest in South China." *The Law & Society Review* 44(1):157–184.

Tocqueville, Alexis de. 1955. *The Old Regime and the French Revolution,* Stuart Gilbert, trans. New York: Anchor Books.

Tsai, Kellee S. 2007. *Capitalism without Democracy: The Private Sector in Contemporary China.* Ithaca, N.Y.: Cornell University Press.

Wang, Feng. 2008. *Boundaries and Categories: Rising Inequality in Post-Socialist Urban China.* Palo Alto, Calif.: Stanford University Press.

Wang, Tianfu and Wang Feng. 2009. "从收入差距到财富鸿沟：城市不同阶层消费差异的深远影响 (From Income Inequality to Wealth Disparity: Implications of Consumption Patterns of Urban Chinese Social Strata)," 领导者 (*Leaders*) 29:73–82.

Whyte, Martin King. 2010. *Myth of the Social Volcano: Perceptions of Inequality and Distributive Injustice in Contemporary China.* Palo Alto, Calif.: Stanford University Press.

Yang, Dali. 2004. *Remaking the Chinese Leviathan: Market Transition and the Politics of Governance in China.* Palo Alto, Calif.: Stanford University Press.

Yu, Jianrong. 2007. "中国的骚乱事件与管治危机：2007年10 月　30 日在美国加州大学伯克利分校的演讲 (Riot Incidents and Control Crisis: Speech at UC Berkeley, October 10, 2007)." *China Elections and Governance,* http://www.chinaelections.org/NewsInfo.asp?NewsID=118361.

Zhang, Xin and Chen Hongjiang. 2008. "绵竹市委书记详述向遇难学生家长下跪原因 (Why Mianzhu City Party Secretary Kneels down to Parents of Student Victims)." http://news.163.com/08/0608/02/4DSOJSI10001124J.html# Zhong Xin. 2008. "公安部长：处置群体事件慎用武器 (Minister of Public Security: Caution Be Taken in Using Weapons When Dealing with Mass Incidents)." *Nanfang Dushibao* November 4, A13.

The Fate of the State after 1989

Eastern Europe and China Compared

DOROTHY J. SOLINGER AND NINA BANDELJ

This volume was born of a project to commemorate the twentieth anniversary of the dramatic events that marked the pivotal year 1989. Our goal was to provide comparative perspectives on trends and outcomes in two broad contexts, the former Soviet bloc and China. That a spring 1989 shock in China was contained by the Communist Party but that jolts that shook Eastern Europe later that year were not similarly addressed by the authorities is the initial, fundamental, difference between these two sets of spaces.

Superficially, the political outcomes of that forbearance left the latter region with what seemed to be a set of new democracies, while China, on the other hand, remained at least nominally socialist. Consequently, one might conjecture that a collection such as this would focus on why democratization took root in some soils but not in others. Thus, it would have seemed likely that comments on the effects of establishing democracy—or the failure to do so— would pervade the chapters by each contributor, even those written by observers who dealt with subjects not explicitly political. Remarkably, in the volume that materialized from this project, the word *democracy* and the stages leading up to it were notably absent from the accounts, except for in the one analysis expressly meant to analyze that process.

Instead, the term that most haunted the chapters was *the state*, broadly conceived as the policymaking organs of the central government, along with the officials who command these organs within a country (to combine the definitions of Skocpol 1985 and Nordlinger 1981). Our contributors thus elaborated on topics such as the old socialist state and its nature, activities, and roles; the leaders of states, both past and present; the issue of whether or not the state made room for civil society before 1989 or how it has done so in the years since; the economic achievements (or lack thereof) of the state at different points in time and the ways in which the state has or has not acted to encourage or, at least, permit the formation of new forms of economic behavior; the state's capacity to handle dissent (or its relinquishment of, or failure at, that enterprise), along with its creation of new modes of dealing with a restive populace; and the state's responsibility for novel societal trends, whether in family formation, toward protest, and in regard to inequality. Even with Akos Rona-Tas's and Yasheng Huang's contributions, chapters 7 and 8, respectively, in which each author discusses the presence of a new private sector within the economy, the state remains important. This is, oddly, the case even where elites chose to encourage more individualized market-based consumer behavior as in Eastern Europe; it is even more the case in China, where, despite official sanction of private and foreign entrepreneurs, these business-people must often yield to the dominance of the state-affiliated companies.

So the tale that threads through the various narratives is really one about the nature of the political unit that has traversed the decades since 1989. Whether this is the same state (though in an updated form) as in China or old states in brand-new incarnations, as in Eastern Europe and Russia, these polities have undergone some fairly foundational metamorphoses. Thus, if the state still defines the types of transmutation occurring in the economic system and if it yet persists in structuring the relations between government and people, it does so in starkly different ways in the two broad contexts that our contributors examine.

Strange to say, the Chinese Cultural Revolution that spanned the years 1966 to 1976 and the bloodbath that occurred in Beijing's Tiananmen Square in spring 1989 stand as springboards for the bigger story, not only about China but also for the overarching comparisons we wish to draw. For, as Joseph Fewsmith discusses in chapter 2, that earlier decade of upheaval and mass societal torment so shook the post-1978 political elite—a great many of whom had been its victims—and so threatened the institutions of the state itself that any later sign of large numbers of citizens in the streets was nearly certain to call for repression, especially when what looked to the leaders like a large-scale, cross-class, multi-site rebellion seemed poised to erupt in 1989. Most Eastern European countries had not experienced popular upheaval on the scale of China's 10-year Cultural Revolution, even if a few resistance movements, such as Poland's Solidarity, played an important role on the Eastern European scene as it unfolded.

In China, despite a decade featuring substantial, if intermittent, periods of intellectual and cultural openness in the 1980s, once the demands for political inclusion and recognition from protesters at Tiananmen Square threatened to spin out of control in April 1989, that behavior caused a "shock" to the leadership, to quote from Barry Naughton in chapter 6; accordingly, a violent clampdown eventuated within a matter of weeks. For history predisposed the toughest instincts among the political elite to win the day, distinguishing the Chinese rulers' extreme reaction to the demonstrations in 1989 from those of their Soviet bloc counterparts who were confronting similar circumstances. A significant measure of economic success and international approval for the country in the 1980s empowered the outraged, conservative Chinese rulers who prevailed in 1989 to act to preserve their own positions (and, as they viewed it, to preserve their state) in the aftermath of the shootings they ordered on June 4. In contrast, the great surprise of the regime transitions in postsocialist Europe, the Baltic States, and Russia was precisely the relative peacefulness of the process, as well as a nearly immediate surrender of the challenged regimes in most places.[1]

In the long term, the Tiananmen episode functioned as a kind of "political meltdown," in Fewsmith's words, in which what had seemed to be growing openness was sharply reversed. At the same time, as characterized by Naughton, the showdown was a "watershed" that "shaped China's future trajectory in nearly every dimension," a conclusion echoed in Huang's chapter. Deeply unsettled, the top officials rallied around a common cause—that of a pullback against progressive reforms—and, within a couple of years, a successful recentralization and concentration of economic resources and power. This was a denouement made practicable by the forced retirement and purging as well as by the dying off of politicians holding alternate views. So the simple plotline of the 20 post-1989 years for China has centered on the sidelining of a set of subordinate, more liberal-minded leaders held responsible for what appeared as open dissent in 1989 (along with the crushing of oppositional social forces, groups that had pinned their hopes on such leaders). The story goes on to underline how that sidelining then served as the impetus for a circling of the wagons at the center of the polity for most of the period after June 1989, a situation that remains in force to this day.

As Naughton notes and as Huang illustrates, the victory of the hardliners at Tiananmen, in turn, lent a new level of clout and energy to officialdom overall, permitting a consolidation of resources at the top of the system and a choice of policies that were at once more heartless but also in some ways more strongarmed by state confidence than what had gone before. An enhanced "priority to state interests," as Fewsmith formulates it, appeared following 1990 and led to further economic growth and to an enhanced capacity for societal management, as charted by Wang Feng and Yang Su in chapter 10. This heightened central authority admitted of some tolerance at times for small-scale apolitical civil groups that were perceived as harmless, as Robert P. Weller details in chapter 4. But the manner in which the most powerful among China's leaders coped with "the street" in 1989 presaged and promoted the trajectory of the enhanced statism (as compared with the 1980s) that followed and that created what these politicians would perceive to be a virtuous circle of statist sway. In this climate, according to Huang's research, a lively private sector might at times have managed to subsist and even to grow, but it did so only within the confines of a much more rigorously supported state sector than before.

In the satellite states of the FSU, and in the new states that broke off from that monolith, a far different sequence unfolded. Instead of a leadership poised to quash most signs of disaffection or disapproval as in China, for the most part the political elite in these places (excepting "authoritarian leaders in advantageous positions" in Armenia, Belarus, and other unreformed former Soviet states, as noted by Valerie Bunce and Sharon Wolchik in chapter 1) in time came to terms with the opposition in one way or another.

Those who remained at the helm in 1989 and thereafter absorbed Western assistance with installing democratic practices—a kind of aid that, as Fewsmith observes, was repeatedly suspected and spurned by top strategist Deng Xiaoping in China. Eastern European leaders assimilated advice on holding elections and were receptive to concepts and models diffused from the outside world. When a significant mass protest was launched, it was for the most part not suppressed; rather, the mobilization behind the protests became the building blocks for styles of rulership that to varying degrees smacked of democracy.

To the contrary, though Chinese intellectuals were conscious of regime changes taking place elsewhere in East Asia and were even, to some extent, aware of such change in Eastern Europe, as Fewsmith recounts, diffusion did not take place. The secondhand knowledge that dissidents in China acquired in the 1980s could by no means match up against the contagious "regional opposition networks" that spread dissident experiences across Eastern Europe and Eurasia, from one former socialist state to another in the two waves of democratic change that Bunce and Wolchik describe. Even decades later, the Internet-provided information that millions of netizens in China acquire about the outside world had not, as of early 2012, made the slightest impact on domestic political institutions.

In the once socialist portions of Europe, a new, but (as compared with the Chinese leaders or with the former leaders of the Soviet bloc) less surefooted elite essayed to exclude members of the former ruling class in some places (as in Katherine Verdery's account in chapter 3), even as in other countries politicians refashioned communist parties or embraced versions of political capitalism that rewarded status holders from the past. Still, significant political transformations took place, as leaders more or less genuinely embraced novel notions of law, justice, and democratic practice, according to Verdery. As measured against the Chinese situation, the shaky underpinnings of an untried, postcommunist world, combined with the EU's influences, formed the backdrop for experimentation in Central and Eastern Europe.

Political tinkering occurred in a context of hasty market building and immediate generalized declines in the economy. As József Böröcz elaborates in chapter 5, new or reborn nations suffered economic contractions following the occurrences of 1989 (in practically every case resulting in an at-least temporary economic crisis), with the collapse of what Böröcz terms the "Soviet bloc's economic integration system." This downslide also was an effect of the dissolution of the Soviet, Yugoslav, and Czechoslovak federations, which produced many smaller and economically weaker states. As each state-owned and state-run economy shrank throughout the region, the state's command of the national economy "eroded by privatization," in the words of Akos Rona-Tas and yielded a much retrenched postsocialist state as of late 2000.

In place of that previous state economy and its ability to redistribute, sudden income inequalities arose and, with them, vast changes in the class structure, phenomena that marked social change in China as well, as Wang Feng and Yang Su document. At the same time, consumer credit became available throughout Eastern Europe and Russia, supplied first by refashioned bank monopolies and, later, by foreign financial institutions (as part and parcel of an influx of foreign investment into the region), catering differentially to the disparate social classes now dividing up society. Rona-Tas views this development as the birth of a new and far-reaching "system of social control," centered on private finance, whose repercussions could well become far less benign than the politically driven apportionments once arranged by the state. As just one instance of the impact of this new configuration, the post-2008 economic crisis that hit these countries hard resulted in the painful exposure of the liabilities associated with the widespread postsocialist embrace of private and public debt accumulation.

Another effect of the diminution in the invasiveness of the states in the region that emerged after 1989, as compared with the era of Communist Party rule, was the set of reversals in family formation observed by Theodore P. Gerber in chapter 9. Whereas once early and nearly universal marriages, high fertility, low divorce rates, and little nonmarital cohabitation and out-of-wedlock childbearing had long marked the area, the postsocialist period has seen a switch in every one of those behaviors. The most likely explanation among those Gerber considers is that the "institutional and policy supports for early marriage and childbearing" provided by the state disappeared, leaving the less well-protected and, therefore, less secure individuals and families who make up the new society far less prone than they were in the past to forge nuptial bonds or to bear offspring early or at all.

It is to be expected that where socialism was vanquished, the party-cum-state amalgam that supported that system would disappear as well, leading to a retrenchment of the former state and on to the appearance of a substantially transformed nonsocialist state. Equally unremarkable is that, in China, where a challenged Communist Party managed to sustain its rule, it not only bolstered some of its powers that had begun to shrink in the 1980s but also focused its efforts on adaptation, in the interest of holding on by whatever means it could (Shambaugh 2008).

Aside from these obvious developments, what the chapters in this volume demonstrate for Eastern Europe is a form of postsocialist state that has extensively repositioned itself in relation to its citizenry. In politics, new leaders in more and more countries across the region acceded to democratic elections in time and grappled with the diminished international economic weight of their nations. At the level of the populace, a consumer society is being born, in which a wealth of individual choice is paired with rising inequality. What people do with their money is entirely their personal choice today, as markets provide output the likes of which the old planned economy could never have produced.

Meanwhile, the state-societal connection has eventuated in a duo of a novel sort from the one that marked the communist era. In this partnership, popular participation often can entail not only voting but also exposing prior perpetrators, rather than, as in the past, simply struggling to preserve one's own innocence in the eyes of the all-powerful state. Family-level decisions are now made in the absence of the paternalistic overseer and provider that the old state had been. The ever-present, meddling—if also supplying—surveillant has been replaced by a looser and more distant entity that has often left citizens to their own devices. In these places, it is not only the state that has become transformed but also the public that has changed in many ways too. Thus, as an entity, "the public" has become less of a mass passively acted upon and more of an individualized and autonomous group of agents than it was before. Thus, the interaction between a less omnipotent state, on the one side, and a less cowed public, on the other, is producing a new set of roles as the two parties interact in new ways. But this altered state is by no means one in the process of fully withering away. Rather it is one that continues to struggle to work out just what its role should be, as it learns about effective democratic governance. At the same time, this new state finds itself sometimes caught up in considerable pressures from the EU and other supranational governance bodies, at other times co-opted by domestic special interests, even as its efforts are often vitiated by the set of informal practices that at this yet transitional stage are endemic to every reach of the system, in both private and public realms. All of these issues deserve more attention than we have space to provide in the present volume.

In China, by way of contrast, although there have been many adjustments, the story is much less one of a state that has stepped back. Instead, there is a force at the helm of the country that holds on to the economy, where the leadership has, if anything, become more intrusive toward political activities on the part of the populace than it was during several periods of the first decade or so after Mao Zedong's passing. While decisively opening up and relaxing its grasp over the economy as a whole—as compared with former times— the political elite reacted to the collision of 1989 by reinforcing its command over the economy's key levers and critical sectors, as well as by bolstering both its ability to act in unison and its capacity to manage social discontent, often with a heavy hand. Even as substantial inequality and a burst of civil associations have each appeared in force (each an indicator of the break that has been made from the more passive, more uniform proletarian-cum-peasant past), the Chinese state of the twenty-first century so far has put its bets on a bolstered, if fine-tuned, bridle on its people and on an alliance with the better-off, all in the interest of extending its rule.

**

The close of the period covered in this volume coincided with a worldwide economic crisis that put the question of the job of the state, especially its role in regulating economic affairs, firmly back on the agenda of both policy makers and scholars everywhere. For the former communist countries of Eastern Europe and Eurasia, which were sharply buffeted by this crisis, the way forward has been complicated since the massive transformations of the prior 20 years has left many skeletons in postsocialist closets. It is easily forgotten that the institutionalization of democracy and the market took many decades, at a minimum, in other parts of the world and surely will require time in these regions as well. The moment in time that this volume adopts as its perspective or vantage point, two decades after the pivotal events of 1989, could well prove to be a critical juncture. In many former Eastern bloc countries, this was a time of recession, high unemployment and soaring sovereign debt, with governance marred by nontransparency and informality; not surprisingly, restive publics began to register support for populist and radical parties. Some even questioned the legitimacy of the economic and political models that Eastern European countries had followed since 1989.

At the other end of the world, an image of a sturdy state in China was bolstered by the crisis, as it weathered the events far better than most countries did, even if this new leviathan was not wholly unaffected. We look forward to insights on the issues of appropriate political models and workable economic patterns that have factored into the transition from socialism as these events unfold further into the future. We hope that researchers intrigued by (post) socialism will continue to take up the unlikely comparison across divergent contexts that we have placed before our readers.

Notes

1. The horrifying civil war in the former Yugoslavia is a glaring exception, but the violence was caused not directly by regime transition but by country secession.

References

Nordlinger, Eric A. 1981. *On the Autonomy of the Democratic State.* Cambridge, Mass.: Harvard University Press.

Shambaugh, David. 2008. *China's Communist Party: Atrophy & Adaptation.* Berkeley: University of California Press.

Skocpol, Theda. 1985. "Bringing the State Back In: Strategies of Analysis in Current Research." In *Bringing the State Back In*, Peter Evans, Dieter Rueschmeyer, and Theda Skocpol, eds. New York: Cambridge University Press.

INDEX

adaptation, 11, 220, 229, 233, 243
Albania:
    democratization, 26
    economic trajectory, 111, 112, 122n11
    hybrid regime, 35, 36
    lustration measures, 69, 70, 72, 80n9
antipolitics, 74
Armenia:
    democratization, 30
    economic trajectory, 116, 117
    hybrid regime of, 35, 36
    lustration measures, 70
    marriage and fertility rates, 199, 201, 203, 206
    suppression of change, 33–34, 241
authoritarian:
    competitive regimes, 28
    government, 64, 142
    leaders, 27, 31–36, 241
    regime, 55, 129
    resilience, 6
    rule, 5, 30, 31, 34, 36, 38, 235
    See also authoritarianism
authoritarianism, 63
    in China, 39, 73
    responsive, 13, 83, 97
Azerbaijan:
    democratization, 30
    economic trajectory, 116, 117
    hybrid regime, 35, 36
    lustration measures, 70
    suppression of change, 33–34

Balkans:
    democratization, 30
    See also specific countries
Baltic States:
    democratization, 4, 25, 31, 35, 36

lustration measures, 69, 70
    See also Estonia; Latvia; Lithuania
Bandelj, Nina, 10, 31, 121n, 211–12
banking, 156, 158, 168, 176
    in China, 139, 181
    retail banking, 151, 157, 167, 170
Bauer-Kornai cycles:
    in Chinese economy, 134–35, 136, 137, 139
    explained, 134
Belarus:
    democratization, 30
    economic trajectory, 116
    hybrid regime of, 35
    lustration measures, 70
    suppression of change, 33–34, 241
    U.S. democracy promotion, 34
blind-eye governance. *See* Chinese state-society relations
Böröcz, József, 13–14, 126, 154, 195, 196, 241–42
Bosnia-Herzegovina, economic trajectory, 113, 114
Bulgaria:
    constitutional court, 71
    democratization first wave, 26, 27
    democratization second wave, 23–24, 27, 37
    economic trajectory, 111, 112, 119, 122n11, 123n15
    lustration measures, 69, 70, 80n9
    marriage and fertility rates, 199, 203
    regime trajectory, 4, 36
    Union of Democratic Forces, 27
Bunce, Valerie, 3, 12, 241

Central Europe. *See* Eastern and Central Europe
Chen, Yun, 49, 50, 131–32, 133, 134, 137